Real LOVE

for WISE MEN AND WOMEN

The truth about sharing Real Love

GREG BAER, M.D.

BLUE RIDGE PRESS

Baer, Greg
    Real Love® for Wise Men and Women
    ISBN 978-1-892319-26-5
    1. Relationships 2. Self-help 3. Psychology
Published by Blue Ridge Press PO Box 3075 Rome, GA 30164
    877-633-3568

Also by Greg Baer, M.D. —

Published by Gotham Books, a division of Penguin USA Group:

Real Love® — The Truth About Finding Unconditional Love and Fulfilling Relationships

Real Love® in Marriage — The Truth About Finding Genuine Happiness Now and Forever

Published by Blue Ridge Press:

Real Love® — The Truth About Finding Unconditional Love and Fulfilling Relationships, Unabridged Audio Book — Seven 60 minute CDs

The Real Love® Companion — Taking Steps Toward a Loving and Happy Life

Real Love® in Dating — The Truth About Finding the Perfect Partner — Book and Unabridged Audio Book

Real Love® in Marriage — Unabridged Audio Book

40 Days to Real Love and Happiness in Your Marriage — A companion Workbook for Real Love in Marriage

Real Love® in Parenting — The Truth About Raising Happy and Responsible Children — Book and Unabridged Audio Book

Real Love® and Freedom for the Soul — Breaking the Chains of Victimhood

Real Love® in the Workplace — Eight Principles for Consistently Effective Leadership in Business

Real Love® and Post-Childhood Stress Disorder — Treating Your Unrecognized Post-Traumatic Stress Disorder

Under the Bridge — a novel

The Truth About Love and Lies — Three 60 minute CDs

The Essentials of Real Love® — Six DVDs, or Six CDs

The Essentials of Real Love® Workbook for DVDs or CDs

The Essentials of Real Love® Bible Workbook for DVDs or CDs

Printed in the United States
10 9 8 7 6 5 4 3 2 1

Contents

❧ Chapter One ❧

What You Want
for Yourself and Others

The Wise Man

After reading *Real Love—The Truth About Finding Unconditional Love and Fulfilling Relationships*, many of you have experienced the happiness that comes from finding Real Love. It is the purpose of this book to offer even more about finding love and about becoming wise men and women yourselves as you learn to share that love. In order to avoid excessive repetition of the principles taught in *Real Love*, I will assume you have read it recently.

At this point, you may be hesitant to think of yourself as a wise man. It may seem strange, intimidating, or arrogant to suppose that you could occupy that role, but becoming a wise man is a natural result of feeling loved and making a decision to share that love with others. A wise man is anyone who feels loved and loving enough in a given moment that he or she can accept and love another person—and you can learn to do that.

First, a word about gender. Because frequent repetition of the phrases *wise men and women, wise man or woman,* and *he or she* can become awkward, I will sometimes use the terms *wise men, wise man,* and *he* when I'm referring to both men and women.

Second, a word about my own experiences as a wise man. In order to illustrate the principles of the book, we'll discuss real situations where those principles were successfully applied. I will use some of my own positive experiences, but I hasten to add that I've also had *many* negative ones, and it's from all of them that I've learned what I'll be sharing with you. I continue to make mistakes and learn from them, as will you.

In the Tale of the Wart King and the Wise Man from Chapter Three of *Real Love*, Real Love moved the Wart King from a place of fear, anger, and loneliness to a condition of peace and happiness, but he was not able to make this powerful transformation by himself. He required the help of someone who could love him, see him clearly, and help him to see himself. When he accepted the love of the Wise Man, his old belief—that he could never feel safe and loved—changed forever. The love of the Wise Man changed the king's view of everything.

We all need wise men in our lives, people who love us without condition and help us see and love others. From the beginning of our lives we needed wise men and women as our parents, grandparents, aunts, uncles, and teachers. But for most of us that didn't happen consistently, not because those people consciously withheld their love from us, but because they didn't have sufficient experience with wise men who loved *them*. They couldn't pass Real Love on to us, because they didn't have it themselves.

We can't go back and change our upbringing, but we can learn how to find wise men now, and we can learn how to become wise men ourselves. We can change the world as we change our own lives and as we love the people around us.

THE CHARACTERISTICS OF A WISE MAN

As a senior medical student, I often had occasion to teach the students who were a year behind me. My *teaching*, however, was possible only because I was also a *student*, learning from physicians with more experience than I. This pattern continued throughout my medical career. Even as I later taught in medical school and lectured other physicians across the country, my teaching was possible only because I was constantly receiving instruction from those who were more knowledgeable.

Similarly, as wise men we're always giving and receiving. While we're loving other people, we also have a continual need to tell the truth about ourselves and receive the love and guidance of other wise men. Throughout the book, as you read about the qualities that identify wise men, and the principles that guide them, always remember the dual process of giving and receiving. If you do, you'll see that each principle and quality can be viewed in *three ways*:

- Personal use. These are the principles you need to *apply* in your own life, and the qualities you need to *acquire*, if you want to be happy yourself and become a wise man for others.
- Identification. These are the qualities you want to *find* in the wise men and women you hope will accept and love you.
- Sharing. These are the principles you want to *teach* to those who are trying to find their own love and happiness.

With an understanding of this three-fold application, you'll know that when I talk, for example, about the importance of faith in telling the truth about *yourself*, I'm also suggesting that you teach this principle to *others* who are learning to tell the truth, and that you look for *wise men* who understand faith as they accept and love you.

Throughout the book, as you read stories of people interacting with wise men, you'll learn more if you imagine yourself in the position of the wise man. In many of the stories, in fact, I will place you in the conversation as the wise man. These real-life examples will help you see how *you* might behave in similar situations, although you will naturally develop a style entirely your own.

A Wise Man Feels Loved

After reading *Real Love*, you probably have a firm intellectual grasp of how unconditional love works. Because you know many friends, relatives, and co-workers who could benefit from these principles, you may wish to help them tell the truth about themselves and feel loved. In the following story, Mark did that with his wife, Dawn.

Like most couples, Mark and Dawn got married because they fell in love and thought their initial glorious feelings would last forever. But their expectations slowly turned into disappointment and resentment, and by the time I met Mark, he and his wife spoke only to argue or conduct necessary family business, or both. Dawn often complained about what Mark did and did not do, and Mark usually responded by getting angry and defending himself. Of course, each of these interactions only bloodied their relationship even more.

After reading about Real Love, Mark realized that Dawn had been attacking him only because she was empty and afraid. One day, when Dawn was bitterly complaining about something Mark hadn't done, he eagerly explained that she wasn't really angry at *him* but was reacting to her own emptiness and fear. Although Mark was correct, and though he did have some positive intent, you might imagine how Dawn reacted to this explanation that her anger was *her* fault, not his. When she exploded and attacked him with additional fury, he tried again to point out what she was doing, but she screamed at him and stomped out of the room.

Mark had expected that Dawn would be grateful for his generous attempt to share his newfound wisdom, so of course he was offended and angry. Later that day he talked to me.

Mark: I don't understand it. I just told her the truth, but then she got angry, like she always does.

Me: I know you meant well, but you didn't give her what she wanted most. You didn't love her.

Mark: How do you know that? You weren't there.

Me: How did you feel when she didn't accept what you were saying? Did you feel like you do now—disappointed and irritated?

Mark: (pause) Well, I guess, but I was just trying to help, and then she goes crazy on me.

Me: If you'd been unconditionally loving—caring about *her* happiness—would you have felt disappointed or angry at her?

There was another long pause as Mark thought about what he'd read and heard. "I guess not."

"Don't feel bad about it," I said. "You just don't feel loved enough yet to be a wise man, but when you do, you'll be able to share that love with other people—including Dawn."

Over a period of weeks, as Mark told the truth about himself to me and several other people, he gradually began to feel more loved. One evening he called me.

Mark: You won't believe what happened with Dawn last night. I'm sitting in the living room, watching a football game, and she comes stomping into the room and says something about how football is more important to me than she is. In fact, she says everything is more important than she is, and I never do anything with her anymore, and never take her anywhere. It was really getting ugly.

Me: You've had those arguments before. What did you do?

Mark: I admit, at first I had this urge to start yelling back at her like I usually do. But this time I thought about *you*. Is that weird? I remembered some of the conversations we've had where I felt accepted by you and some of the other guys I've been talking to, and when I thought of that, I didn't feel like I had to defend myself anymore with Dawn. And I remembered that you said she uses anger as a Getting and Protecting Behavior, because she's empty and afraid. Am I making any sense?

Me: Sure. We only attack people to protect ourselves when we feel unloved and afraid. The whole reason you and Dawn have always fought is that neither of you has felt unconditionally loved—not just by each other but by anyone. Dawn attacked you last night only because she didn't feel loved and was trying to get you to love her. If you'd felt empty, you would've protected yourself by getting angry, but you remembered that you *are* loved, and then you didn't need to defend yourself anymore. That's a miracle. So then what happened?

Mark: Once I didn't feel afraid or angry, it was easy to see what she needed. I got up, turned off the television, and put my arms around her. I hugged her and told her she was right—I *haven't* spent much time with her—not for a long time. And I told her I was learning how to love her—that's why I've been spending time with you guys.

Me: What did she say?

Mark: Nothing. She just cried and let me hold her.

Me: Do you remember when I told you that eventually you'd be a wise man?

Mark: Sure.

Me: That's what you did last night with Dawn. You felt loved enough that for a few moments, you were a wise man.

Mark: Dawn sure liked it—a lot—and I did, too.

Mark was able to be a wise man for his wife only because he'd made the necessary preparations *before* their interaction. That is how we become wise men. There's no formal school, no certification. We just exercise the faith required to tell the truth about ourselves, and then we feel the love we're offered. As we feel loved and lose our emptiness and fear, we *naturally* acquire the ability to see, accept, and love other people. Mark didn't even realize he was being a wise man. In the beginning, his ability to do that lasted only for a few minutes, but as he continued to feel loved, he acquired the ability to accept and love his wife and others for longer periods. We can all do the same.

A Wise Man Sees Other People Clearly

Throughout *Real Love*, beginning in Chapter Three, I talk about the process of feeling loved: Truth → Seen → Accepted → Loved. For years Dawn didn't feel accepted and loved by Mark because they weren't taking the first two steps of this process (Truth → Seen) together. Dawn wasn't telling the truth about herself, and Mark was quite blind to the truth about her. Blindness is caused by two things: emptiness and fear. If I'm empty, I won't be able to clearly see who *you* really are. I'll see only what I *want from you*. If I'm starving to death, for example, I'll see you only in terms of whether you can give me food. Similarly, if I'm afraid of you, I'll see only what you might *do to me*. If you're holding a gun to my head, that's the only thing I'll see about you.

Because Mark had never felt loved, he could see only what Dawn might do *for* him or *to* him. After he felt the unconditional love of several wise men, he lost his emptiness and fear to the point that he was no longer entirely blinded and could begin to see and accept her.

Being a wise man is not a technique—it's not a matter of cleverness or manipulating people. In Chapter Six of *Real Love* I describe the process Loved → Seeing → Accepting → Loving. When we feel loved ourselves, we naturally gain the ability to be wise, as Mark did. We do not have to wait, however, until we're completely filled with Real Love before we can move on to the steps of seeing, accepting, and loving others. Notice that Mark was able to respond in a loving way to Dawn not only because he felt loved but also because he *remembered* that she was just empty and afraid and using Getting and Protecting Behaviors. Even when we have only a little Real Love ourselves, a *knowledge* of true principles (seeing clearly) can help us take giant strides toward accepting and loving, as illustrated further in the following story.

Imagine that you and I are having a pleasant lunch together by the side of a large pool. It's a lovely day, and we're having a great time, but then someone in the pool starts splashing you—first on your shoes, then higher up on your pants or legs. You can't see who's splashing you because there's a deck chair between you and the person in the pool. At first you ignore it, but you're really starting to get wet, and finally you become irritated and get up from your chair to say something to this idiot who's being so thoughtless. As you stand up, you look over the chair that was in your way, and you see that the man splashing you is *drowning*. He's splashing you only because he's thrashing and kicking in the water to keep his head from going under.

Are you still mad at him? Of course not. As soon as you see *why* he's splashing you, you not only lose your irritation, but you immediately become concerned about him, and you help him out of the water.

When we believe people are inconsiderate and unkind because they're trying to hurt us, we feel even more unloved and react with Getting and Protecting Behaviors. You experienced that when you were irritated as the man first began to splash you. When you stood up and could *see* more clearly, however, you changed in an instant from empty and angry to accepting (loss of anger) and loving (acting to help him): Loved → Seeing → Accepting → Loving. You didn't have to think about the process. You simply became more accepting and loving as you saw the truth clearly.

When you saw the man in the water more clearly, and then accepted and loved him, you also felt more *loved* yourself—you lost your anger and felt the kind of peace and happiness that always follow the presence of Real Love. As I describe in Chapter Six of *Real Love*, when we fill our buckets with love, we are better able to pour it out for the benefit of others. But as we pour, Real Love somehow multiplies miraculously and leaves us with more than we had originally. We can see, therefore, that the process of Loved → Seeing → Accepting → Loving is not linear, but circular, as depicted in the following diagram.

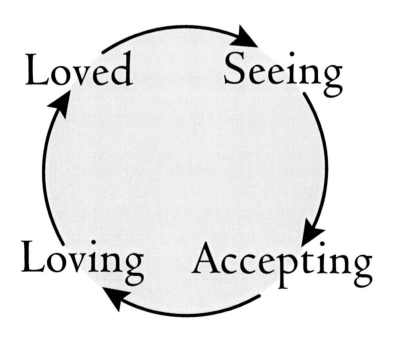

Feeling loved leads to seeing, accepting, and loving, and when we're loving we *feel* more Real Love, which perpetuates and amplifies this healthy cycle. This is a principle we must understand for ourselves as wise men, and which we must teach to others as they're learning to feel loved and loving.

A Wise Man is Loving

Accepting people means you don't get afraid or angry or react with other Getting and Protecting Behaviors when people behave badly. *Loving* people is a more active concern for their happiness and is often accompanied by some kind of service. Loving is a result of seeing and accepting and consciously making loving choices. Loving *includes* accepting. There are many ways we can show our love for others. We can:

- Simply decide not to use our own Getting and Protecting Behaviors when other people use theirs
- Say something kind and supportive
- Touch them gently on the hand
- Look them in the eye as they speak
- Perform some act of service we know they'd enjoy
- Cooperate with their requests, even when they're being critical (which does not mean you have to do *everything* someone wants)
- Take full responsibility for our own mistakes in a situation without bringing up theirs

The potential list of kind acts is endless, and we can all think of things that would help other people feel our concern for them. Loving people, however, often involves more than just offering our help and being "nice." In order to genuinely care about the happiness of other people, we must remember that they cannot feel loved and happy without telling the truth about themselves: Truth → Seen → Accepted → Loved. No matter how much love we offer to others, they will not feel it until they are truthful.

For most people, however, telling the truth is frightening. Because of their past experiences, they cannot imagine that they will ever be accepted with their mistakes and flaws. Without help, most people will continue their familiar pattern of hiding and using other Getting and Protecting Behaviors for their entire lives. If we love them, we will help them tell the truth, although our efforts do need to be tempered with knowing when and with whom we do this. We'll talk more about that in Chapter Four.

We need to realize that our attempts to help people be truthful may not be well-received. Earlier we talked about the man drowning in a pool. Now imagine that you find another man drowning, and he's your friend. Of course, you don't want him to drown, so you find a rope and throw it out to him. The throw is perfect, and the rope comes to rest right beside his head. But in his panicked condition he thinks the rope is a snake, so he screams and tries to get away from it. Next you throw him a board, hoping he can grab hold and float to the side of the pool. But the board hits him on the head, and he screams obscenities at you as he thrashes even harder. Finally, you jump into the water and swim out to help him, but he grabs your head, pulls you under, and you both drown.

Now imagine that you have a friend who is often angry. Although other people are irritated by his anger, you realize that he's just drowning in the middle of a pool and doing the only things he knows to keep his head above water. As he kicks and flails his arms, however, he splashes water on everyone around him— his boss, wife, children, and friends, including you. Occasionally, he even hits people who swim nearby. In response, other people yell at him, or kick him, or avoid him altogether. Of course, those behaviors only make him feel even more desperate, and he thrashes all the harder.

Because you care about your friend, you want to help him, and you know that until he sees the cause of his anger, and quits blaming others for it, he will remain unhappy. What can you do? Most of us would do nothing, because we've learned from extensive past experience that other people often get offended and defend themselves when anyone offers advice, which they perceive as criticism. Sometimes saying nothing *is* the best thing to do, but if we really care about someone's happiness, how can we stand there on the side of the pool and watch that person drown?

You decide to help your friend see the truth about himself, effectively throwing him a rope or flotation device. Even though you present the truth with love and skill, he may perceive your words as threatening and will then push you away—like a snake. At other times, your attempts may be a little clumsy—hitting him on the head with a board—and he'll become even more angry. Or you may react with your own Getting and Protecting Behaviors—jumping into the pool with him—and then you'll both drown.

In subsequent chapters, we'll describe the many ways you can best extend the truth to people who are drowning, and what to do when they resist you. Continuing to hit them on the head with a board is usually unproductive, and it's not wise to jump into the water where they can drown you. Sometimes there is no way you can help. Some people will resist you no matter what you do, and you do not have the right to insist that they accept what you offer. But we often *can* find an effective way to tell the truth to others, and of course it always involves acceptance and love. The Wart King resisted many of the Wise Man's efforts to love him, but the Wise Man persisted and eventually succeeded in helping the king feel loved.

For a wise man, Real Love and telling the truth are inseparable. A wise man's entire mission can be summed up in two words: *love* and *teach*. People need to see the truth about themselves and learn the true principles that lead to happiness and loving relationships, and they learn best when the teacher is also loving. If you can love and teach together, you will greatly improve the likelihood of increasing Real Love in the lives of others—and for yourself. You will be a wise man.

Why a Wise Man Loves

When people say to us, "I love you because ..." we can hardly wait to hear what follows: "... you're so handsome/clever/beautiful/strong/funny." All our lives we've heard people describe the qualities that make people lovable, and we've come to believe that in order to be loved ourselves, we must possess those qualities. How delighted we are when someone tells us that we are indeed worthy of their affection. But that is *conditional* love, not Real Love, which is caring about someone's happiness without any concern for what we'll get for ourselves, and without any standard that must be met by the person we love. Still, many people ask, "But if a wise man doesn't love me because of my intelligence or appearance or because I do something for him, why *would* he or she love me?" Simply because you *need* it.

Let's continue the metaphor of your drowning friend. Why do you throw him a rope and try to help him out of the pool? Does he have to pay you before you'll help him? Or say something nice to you? Or tell a clever joke to make you laugh? No, you pull him from the water just because he *needs* it. And that's why we love people unconditionally, because they need it.

What if you don't really know someone? Can you still unconditionally love him or her? What's the most important thing you could know about someone? His favorite football team? Where she works? His favorite hobby? Where she likes to shop? Would that help you to love him or her *unconditionally*? The most important characteristic about each of us is that we need to be loved. That's also the second through tenth most important characteristic, and it's all you need to know as a wise man to love someone.

FINDING AND CREATING WISE MEN

We've established that in the process of becoming wise men ourselves, we need to find people to be wise men *for us*. We don't have to climb mountains to find them, as the Wart King did. Wise men are naturally and irresistibly drawn to the truth, and if we'll tell the truth about ourselves, we'll find wise men and women all around us. Of course, telling the truth requires faith on our part, because we simply can't know which people will accept us until we actually take the risk of telling people who we are. You can't win the lottery until you take the risk of parting with your money and buy a ticket.

Tell the Truth to Whom?

You can maximize your chances of finding a wise man by looking for people who feel loved, who see people clearly, and who are genuinely happy. Few people possess these qualities all the time, but we can look for people who demonstrate them enough that we can have some degree of confidence in their ability to accept us when we tell the truth.

An important quality for potential wise men is that they don't need you to make them happy. Now, it's true that we all need *someone* to love us—even many people—but a wise man recognizes that he or she does not have the right to require love from any one person, like you, or group of people. How do you know when people need you and will therefore be likely to use you instead of seeing you? It's usually easy. They use Getting Behaviors. To get Imitation Love, they attack, lie, act like victims, and cling. The following behaviors are just a few examples of people demonstrating a need to use you.

- When people express disappointment in the things you do, you *know* they have expectations and need you to make them happy.
- They regularly broadcast their virtues and accomplishments. People only do that when they need your praise.
- They have a strong need to be right, demonstrating a need for praise and power. They want you to be on their *side*.
- They're quick to give advice and want to know whether you followed it. They're also offended if you don't do as they suggest. They're enjoying Imitation Love in the form of praise and power.

People who behave in these ways are not bad, but they do *need* something from you, which makes them incapable of seeing you. Also keep in mind that when *you* demonstrate these behaviors, you're not capable of being a wise man for others.

Unfortunately, we do tend to seek unconditional acceptance from people who need us. For example, we may choose our spouses. It seems logical that we should be able to pour out our hearts to our spouses and expect them to see and accept us—after all, didn't we exchange vows to love each other more than anyone else? Yes, but if two people have not been sufficiently loved unconditionally, it doesn't matter what promises they've made to each other—they still don't have the Real Love their partner needs, and all their expectations to the contrary can lead only to disappointment and frustration. Spouses *can* be wise men for each other—a wonderful experience—but that is *sometimes* not possible in the beginning when they're both relatively empty and desperately need each other.

Similarly, it's tempting to tell our life's story to an employee or one of our children, because those people are convenient and already familiar with us. But those people *need* us, and that affects their ability to see us clearly.

What to Say—and When

Throughout *Real Love*, especially in Chapter Four in the section entitled "Telling the Truth About Yourself," I give examples of what you can say to find a wise man. I suggest you review them and practice them. It's not as important that you say the "right" words as it is that you persist in trying to share who you are, and you'll have many opportunities to do that. We're all commonly asked, for example, how we're doing. Instead of just saying, "Fine," describe a recent event where you later realized you were using Getting and Protecting Behaviors. You don't have to use those terms, but you can still describe how you were wrong in a situation. Certainly I don't recommend doing this with everyone who asks you how you are, but if you'll do it occasionally, you'll find people who are interested in the truth about you.

We don't share who we really are because we're afraid people won't like us, and then we'll feel unloved and alone. But as soon as we hide who we are, we *guarantee* that we'll feel unloved and alone. You really have nothing to lose by taking the tiny risk of telling the truth. Finding wise men can sometimes be difficult. It may take patience, but it's well worth the search. You're creating the opportunities to feel loved and change your life.

As we find wise men, we need to tell the truth about ourselves more frequently and more directly. After a lifetime of insufficient Real Love, we need more than an occasional experience with love before we can find the happiness we're looking for. If we don't feed our bodies every day, we become weak and can even die. There is no less urgency about feeding our souls. In the beginning we need to make contact with a wise man every day. Get in the habit of making regular phone calls and, even better, meet with wise men in person. That personal contact is far better than talking to a faceless voice on the phone. In our society we tend to depersonalize our interactions as much as possible, using the phone and the Internet.

Creating a Wise Man

You find wise men by telling the truth about yourself. You *create* them in the same way. When you are truthful at first, you won't know for certain whether people will unconditionally accept you. *They won't know, either.* Most of the people around you have no idea whether they're capable of being wise men. They find that out, and they practice their skills, only as people like you share the truth about themselves. Without your faith and courage, many people won't be given the opportunity to see, accept, and love others.

I've read many accounts of men who were decorated as heroes in battle. They did extraordinary things as they protected and rescued their comrades under the most dangerous and frightening conditions. In none of these cases do I recall these men being identified as heroes beforehand. They didn't *plan* to do something grand and brave. They just did what had to be done. A need arose, and they responded.

And that is how wise men are created. They come forward when there is a need. When you tell the truth, some people will respond with acceptance. We all have an inborn desire to love one another, and if in a given moment we're not empty and afraid, we will naturally accept and love people when they're telling the truth. As we all tell the truth about ourselves, we help one another develop our natural tendency to accept and love people.

Faith

There's a difference between *being* loved and *feeling* loved. We can be unconditionally loved on many occasions but never feel it if we don't exercise the faith to *accept* the love we're given. In Chapter Six we'll discuss this principle in greater detail.

Identifying—Not Capturing—a Wise Man

If you want to feel loved, you can only make the truth about yourself available and then wait to *learn* who is capable of loving you. You're simply creating *opportunities* for wise men to be attracted to you and love you. It never works to *get* a particular person to love you. If you're truthful with someone and *expect* him or her to accept you, your expectations will destroy any possibility of feeling loved by that person, because everything you get from him or her will feel like it was given only in response to your demands, not offered freely. In addition, you'll almost certainly do something to manipulate that person to like you, which again makes his or her response feel like Imitation Love.

The Gender of a Wise Man

If you feel sexual attraction toward people who are sharing themselves with you, you won't see them clearly. You'll see them as objects who can do something *for* you. Do not try to be a wise man for someone if you feel sexual attraction for him or her— with the exception of your spouse. Don't misunderstand, you can unconditionally love someone who happens to *be* sexually attractive, but not if you *feel* attracted to them in a sexual way. Considerable honesty is required to make that assessment.

For similar reasons, you must realize that someone who is sexually attractive to you cannot be a wise man for you. Even if that person actually offers Real Love, you'll receive it as sexual approval or attention, and you'll likely manipulate him or her to get those things.

The Changing Relationship with a Wise Man

Our relationship with a particular wise man will change from day to day, and over longer periods. Our first interactions with wise men are often fearful and tentative. With practice and positive experiences, we become more courageous and are able to tell the truth more boldly. As we first taste unconditional love from someone, it's not unusual to regard that person as a kind of parent.

That's natural, since the ability to love us unconditionally is the primary quality of an ideal parent. With time, as you feel more loved and confident, your relationship with a particular wise man will change. Eventually, there will be times when you'll feel more like a peer than a child. You'll feel loved enough to see and accept the wise man, and on those occasions *you* will be a wise man for him or her. That's how it's supposed to be. We learn from and practice on each other. Real wise men will welcome these changes. They won't want to keep you from growing.

On some occasions we'll have expectations of wise men that remain unfulfilled, and then we might feel disillusioned or resentful, because we didn't get what we wanted. Don't give up. Keep giving people the opportunity to see you and accept you, and it will pay off.

LEARNING TO BECOME A WISE MAN

A wise man does not become truthful, loved, loving, happy, and unafraid overnight. Remember what it was like to take your first few swings at a baseball? Or drive a car with a clutch for the first time? Or say your first few sentences in a foreign language? We learn to do all those things with *practice*, and that's also how we learn to see, accept, and love other people. The more we practice loving, the better we can do it. It's a gradual process, and in the beginning we're naturally pretty clumsy, as we are with most unfamiliar things. So we have a choice when faced with the unfamiliar: We can give up when the reward isn't immediately sufficient, or we can persist through the awkward moments until we become comfortable with our new abilities and experience the rewards that come with doing a worthwhile thing well.

Learning to see people and love them is not a process you have to suffer through while gritting your teeth. You can enjoy it if you accept the fact that you will make lots of mistakes. At times you'll become empty and afraid, and the Getting and Protecting Behaviors you use will have a negative effect on other people. That's unavoidable. You learn to love people only by interacting with them, and because learning involves making mistakes, you *will* inconvenience and hurt people as you learn. It's the price we all pay for living in a world where we make our own choices and learn from one another.

Being a wise man isn't something you campaign for or earn. On the other hand, it's not an accident, either. To become a wise man or woman, you must consciously tell the truth about yourself and feel loved by other wise men and women. As I've said, you can't give what you don't have. And you must make a conscious effort to practice seeing, accepting, and loving other people. You can't expect to become a wise man while you simply sit back and receive the love of others. Almost every person around you carries a degree of emptiness and fear. Virtually every time you interact with anyone, therefore, you have an opportunity to practice loving and being wise.

In the moments we feel loved, we're not blinded by emptiness and fear, and then we can be loving, but on some occasions we simply *forget* that we're loved. That might happen for no apparent reason, or it might be precipitated by emotional or physical stress—the anger of another person, for example, or our own exhaustion. Then we become empty and afraid again, and instead of being loving toward others, we protect ourselves and manipulate them for Imitation Love.

We don't need to feel guilty about the times we lose our ability to be wise men. We're just imperfect and learning. But we do need to *recognize* those times, so that instead of trying to help other people—at which times we tend to cause more damage with our Getting and Protecting Behaviors—we can tell the truth about ourselves and get the Real Love we need.

At times you may feel loved enough to respond lovingly to some people but not others. Some people are so critical and angry that you'll become empty and afraid and will react with Protecting Behaviors. You certainly can't function as a wise man when you're protecting yourself. Our capacity to feel loved and to love others will grow with experience and practice. Eventually, you'll be able to see, accept, and love people with greater frequency and for longer periods. You'll be capable of loving people in situations that would be impossible for you now. Don't waste time and energy feeling bad about the times you can't be loving. Just be honest about those times, learn from them, and do what it takes to get the love you need.

Also recognize that other people may function only intermittently as wise men for *you*. Don't look for someone capable of accepting and loving you all the time. Just as you'll make mistakes as you're learning to be a wise man, others will do likewise as they're learning.

Gerald learned about being an intermittent wise man as he interacted with John. One day John called Gerald to talk about some events in his life, and after a few moments Gerald said, "You know, I'm just not listening to you as well as you need. I have some other things on my mind, and I'm thinking more about those than you. Can we talk tomorrow?"

Gerald recognized that he couldn't always be a wise man, and he had the courage and integrity to express that. John didn't take it as a rejection. He chose instead to be grateful for the times Gerald *could* accept him, and he called back later. Intermittent Real Love is still Real Love, and you'll feel it if you have faith in it. At other times, Gerald did not recognize his inability to be loving, but John often did, and on those occasions John didn't push Gerald to give him what he needed.

Don't be in a great hurry to become a wise man. Sometimes you'll fall on your face and do a lousy job. Just recognize that you've fallen and get back up. All this takes time. Be patient. You can do it. Remember that wise men are ordinary people—butchers, bakers, candlestick makers—like you and I.

The Rewards of Being a Wise Man

Why should you want to be a wise man or woman and expose yourself to all these potential mistakes? If you have any inkling that it will put you in a superior position to anyone, or that people will admire you for being wise, give up the quest now. There are, however, two healthy rewards that come from pursuing the path of becoming a wise man:

- You'll feel a great deal more Real Love in your own life. First, the *preparation* for seeing, accepting, and loving other people requires that you feel more loved yourself. Second, as I've previously described, when you share with others the love from your bucket, you'll find that you have more than you started with.

- As you share Real Love with others, they can experience the same kind of joy you have. The benefit to them is obvious, but it will also bring great happiness to you. The joy of being loved is indescribable, but the joy of loving others is even greater.

THE IMITATION WISE MAN

The fear, anger, and loneliness we see all around us are ample and undeniable testimony of the relative absence of wise men in our midst. If wise men had embraced us with sufficient Real Love from the time we were children, we'd have no need for the Getting and Protecting Behaviors that now seriously interfere with our happiness. Where were the wise men we needed to see and love us? Where are they now?

We've certainly known plenty of people who have occupied the *position* of wise man in our lives—parents, teachers, counselors, ministers, public officials, doctors, lawyers, supervisors, and even friends. Whenever anyone is in a position to accept us and care about us, they occupy the position of wise man. But the position alone doesn't make anyone capable of actually *being* a wise man, which requires the ability to love. The people who occupied that position for most of us—the people we expected to love us—were not sufficiently loved unconditionally themselves, so they couldn't give us what they didn't have. No one intentionally withheld Real Love from us.

Unfortunately, people in caring positions rarely recognize their inability to be loving, so they continue to function in their positions while crippled by their own emptiness and fear. Instead of offering Real Love ("I care how *you* feel"), they're concerned about how other people make *them* feel. These people are imitation wise men.

Just as Real Love has its imitations, so does the real wise man. A real wise man sees other people clearly and cares about their happiness. An imitation wise man likes how other people make him feel, and he "loves" them more when they do what he wants. Instead of giving Real Love, an imitation wise man seeks Imitation Love. Using those criteria, how many of us can say we haven't qualified on countless occasions as imitation wise men? We don't do this intentionally—we're just filling our own emptiness and protecting ourselves from pain. That doesn't make us bad, but it does make us worthless as wise men. We can't see other people clearly while we're using them to fill our own needs.

How can you know whether you're being a real wise man or just an imitation of one? That can be difficult, because if you're empty and afraid, not only can you not see the needs of others, but you can't recognize the truth about your own behavior. We have a tendency to convince ourselves that we genuinely care about the happiness of others when we don't, because we know we *should* be loving, and we feel better about ourselves when we believe we are. It's easier to believe we have the good qualities we don't, then we don't have to make the effort to change.

This self-deception is a sticky problem indeed. Fortunately, there are two reliable signs that tell us we're not being unconditionally loving: *disappointment* and *anger*. I've heard a bushel of justifications for these two feelings, but we feel disappointed and angry only when things don't go *our* way, and that means at those times we can't be genuinely concerned for the happiness of other people. When you feel disappointed or angry, you're not permanently disqualified as a wise man, but *while* you're having those feelings, you simply can't be loving enough to see, accept, and unconditionally love others.

Another reliable indication that we're being selfish is the presence of any of the Getting and Protecting Behaviors. If we're lying, attacking, acting like victims, clinging, or running as we interact with someone, it's obvious that we're concerned about our own well-being and not the happiness of the other person.

Of course, even these signs of selfishness are helpful only if we're honest about them to some degree. You can still lie to yourself—consciously or not—about your disappointment and anger and all your Getting and Protecting Behaviors. I've seen people deny their anger while their voices were raised, their faces were red, and the veins in their necks were bulging. We must constantly examine ourselves for signs of selfishness, and a willingness to see them is a great start.

When we do identify that we're incapable of being wise men, we don't need to feel guilty. We just need to understand that we can't see other people clearly at those times. We need to step out of the way and not try to help anyone—we'll just make things worse. We can then get the Real Love we need ourselves and regain the ability to be loving.

Another way to identify our ineligibility as wise men is to recognize when we're using Imitation Love in its various forms— praise, power, pleasure, and safety. We use Imitation Love only when we're feeling unloved and empty, and at such times we are not capable of seeing, accepting, and loving other people. For the remainder of the chapter, we'll discuss how the use of Imitation Love interferes with our ability to function as wise men. The more familiar we are with these distractions, the better equipped we become to avoid them.

The Imitation Wise Man Seeks Praise

In the absence of sufficient Real Love, praise feels great. We get addicted to it, in fact. It's shallow and fleeting, but it feels a lot better than being ignored and alone. We love to hear positive things about ourselves—"You're beautiful." "You're so strong." "I wish I was as smart as you." "I couldn't have done this without you. Thank you."—and when we hear those words, we feel more worthwhile. Without thinking about it, we manipulate people to keep giving us the praise we want.

It should be obvious that we can't function as wise men when we're trying to manipulate people for praise and gratitude. We'll see this illustrated as we watch Mitch, a high school teacher.

Under Mitch's supervision are dozens of young people who sorely need to be seen and loved. Like most teenagers, they've been accepted only when they were "good," which has left them feeling empty and alone. They've responded as you might expect: they attempt to fill their lives with Imitation Love in the form of anger (power), sex, drugs, and the conditional approval of their peers.

Mitch has learned about Real Love and is trying to be a wise man to his students, but no matter what he does, almost every classroom experience is frustrating. He finally talks to me about it.

Mitch: "I just don't get it. I understand that they need me to see them and accept them—and I try to do that—but I don't get ten minutes into class before I want to hit one of them."

Me: "What's the problem?"

Mitch: "I'm not sure, but I know that I work real hard to prepare a great class, and they just don't . . ."

As soon as Mitch says "*they* don't," he's blaming his students for the problems he's having. We only blame people when they fail to meet our *expectations*, and invariably what we want most from them is their *love*. We may call it something else—respect, cooperation, gratitude, and so on—but it's still a form of "love" that we want. Of course, Mitch doesn't realize he has this blinding need. We rarely do.

Mitch has very little experience with Real Love, so the "love" he's looking for from his students is Imitation, and he communicates the kind of Imitation Love he wants when he talks about how hard he's worked to prepare for the class. I ask him about that: "They don't appreciate what you do for them, do they?"

"Well, no, they don't," he says. "They talk constantly, and they don't seem to pay attention to anything I say."

Me: Name the one person in the class who bothers you the most.

Mitch: Ricky. The kid never shuts up. He's always flapping his lips. He—

Me: I get the picture. And *why* does he do all that?

I would not have asked Mitch this question if he hadn't already read *Real Love*. After a long pause and a sigh, he says, "He does it because he doesn't feel loved, and getting any kind of attention is better than no attention at all. It's easy to forget about that when this kid is bothering me."

Me: "Ricky doesn't feel unconditionally loved by anybody—not at home, not at school, not anywhere. So he does whatever it takes to *buy* Imitation Love wherever he goes. He does it by being loud, brash, cool, whatever. When he acts like that, he gets the praise of his classmates and some sense of power. But what he really wants is someone to genuinely see him and accept him—even though he doesn't realize that's what he wants. Then you come along as his teacher, and what do you do?"

Mitch: I don't accept him, either.

Me: No, you don't. Even worse, you insist that this kid somehow communicate to you that you're doing a great job. You want him to praise you and make you feel in control, which gives you a sense of power. Those are both forms of Imitation Love you want in order to make *you* feel better. He senses that you want something from him. He needs a wise man, and you're being an *imitation* wise man. It's no wonder he doesn't want to listen to you. Make sense?

Mitch: It does now. I'm embarrassed.

Me: Oh, don't be embarrassed that you're learning something. You're *supposed* to make mistakes while you're learning. You just didn't feel loved enough to be able to see and accept Ricky or the rest of the class. As you get more Real Love for yourself, you'll be able to do that.

Mitch is visibly relieved. "So what can I do?" he asks. "Do I just let him talk during class and disrupt everything?"

"No. First, keep preparing those great lessons you give. And there are several teaching techniques we can talk about later—talking to him individually, natural consequences for his behavior, and so on—but what matters most now is that *you* get the love you need so you'll have something to give Ricky and the rest of the class. He *will* feel the difference as soon as you're not expecting something from him and you're not angry at him."

Mitch continues to tell the truth about himself to other men. He admits that he's been selfish with his students and more concerned about what he was getting than what he was giving. As he begins to feel more loved himself, he loses much of his need to be praised by his students. He talks to me about his recent experiences.

> Mitch: It's like I'm teaching a different class. They don't act the same at all. For days they've really been listening to me, and they're participating in discussions. I can't believe it. I thought they were stupid beyond hope, but now I see that the problems we've been having were really my fault all along.
>
> Me: You're feeling much happier—it's obvious just looking at you—and that's why you don't need the kids to give you something. What about Ricky?
>
> Mitch: The first time he said something rude, I knew he was just looking for attention, so I gave him the kind he needs instead of the kind he usually gets. I said I really wanted to know what *he* thought about the topic we were discussing. He said something kind of smart-mouthed, but I didn't quit. I pointed out the insights in what he'd said and thanked him for them. He quit being rude. Eventually he started to make real contributions.

Real Love feels so much better—and lasts much longer—than praise. During the moments we feel loved, we're not blinded by emptiness and fear, and then we can choose to see and accept other people.

Gratitude as Praise

When people first experience Real Love, they're often quite grateful to the wise men who help them discover that amazing feeling. When you are that wise man, you may hear words like, "I've never had anyone listen to me like this before. This feels incredible. I can't thank you enough." When you hear these expressions of gratitude, you may have a tendency to believe that you're pretty wonderful, and in those moments, you'll be swallowing a big dose of Imitation Love. Gratitude is natural, and even healthy on many occasions, but you can't see people clearly when you're flattered by it. You will have such times, but don't worry about it. Just recognize it, learn from it, and move on to the next experience, wiser and better prepared to be selfless and loving.

It's easier to resist the distraction of gratitude when we recognize that there are many factors that combine to determine whether a person learns and grows: their upbringing, their own choices, and other causes we know little about—genetics, for example. A wise man does not *cause* the change in anyone's life—he only provides an *opportunity* for change as he loves and teaches.

So what *can* you say when someone is effusively grateful to you for the love you've given them? Just say, "I'm happy for you." If you mean that, you're saying that your pleasure derives from *their* happiness, not from the gratitude you're being offered.

The Real Meaning of Praise

Praise is less distracting when we understand what it really means. When praise comes from someone who is unconditionally loving, it can be a useful piece of information about our performance—in school, our careers, and so on. But when it comes from people who don't feel unconditionally loved—which includes almost everyone—praise usually means this: "You've done something that makes *me* feel good." I'm certainly not saying there's anything wrong with enjoying how other people contribute to our happiness, but I am saying that when people who don't feel loved compliment us, they're not saying anything about *us* at all. They're praising us so we'll continue to behave in a way that makes *them* feel good.

Real wise men need to understand that *most* praise is just a reflection of the emptiness of those who give it. Eventually, wise men who are filled with Real Love receive praise and criticism with equal weight. They evaluate both, but they become neither excited by the former nor discouraged by the latter.

The Imitation Wise Man Seeks Power

When we feel empty and alone, we'll do almost anything to get a temporary feeling of connection to people that will eliminate the pain of our loneliness. If I can't have your genuine love, I *can* try to make you do what I want, and in that moment I'll feel a brief connection to you, however unhealthy it might be. I will also experience the rush of power that comes from holding you like a tool in my hand. When I command your obedience and fear, I briefly feel less alone in the world. It's a shallow and forced relationship, but without Real Love it can often seem far better than nothing at all.

I've met very few leaders who didn't have a need to control people, from which they get a sense of power. We see this need in many imitation wise men in our lives:

- We hope our supervisors at work will see us clearly, understand us, accept us, and help us. But instead they often use us to further their own power.
- Children of all ages desperately hope their parents will unconditionally accept and love them, but parents frequently exercise their awesome power in ways that make children feel controlled, not accepted.
- We look to leaders in our schools and in government for protection and understanding, but often we find that they're only interested in protecting themselves and using us to feel powerful.

The list is endless. At every turn, we hope to be accepted and loved by people in the position of wise man, but instead these people use their position to feel important themselves. They do this— almost always unintentionally—because power temporarily fills an emptiness created by the lack of Real Love in their lives. As these people fail to see, accept, and love the people who come to them for love and guidance, the world is largely deprived of loving leadership, and people everywhere stumble about in blindness and pain.

These imitation wise men who use power in unhealthy ways are not just a bunch of *other people*. *We* often do the same. Although we don't usually *intend* to control people, most of us still do it every day. We vigorously compete for advancement at work, not just for the benefits of increased income or career opportunities, but so we can be "in charge." We like to control other people, including our spouses and children. We prove how much we like to control the members of our family, for example, each time we act disappointed and irritated when they *don't* do things our way. When our desire is for power, we cannot love other people.

As you attempt to share your love with others, some people will eventually put their trust in you and place you in the position of wise man. That is a powerful assignment, and one you can easily abuse. Watch carefully for any tendency you might have to insist that people take your advice or otherwise do what you want. When people are literally frozen in place by indecision, I do occasionally give specific advice about *options* available to them. Many people can't see any of the wiser choices they could make, and they might benefit from a description of some of them. But I caution that wise men can easily come to enjoy the power of advising and guiding people. We need to beware of that pleasure and be slow to tell people what to do with their lives, other than to suggest that they tell the truth about themselves and find the love they need.

The Imitation Wise Man Seeks Safety

Without Real Love, we're in a constant state of emptiness and pain, and we're understandably afraid of anything that could add to our anguish. Of course, that means we're afraid of almost everything. Protecting ourselves is then quite natural, but as we engage in Protecting Behaviors, we're worthless as wise men. That doesn't make us bad human beings, but we can't clearly see and accept other people while we're concentrating on achieving safety for ourselves. When we realize that we're using Protecting Behaviors, we must tell the truth about it—at least to ourselves, and preferably to someone capable of loving us—and realize that in that moment we are not feeling loved enough to be wise men. We can see the effect of seeking safety as we watch Elaine and Joan.

Elaine is an angry woman. She heaps blame and criticism on everyone around her, and naturally they avoid her. One day, when she tells her friend Joan what's wrong with everyone on the planet, Joan says, "Elaine, you keep blaming everyone else for how you feel, but other people are not *making* you angry. How you feel and behave is a choice, and you'll be much happier when you realize that."

Elaine's eyes open wide as she says, "You're just like everybody else! You don't care about me, either."

Joan isn't prepared for Elaine's anger and says, "I'm only trying to help. You don't have to get angry at me!"

At this point, Joan completely loses her ability to be a wise woman. She's hurt and achieves her own safety by acting like a victim and getting angry. In the process of defending herself, she can't possibly be concerned primarily about Elaine's happiness, and then Elaine feels even more empty and afraid. Their conversation becomes an argument.

One way we protect ourselves and achieve safety is to insist on being right. We've been taught from infancy that when we're wrong, we're more likely to be criticized—and certainly less likely to be accepted and loved—so we cover up our mistakes and try to look good all the time. We claim to be right when we're not, and in the process we feel a little safer, but we make it impossible to feel loved ourselves and to care about the happiness of others.

Real safety comes from feeling loved and from loving other people. Wise men do not need to defend themselves. You will experience many occasions when people need to hear the truth even though they're resistant to it, and that will require faith and courage on your part. You won't be up to the task if you're concerned about their criticism, anger, or sometimes even their momentary discomfort. If you're afraid of what other people will say to you or think about you, you can't be a wise man in those moments. On some occasions you do need to refrain from speaking, but wise men determine those times according to what is effective, not in response to their own fears.

Chapter Summary

- Being a wise man is not a technique. We become wise men and women as we tell the truth about ourselves, feel loved, and make conscious decisions to love other people.
- When we feel enough Real Love to eliminate the blindness caused by emptiness and fear, we can see that other people use Getting and Protecting Behaviors only when they lack Real Love. When we understand that, we can love people, instead of reacting to them with our own Getting and Protecting Behaviors.
- Because people have to tell the truth about themselves to feel loved (Truth → Seen → Accepted → Loved), genuine loving often involves helping people be truthful.
- A wise man loves and teaches. The two functions are inseparable.
- We find wise men by telling the truth about ourselves and simply waiting to find those who can accept and love us. As we're truthful, we also help *create* wise men by giving them the opportunity to practice loving.
- As we're learning to be wise men, we will make many mistakes. The learning process requires time, faith, patience, and persistence.
- Although many of us occupy the *position* of wise man, we cannot actually *function* as wise men if we don't feel loved and cannot see, accept, and love others.
- Imitation wise men are not primarily concerned about the happiness of others, but are interested instead in the many forms of Imitation Love they can manipulate other people to give them. When we are empty or afraid or using Getting and Protecting Behaviors, we can only function as imitation wise men.

~ **Chapter Two** ~

The Crucible

Group Meetings

If you have a sincere interest in finding Real Love and learning how to share that love with others, your efforts will be far more successful if you intentionally associate as often as possible with people who have the same interest. When two or more people are consciously making an effort to tell the truth about themselves and be wise men for each other, I call them a group of wise men, or a group of wise men and women, or a loving group, or—more often—simply a *group*. A group is just a loose association of people with the common interest I've described. A group is not a place. You don't have to *join* a group; if you're deliberately involved in the process of giving and receiving Real Love, you're already in a group, whatever your numbers or location.

How do groups form? Let me describe a pattern common to most. One person reads *Real Love: The Truth About Finding Unconditional Love and Fulfilling Relationships*—or hears the principles of Real Love at a seminar or on a recording—and then she shares the truth about herself with several friends and discovers that one or more of them are interested in seeing and accepting her. They also want to share the truth about themselves. As these friends continue to talk about themselves and the principles of Real Love, they become a group. A group is not therapy. It's not a cult. It doesn't make arrogant claims to fix people. It's not exclusive, does not require loyalty or money from its members, and is not characterized by a formal organization.

Groups exist only to increase the opportunities of its members to be seen and loved. I need all the wise men I can get, and I love the time I spend in groups of loving men and women. For most people, a group becomes a loving family, healing the wounds of the past and changing their lives forever.

I refer to groups of *wise men* not because everyone in the group is loving—or *anyone* in the group, for that matter—but because these men and women are *consciously trying* to see and love others.

Throughout the book, I will give examples of men and women being seen and loved in groups. No formal setting or time is required for doing this. People can give and accept Real Love while talking on the phone, waiting for a bus, jogging in the park, standing in a supermarket line, sitting in a car on the way to work, and so on.

Once you find people interested in telling the truth and experiencing Real Love, you could allow loving experiences with them to just *happen*. Or you could actually *create* these experiences by arranging regular times and places to meet with these developing wise men. These planned gatherings are *group meetings*.

Although you can have loving experiences anywhere, in group meetings you can share who you are with more people in less time, and you learn more as you listen to the many experiences of others and watch the effect of Real Love in their lives. You also have more opportunities to accept and love other people. The effect of association with one wise man can be life-changing. Group meetings simply make it possible to multiply that effect. Again, although group meetings can be a powerful tool, they are not required in order to feel loved and happy. In your efforts to be a wise man, you can apply all the principles in this book in a loving group without attending a scheduled group meeting.

THE STRUCTURE OF GROUP MEETINGS

After attending hundreds of group meetings over the years, I've learned some elements of form and function that contribute to successful meetings, which we'll now discuss. You'll learn by your own experience, however, what works best for your meetings, and each group will have its own style.

Who Comes to a Group Meeting?

As you tell the truth about yourself, you'll attract those who are capable of seeing and accepting you, and who want to be seen and accepted themselves. When you're confident you've found such a person, you can invite him or her to a meeting. That's how meetings happen.

People don't exist for the purpose of attending meetings; meetings exist for the benefit of those who attend. For that reason, people should not feel obligated to attend meetings. Groups are bound together by a mutual interest in Real Love, not by duty. You should therefore feel free to go to meetings whenever you wish, not when other people want you to.

Some people who attend meetings appear to have no interest in telling the truth about themselves, and you may wonder whether they should continue to attend, as Robin did when she called me one evening.

> Robin: There's a woman in our group who just won't be honest about herself. What's the best way to ask her to leave?
>
> Me: Why would you want her to?
>
> Robin: The purpose of a group is to tell the truth about ourselves, isn't it?
>
> Me: Yes, and how does she interfere with *your* ability to do that? Remember the Law of Choice? This woman has a right to make her own choices. You can't control hers, only yours.

Robin: But she just sits there saying nothing, or she wastes everybody's time by lying about her Getting and Protecting Behaviors.

Me: You're thinking about *yourself* and how she inconveniences you, instead of thinking about how you can accept and love *her* while she's lying, resisting, or whatever. It's easy to accept people when they're doing what we want, but we don't really grow as wise men until we start accepting people when it's more difficult. In addition, she can't feel loved and safe if she feels like you're criticizing her—which you are. You can only give her an *opportunity* to tell the truth and feel loved, but instead you're *expecting* it, and she feels that. Your expectations are making *you* unhappy, too.

Robin: So what if she never does tell the truth, even if we accept her?

Me: Just keep sharing who *you* are. That will give her an example to follow. And when you feel sufficiently loving—and only then—you can begin to share what you think is true about *her*. If you tell the truth about her while you feel critical, she'll feel that and will only defend herself. As you tell the truth consistently—about you and about her—one of two things will almost certainly happen: either she'll feel more like being truthful, *or* she'll feel more and more uncomfortable in a truthful atmosphere and will choose to leave the group.

People who lie about themselves are the very ones who have the greatest need to come to a meeting. We need to accept and love them, not exclude them. There are *rare* occasions when it might be appropriate to ask someone to leave a meeting, such as when he or she is physically or verbally abusive.

Open or Closed Meetings?

In a closed meeting, no one attends without an invitation from other group members, while an open meeting may be attended by anyone. The primary purpose of making a meeting closed is safety.

I'm not saying that feeling safe is bad, but it's often achieved at the expense of learning and growing. Our principal objection to open meetings is the possibility of exposing ourselves to people we're not familiar with—people who might reject us, laugh at us, criticize us—but we grow only as we share who we are with other people, and the more the better.

Some people object to open meetings because they claim that when each person attends for the first time, everyone in the group has to explain his or her whole history to the newcomer. Not true. We can be seen and loved with whatever feelings and behavior we're experiencing in the moment. You don't need to know my entire past to see me well.

There are exceptions to my recommendation for open meetings. If you're new to the process of telling the truth and feeling loved, some of the people close to you can seem threatening. You have much greater expectations of your wife, for example, than you do of a stranger. So if your wife is in a meeting with you, you *might* be reluctant to tell the truth about yourself, because you'd be far more disappointed if she didn't accept you. We have more to lose with people close to us than with others, and we're often not willing to take risks with them.

For that reason, some people initially may not want to tell the truth about themselves with their spouse in the room—or their boss, or one of their children, or a co-worker. In those cases, I suggest you tell the partner (spouse, boss) to find another group meeting. Eventually, the people who intimidate us may be able to attend the same meeting, but only with mutual agreement. As we feel more loved, we eventually feel comfortable sharing the truth about ourselves with almost anyone.

How Many People Should Be in a Meeting?

In the beginning you may have meetings with only you and one other person. That can still be a powerful experience, but when more people attend, there is simply a greater statistical likelihood that one or more of them will feel loved enough to be a wise man when you speak. When there are too many people in a group, however, each person has less time to speak and be seen. You may also experience a loss of intimacy in a large group meeting. When the group gets large enough that people don't get a sufficient opportunity to speak in the time allotted, I suggest you split the group into two smaller ones. You'll figure out what works best for you.

Where Should You Meet?

I've seen meetings conducted in homes, apartments, auditoriums, offices, and outside under a tree. I suggest a few criteria for choosing a meeting place:

- Convenience. More people will come if the location is fairly central to the majority.
- Absence of interruptions. Homes and places of business can be great meeting places, but not if there's a likelihood of interruption from people not in the group. People find it hard enough to talk about themselves without worrying about when the next child, customer, or passerby will open the door.
- Cost. If at all possible, choose a place that can be used without cost. Don't let money get in the way of people having an opportunity to feel loved.

How Often Should You Meet?

The goal of these meetings is to create opportunities for us to feel loved and loving. How could we do that too often? I suggest that group meetings be held once a week.

How Long Should A Meeting Last?

If meetings are too short, people don't have enough time to speak and be seen. If meetings are too long, they become a burden. You'll come up with what's right for you, but most meetings I've attended lasted two hours.

Agree on a starting and stopping time and remember that running overtime is inconsiderate of people who have to be somewhere else. If people have more to say when the time arrives to end the meeting, they can get together later in the week or by phone.

Age

I've seen group meetings that included people from ages eighteen to eighty. You'll learn what's most effective for you.

Special Groups

Many support groups are focused on some common wound or problem: rape, alcoholism, abusive parents, and so on. I recommend that loving groups not have such a focus. Although we do need to discuss our wounds to some extent, emphasizing them tends to encourage us to feel and act like victims. Real Love is what we need most, and as we find it and share it, we enjoy the happiness we're really looking for, regardless of our old wounds. I'm not saying there's no place for special support groups, only that *groups of wise men* are more effective without such an emphasis.

HOW GROUP MEETINGS FUNCTION

No certifying organization will ever come around to approve your meetings, so you can do whatever you want with them. Some principles and guidelines, however, can contribute significantly to the success of your meetings.

The Purpose of Meetings

Group meetings exist to provide opportunities for people to tell the truth about themselves. In this book and in *Real Love* you'll find many examples of people doing that, in and out of meetings. You might consider these as possible models for your interactions in meetings.

Confusion About the Purpose of Group Meetings

When people are in pain, we have a natural—and mostly well-intentioned—desire to help them feel better. When people describe the unpleasant things others have done to them, for example, we're often tempted to temporarily relieve their pain by sympathizing with them or criticizing the people who have hurt them. But in order to feel unconditionally loved, people have to tell the truth about *themselves*—about their own emptiness, fear, and Getting and Protecting Behaviors, not just the injuries they've suffered—and that may require moments of *discomfort*. That takes courage and faith on their part—*and on yours* as you help them be truthful.

The primary goal of some support groups is safety. They're careful that no one's feelings are ever hurt, but, unfortunately, that means they often don't take the risks necessary for real change. People can't feel genuinely accepted by you until they stop denying their fear and anger and allow you to see who they really are. You have to take the risk that they might not like what you say, which means they might not like *you*. If you're only interested in their safety—and your own—they'll stay the same. Being safe often keeps us unloved and alone, and can therefore be deadly.

Remember that a wise man doesn't just tell the truth. He or she *loves* and teaches. As we help people tell the truth about themselves, compassion should never be neglected. But compassion is different from the sympathy we often give to victims. Any time people believe they've been the object of injustice or unkindness, they tend to act like victims to win the sympathy of those around them. Although some people *have been* genuinely injured—survivors of incest, parents of children killed by drunk drivers, rape victims, and so on—only misery can result from *acting like victims*. Victimhood is a virtual institution in this country. We've been taught that we *must* give sympathy to anyone who demands it. We support each other in the belief that victims are always justified in their anger and their claims of helplessness. But as we do that, we fail to recognize the power of choice, responsibility, truth, and love. We often cripple people by giving them sympathy, when their true need is for telling the truth about themselves and feeling the genuine compassion found in Real Love.

Confidentiality

In group meetings, people are sharing the intimate details of their lives, and they're doing it for the purpose of feeling seen, accepted, and loved. It would be unproductive and unkind for group members to share what they hear in a meeting with anyone who was not capable of being accepting and loving. For that reason, everything spoken in a meeting is confidential.

The Role of the Books, *Real Love* and *Real Love for Wise Men and Women*

In group meetings I have found these two books to be useful in several ways:

- For introduction. You know many people who could benefit from attending a group meeting, but if you invite them without some kind of preparation, they might not be interested—after all, they do have other demands on their time. They might even be threatened—what if this is some weird kind of therapy or cult? After they've read *Real Love*, however, many people will see the possible benefit of meeting with people interested in those principles.
- For orientation. When people are new to a group, they're often confused by the new principles and language. After reading one or both of the books, most people feel much more comfortable.
- For direction. Many people have difficulty starting the process of telling the truth about themselves, but as they read examples of truth-telling in the books, they have a better idea of what the truth looks like and can often summon the courage to share examples from their own lives. The books will also help you see how you might respond to these people.

Never feel obligated to do anything the way I suggest. It's your group, your meeting, and your life. People need to feel loved, and books can't do that. You'll come up with ways to love people that will work best for you.

Who Leads the Group?

Countless conflicts have begun with more than one person wanting to be the leader of an organization, and they've often resulted in the destruction of social groups, families, businesses, and even countries. Most men and women want to lead so they can look good, control people, be praised, be right, and be powerful. People compete with frightening intensity to be president of the country club, chairman of the parent-teacher association, and so on, all to win Imitation Love in the form of praise and power.

Groups of wise men are formed for the purpose of telling the truth and sharing unconditional love, and that answers the question, "Who leads?" A group doesn't need a boss, only wise men and women, and they're not appointed, formally educated, graduated, or elected. They simply develop with experience. Whoever can see, accept, and love another person in the group in a given moment is a wise man, and that has little to do with age, time in the group, education, or title. Every person in a meeting may be a wise man, or there may be only one, or none.

If you're eager to lead a group, that usually means you want something for yourself—to be seen by others as wise and good, or to be in control. If you have a need for praise and power, you'll focus on your own needs and will not be able to see or accept others.

Occasionally, people who don't understand the purpose of a group will attempt to present themselves as much wiser than they are. They may offer excessive advice, try to control the flow of the meeting, and otherwise attempt to get praise and power. Such people are imitation wise men, as described in Chapter One. Don't be impatient or angry with them. Continue to tell the truth about *yourself* and learn to be loving. When you're feeling accepting, you might suggest that the imitation wise man consider the possibility that he or she is controlling people and looking for Imitation Love. Truly loving people—real wise men—will eventually become obvious, and imitation wise men will be apparent by contrast.

How to Begin a Meeting—The Check-In

Most people can tell the truth quite well once they get started, but they may need help making the initial moves. To facilitate that, you can use a simple *check-in*, where people start the meeting by saying how they feel in that moment, or how they've felt during the past week. Following are a few examples of what you might say:

- "I'm Mike. This is my first group meeting, and I feel nervous."
- "I'm excited to talk about what I've learned this week. I've had some very positive, loving experiences."
- "Michelle. I've been angry all week, but right now I mostly feel afraid, because I know I'll be talking about myself later in the meeting."
- "I'm a little anxious, but I'm also happy to be here with people who can see me."
- "I'm Mary. I don't know how I feel. Maybe confused. I'm not exactly sure why I'm here. Maybe I'm looking for something different."

The check-in takes less than a minute per person and creates an opportunity for everyone to be seen for a moment. No one is obligated to speak during a check-in, and there's no rigid format for it. If everyone in the meeting knows one another, for example, there's no need for anyone to say his or her name.

The Body of the Meeting—Telling the Truth

After the check-in, people tell the truth about themselves and begin the process of feeling accepted and loved. As one person— the speaker—tells the truth about himself or herself, everyone else becomes a listener and remembers the Rules of Seeing from Chapter Four of *Real Love*. Throughout that book, and in this one, I discuss many examples of what people can say about themselves.

Certainly no one ever has to speak in a group meeting, but if they don't, they'll miss out on powerful opportunities to feel accepted and loved. Sometimes we can help them begin the process, as a wise man does here in a group meeting with Seth.

Although Seth is attending his fourth meeting, he's now speaking for the first time, during the check-in. "I'm Seth," he says. "I guess I feel a little anxious. It's been a hard week."

After everyone checks in, several people talk about themselves. An hour into the meeting, Seth still hasn't spoken, so a wise man finally says, "Seth, during the check-in, you said you were anxious. You don't have to talk about that if you don't want, but if you do, you'll give people a chance to see you."

Seth: I'm not sure.

Wise man: Again, it's up to you, but isn't that why you're here?

Seth: (pause) I guess it is—okay.

Wise man: You said you had a hard week. What happened?

Seth begins to describe how several people were inconsiderate of him in the past several days. Rather than offer him the sympathy he's seeking, two men in the group help Seth see the real cause of his anger. He tells the truth about his Getting and Protecting Behaviors and has a wonderful experience as he feels the acceptance of group members.

People can sit and say nothing in group meetings for as long as they want, but from time to time, loving wise men will give them an opportunity to speak. On some occasions, part or all of the meeting might be devoted to doing the exercises in Chapter Eleven, which are designed to help people tell the truth about themselves and feel seen.

The Truth About Interactions Within the Group

In group meetings, we tend to talk about the Getting and Protecting Behaviors we use with people *outside* the meeting, but it can also be quite useful to talk about our feelings and behavior toward people *in* the meeting. Imagine, for example, that you're attending a group meeting, and you decide to tell a man in the meeting about the anger you feel toward him. You're anxious, because in the past you've experienced almost uniformly negative results from doing this—or you've hidden your feelings entirely.

Here in the group, however, you've all declared with your attendance that you want to learn how to feel loved and loving, so it's much more likely that this man will understand that your anger is a reaction to your own longstanding fears and has little to do with anything he's done—even though he may indeed have made a mistake. With that understanding he can refrain from defending himself and instead can offer you the acceptance and love you need. It feels especially wonderful to be accepted and loved by someone *while* you're angry at him or her—a welcome change from the reactions we usually get.

There is a possibility that this man won't feel loved or loving enough to accept you in the moment you share your anger, but there will almost certainly be other wise men in the group who *can* accept and love you. Real Love from any source is healing and gratifying.

When People Monopolize Meeting Time

Some people have a tendency to talk on and on, taking up a disproportionate segment of the time allotted for a meeting. Certainly we need to genuinely listen to anyone as he or she speaks, but long monologues are rarely useful to anyone. Most people talk excessively only when they're convincing you of something—that they've been injured, that they're right, that they're worth accepting, or combinations thereof. When they do that—instead of telling the truth about their emptiness, fear, and Getting and Protecting Behaviors—they can't feel love from you, even if you offer it. On those occasions, you might ask them questions that give them an opportunity to see the truth. If that's unsuccessful, you could actually tell them what you see. With either approach, most people will then either tell the truth about themselves or be quiet.

When someone is new to the group, he or she might require more time than most people, but you don't have to learn everything about a person's life to understand a great deal about them. Help him or her focus on the truths that are most important, and your meetings will be more effective.

Socializing

In some group meetings, considerable time is occupied by light conversations about jobs, football, shopping, articles in the newspaper, and so on. This often happens because people are unconsciously avoiding more difficult, even frightening, subjects: their emptiness, fear, and Getting and Protecting Behaviors. There's nothing wrong with light conversation—it's a source of considerable pleasure in our lives—but you can have these conversations anywhere. I'm not suggesting that group meetings are formal, serious affairs, but they are a special opportunity to do something different and life-changing. We often detract from the higher goal when we use valuable meeting time to have the same conversations we've always had.

Ending the Meeting—The Check-Out

The meeting closes with a check-out, which is much like the check-in. Each person briefly—less than 30 seconds—says how he or she feels at the close of the meeting. Some examples:

- "I had a lot of things to do tonight, so I wasn't going to come. But I'm glad I did—I'm feeling less alone and more peaceful than I did before I got here."
- "I'm still angry at my wife, but it's less now than when we started the meeting. I'm glad I talked about it. You all helped me understand better that it's not her fault."

No one has to participate in the check-out–nor are you required to have one at all. It's just another opportunity for everyone to feel seen.

A School for Wise Men

You won't learn how to be a wise man from a book. You'll learn from experience. Meetings are a great opportunity to practice the principles you're learning. Make use of them. After any interaction between a speaker and a wise man, ask questions if you wonder why something was said or done. We can learn a great deal as we see other people tell the truth and get accepted. We also learn as we see others use Getting and Protecting Behaviors. We're all remarkably similar and have much to teach one another.

Don't be afraid of making mistakes. You don't have to be perfect while trying to see and love people. Sometimes you'll say something as a wise man that appears to have no positive effect whatever on the person you're trying to see and accept. He or she may even react badly and become more afraid or angry. Perhaps you weren't feeling as loved and loving as you'd thought. Or you *were* loving and the other person simply wasn't in a position to accept what you said. Or a little of both. You'll make a lot of mistakes. Learn from them.

After the Meeting—Phone Calls and Other Contacts

Most of us have been feeling unloved and alone—to varying degrees—for a lifetime. After all those years of unloving experiences, we've generated a considerable momentum taking us away from the happiness we want. We've become like supertankers moving swiftly through the water in the wrong direction. Changing the direction of such a large ship requires miles of ocean and a great deal of energy. Similarly, our lives often change significantly only after persistent effort and long periods of consistently positive experiences.

Once-a-week group meetings alone are rarely enough to turn our supertankers around. We need more opportunities than that to accept and give the Real Love we need. Effective groups create lists of the phone numbers and e-mail addresses of all the members— with their permission, of course. The people on this list become an extended family, a lifeline, to one another. Whenever people feel afraid, angry, lost, or alone, they simply call someone from the group and talk about their feelings or behavior. Or they arrange to meet in person with other members. As they feel accepted, *their feelings change.* It really is that simple. The more loving experiences you have with others, the greater the change you will feel in your life. Real Love leads to genuine happiness, and we find that love by creating interactions with loving people.

In the beginning of my own process of feeling loved, I made a lot of phone calls to members of the group—sometimes three or four *every day*. Without those positive experiences, I often went back to using Getting and Protecting Behaviors. Even though these calls and other contacts are necessary and hugely beneficial, they can be difficult in the beginning. Most of us—especially men— are not accustomed to reaching out and sharing our feelings and behavior with others. Initially I was nervous about making these calls. It was embarrassing—here I was a middle-aged man who couldn't begin a truthful conversation with another human being. Like a frightened teenager arranging his first date, I sometimes sat at my desk punching in the first few digits of a phone number five times or more before I had the courage to actually complete the call. I was terrified that someone would communicate that he or she didn't have time to talk to me, which might imply that I wasn't worth talking to. I was afraid that when I said who I was, the person on the other end would say, "Greg *who?*" which would prove that I wasn't worth remembering. Most of us have similar fears. But I made the calls, and it was well worth it.

I also didn't know exactly what to say when I called. What I really needed to say, but couldn't, was this: "I'm empty and afraid. I need you to love me." That's what most people need to say, but they don't have either the courage or the insight to do that.

So what *can* you say when you call someone from the group for the first time? How do you get the love you need? Keep it simple and follow some of the guidelines and examples in this book and in *Real Love*—but *make the call*. You can't increase your feelings of acceptance and love while you sit alone in your house. Remember that you're calling someone who's a member of a group of wise men. They know what it's like to make a call like this. They know you're nervous.

Make the call and say, "Hello, this is _____. I'm calling because, well, I don't know why exactly, but I heard it was a good thing to do. I don't really know what to say." People in a group who have any experience telling the truth will know how to help you. They'll ask how you're feeling and what you've been learning. They might ask you to talk about any experiences you've had lately with being angry or afraid. And with a little time and experience, other people in the group will be calling *you* to be seen and accepted.

Sometimes phone calls—and other contacts—are easier if you ask in a meeting whether anyone has experience with these calls. You could also ask who has the time to take your calls or meet with you, and you could go a step farther and arrange the day(s) and time(s) you'll be calling or meeting with people.

You'll have a lot to talk about. People in the group will accept you and love you, and *that's* what you really want. These experiences with loving men and women will change your life. Have as many of them as you can. You eat every day. Have love interactions with wise men and women every day, too.

The Ups and Downs of Group Meetings

In the beginning you may have only two people attending a meeting. As you tell the truth about yourself to more people, and as they see your happiness, you'll attract more people. Some groups form easily. You may know a dozen people who have just read *Real Love* or attended a seminar on the subject. You'll all arrange to meet weekly at someone's home, and the group will flourish for years, even divide as others join in.

But many group meetings don't happen that easily, because even though most people don't feel loved or genuinely happy much of the time, they're *accustomed* to it and tend to resist doing anything different—like a group meeting—where they could look stupid, be hurt, or just waste their time. You may know many people who could benefit greatly from being with wise men and women, but remember that fear is a powerful motivation, one that often prevents us from doing things that would help us.

Genuinely changing our lives takes time and effort, and many people lose interest in anything that doesn't offer a quick fix. Most of us want a cute technique that will give us instant happiness. We want to take a pill and wake up happy. Even when indescribable rewards are available, we're not willing to make the consistent effort required, so you will see many people come and go in these meetings. People will commit to attend but will not show up. Sometimes you might be the only person there. Do not get discouraged. Starting something new requires faith, persistence, and courage. In the beginning of my own experiences with meetings, I simply reminded myself that I was not willing to settle for the same level of happiness I'd known in the past. I made a commitment to do whatever it took to create the life-giving experiences that come from receiving and giving Real Love. A similar commitment on your part will yield profound results.

Chapter Summary

- A group consists of two or more people who are consciously making an effort to tell the truth about themselves, find Real Love, and share that love with each other.
- When people in a group practice being loved and loving at a regular time and place, that is a group meeting.
- We need to interact with group members as often as possible—in meetings and outside them.
- Meetings are generally held weekly and last two hours. They are led by wise men—those who are capable of seeing and accepting other people at the meeting. Meetings can include any number of people, can be held at any location, and generally include members of all ages.

∾ Chapter Three ∾

The Foundation of Wisdom

The Laws of Choice and Responsibility

Diane is complaining angrily about her husband, Ken, saying that whenever she doesn't do what he wants, he becomes impatient and irritated. "He's angry all the time," she says, "and he talks to me like I'm some kind of servant. He wouldn't talk to anybody else in that tone of voice."

"He has the right to do that," I reply.

If eyes could flash real fire, I'd be toast.

Diane: You're saying it's *all right* for him to talk to me like that?

Me: Not at all. I didn't say his behavior was *acceptable*. I said he has the *right* to make his own choices.

Diane: I can't believe you're saying this. Nobody has the right to act like that.

Me: So if you could, you'd make him stop, right?

Diane: Yes.

Me: That's understandable, but where would that end? If *you* can stop people when they're doing something you don't like, shouldn't the rest of us have the same power?

Diane: (pause) I guess so.

Me: And how would you like it if everyone around you could control you whenever you did something they didn't like?

Diane: (frowning) I wouldn't. I never thought about it like that.

Me: Most of us don't think about the consequences of controlling people. When you're in pain, all you can think about is getting rid of *your* pain, and if other people won't help you, you feel justified in trying to *make* them. But people really do get to make their own choices—even when you don't like them. That's the Law of Choice. The alternative is unthinkable: The whole world would become a stage of puppets controlling each other, and ultimately who would be in charge of all that controlling?

We must not interfere with the right other people have to make their own choices, nor should we give up our own right to choose—either to others, or to fate. The power of making choices is illustrated in the poem, Winds of Fate, by Ella Wheeler Wilcox:

One ship drives east and another drives west
With the selfsame winds that blow.
'Tis the set of the sails
And not the gales
Which tell us the way to go.
Like the winds of the sea are the ways of fate,
As we voyage along through life:
'Tis the set of a soul
That decides its goal,
And not the calm or the strife.
Ella Wilcox

Our choices determine who we are. The Law of Choice is the foundation of happiness and human relationships. Without it, our existence would be meaningless. We'd become unthinking lumps of clay in the hands of those who controlled us. From the Law of Choice spring the principles that will help you find happiness and share it with others. In this chapter, we'll talk about these principles, as follows:

- The nature of relationships
- The choices we can make in any situation or relationship
- The Law of Expectations
- We always have the right to make our own choices.
- A new understanding of fairness
- How our behavior often can be explained by a failure to understand the Law of Choice
- How our choices are affected by past experience
- Other people never make us angry.
- How loving is the natural result of understanding the Law of Choice
- We are responsible for our choices.

THE NATURE OF RELATIONSHIPS

A relationship is the natural result of people making independent choices. Diane wanted to control Ken's choices in order to make her life more convenient, but the instant she tried to stop him from making independent choices, she no longer had a relationship with *Ken*. She could only have a relationship with a puppet being controlled by herself. Ken—as he really was—disappeared, and she became *alone*.

Most of us do what Diane did. We've been trying to control people for so long, we no longer even recognize that we do it. We use praise, subtle hints, persuasion, money, power, and sex to get our spouses, children, co-workers, and others to give us the love, attention, obedience, and praise we want. But the instant we modify the behavior of others to *get* what we want, they're not making independent decisions anymore. We've made them into objects we control, and then we're alone.

We can only have fulfilling relationships as we understand the Law of Choice. We must allow people to make their own choices— including the ones we don't like. Most relationships suffer because one or both partners want to control the other. (I define a partner as anyone with whom we interact, however briefly.)

We often don't realize we're trying to control other people, but that's what we're doing whenever we try to *get* something from them. As a wise man, you need to recognize that the word *getting* is an unconscious code for the word *controlling*, which always plays a role in unhappy relationships. When two people understand and respect the Law of Choice, they accept each other's choices and find that a loving relationship follows with relative ease. When you really accept your partners' right to choose, why would you ever get angry—or act like a victim, or withdraw—when they make any decision?

THE CHOICES WE CAN MAKE IN ANY SITUATION OR RELATIONSHIP

Diane and I continue our conversation from above until she understands that she really doesn't have the right to control her husband. She sees that when she tries to do that, their relationship always suffers.

Diane: So what *can* I do? I *hate* it when he talks to me like that.

Me: After you give up the right to change him, there are only three choices to be made: You can live with him and like it, live with him and hate it, or leave him. Do you see another choice?

Diane: (pause) Not really, no.

Me: So let's go through the choices one at a time. Do you want to leave your husband?

Diane: Sometimes.

Me: (laughing) I understand that feeling, but make a choice. Do you choose to leave him?

Diane: I'm not sure.

Me: If you leave Ken now, what have you got? Nothing—no relationship. And what have you learned? Nothing. If you leave this relationship without learning how to be loving, you're virtually certain to have the same problems in the next one.

Diane: I see what you mean.

Me: We can always come back to the possibility of you leaving Ken, but for now let's move on to the other two choices. First, "live with him and hate it." You *could* stay in your marriage just like it is and hate every minute of it for the rest of your life.

Diane: I don't think I want to do that.

Me: Living with him and hating it would be like choosing to sit in a messy diaper and complaining about it—pretty stupid. But lots of people live in relationships like that. They can't change their partners, so they stay with them and resent them. Doesn't that actually describe what you're doing with Ken most of the time?

Diane: I guess so. That diaper picture isn't pretty, but it's true.

Me: So what's the third choice? You could live with him and learn to *like* it. You could learn to have a completely different kind of relationship, one you can enjoy.

Diane: And how can I do that?

Me: It's not complicated. Your marriage is missing only one thing—the one thing people want most in all the world—unconditional love. When you have that, you'll be happy.

I explain to Diane what Real Love is, and how people behave when they don't have enough of it.

Me: Before you were married, neither of you had enough Real Love to be genuinely happy. When you got married, you both expected that your partner would make you happy, but neither of you had what the other needed most. You were virtually doomed before you started.

Diane: This is a lot to think about, but it does seem to explain things about our relationship that have been confusing me for a long time. So what can I do now? I'm not sure I've ever felt Real Love. Part of me isn't sure it even exists.

Me: I've seen Real Love many times, and I've seen it change the lives of hundreds of people like yourself. If you're willing to learn, you can find it. What have you got to lose? You certainly don't like what you have now.

People usually want to control their partners. They prove that with their disappointment and anger. As a wise man, you first need to teach them that *they do not have that choice* and that they cannot be happy while they try to make it. Teach them the Law of Choice, and help them see that one of three choices available to them—live with it and hate it—is always stupid. It guarantees unhappiness every time. When people whine and complain about their partners, they're making this choice.

Leaving the relationship *is* occasionally the right choice, but rarely in the beginning and only as a last resort in a marriage. How can we justify leaving a relationship before we've acquired the one thing that's necessary to make the relationship succeed? In almost every case the best choice is to live with it and like it. When we do that, we create the opportunity to feel loved and to unconditionally love our partners. We make it possible to find the happiness we've been looking for all our lives. Shortly we'll talk about choices we can make *within* the choice of living with it and liking it.

When people tell you they're determined to leave a relationship, they're just saying they're afraid and don't know another way out of their pain. They don't know that unconditional love is the only way to genuinely eliminate the pain of emptiness and fear. As a wise man, you are *not* there to tell people whether to leave a relationship or stay in it, only to do what wise men always do: Love people and tell them the truth. Help them see that when they find Real Love, they'll have the one ingredient that will make them happy and infuse life into all their relationships.

THE LAW OF EXPECTATIONS

It's clear that we're controlling people if we chain them hand and foot, put a ring in their nose, and lead them around as we wish. We know *that's* wrong, but most of us use a more subtle way of controlling people, and we use it every day. We control them with our *expectations*.

What happens when people don't do exactly what we want? We sigh and change our facial expression, tone of voice, and body language to communicate that we're disappointed in their performance. We saw this pattern of expectations, disappointment, and manipulation from the time we were very young. When we failed to meet the demands of our parents, teachers, friends, and others, they often used their expressions of disappointment as a way to change our behavior. That was usually unconscious, but they still knew that often we would do what they wanted in order to avoid their disapproval. Now *we* use the same unconscious manipulation with others when our own expectations are not met. We use anger in a similar way. If I express irritation at you for the way you're acting, I know that your fear of my disapproval may motivate you to behave in the way I expect.

When I expect you to change your behavior for my convenience, I'm demanding that you change who you are to make me happy. I'm arrogantly expecting you to sacrifice *your* happiness for *mine*. But I never have the right to expect you to do anything for me, nor do you have the right to expect me to do anything for you. That is the Law of Expectations, which naturally follows the Law of Choice. When I accept that you have the right to make your own choices, how could I ever expect that you would give up that right to do what I want?

Promises—An Exception to the Law of Choice

I've categorically stated that we *never* have the right to expectations only because I want to emphasize how devastating expectations are to relationships. There is an exception, however, to the Law of Expectations—a promise. The expectations associated with promises can actually be quite productive. Imagine, for example, that you're planning a picnic with several friends, and you ask each of them to bring a single dish in sufficient quantity to feed everyone. They all agree, so now you have a right to expect that they'll do as they've promised. Without that expectation, you'd have to bring enough of all the dishes for everyone, which could result in needless duplication of effort and resources. Or you could just throw the dice and hope for the best, but in that case you have the potential for some dishes not arriving. You might, for example, have hot dogs show up but no mustard and relish—a crime by any standard.

So expectations can actually be beneficial when associated with promises. Regrettably, however, most of us have enormous expectations of other people even when we have no promise from them. We expect people, for example, to make our lives convenient all the time, and we prove that every time we become disappointed or irritated when they don't do what we want—when our spouses aren't attentive, our children are slow to obey us, or other drivers on the road fail to realize that we're far more important than they are.

Some expectations are wrong even when a promise is made. A spouse, for example, may say, "But when we got married, part of the agreement was that my partner would love me. In fact, he/she promised me right there in front of God and everybody." Although in many circumstances expectations are justifiable when promises are made, we never have the right to expect other people to *love* us or make us happy, *even when they promise to do so.* Unconditional love can only be *freely* given and received. When we *expect* love, we ruin the possibility that we can feel unconditionally accepted or happy.

We can experience Real Love only when we tell the truth about ourselves and wait for *someone*—perhaps many people—to unconditionally accept and love us. That *will* happen, but we don't get to choose *who* that person—or people—will be. We need to identify our expectations that specific people love us, and we can do that by recognizing our disappointment and anger. Almost without exception, these two feelings are signs that we're expecting but not getting the Real or Imitation Love we want from a particular person. Of course, these expectations are usually unconscious, but they're still quite intense, and the subsequent disappointment and anger are very real.

When we can identify our unreasonable expectations that specific people love us, we can quit making destructive demands and begin to focus on telling the truth about ourselves. We can allow people to love us unconditionally when they wish, and then whatever acceptance we're offered is real, which feels wonderful.

I can further illustrate healthy and unhealthy expectations as I introduce you to Adam and Samantha, who have been married for twelve years, have two children, and both work outside the home.

Because Adam works full time and Samantha part time, they've agreed that she will have a meal prepared (or brought in) each evening and will also do the housekeeping. On many occasions, when Samantha fails to have the food prepared, or when the house is a mess, Adam says something unkind, and then she gets irritated about it.

Does Adam have a right to expect Samantha to fix meals and clean the house? Yes, because she agreed—promised—to perform those tasks. She agreed mostly in order to avoid Adam's disapproval, but she still agreed, and Adam therefore has a right to his expectations about the completion of those tasks.

Adam is making two mistakes here: First, he is disappointed and angry, which is always wrong, as I discuss in *Real Love* and again later in this chapter. Second, he not only expected her to do her work but also to make him *happy*. Every time we become disappointed or angry with people, we're declaring our expectation that they will add to our happiness in some way, or at least not detract from it. Even though we may reasonably have expectations that our partner accomplish certain tasks, we cannot expect him or her to make us happy. After childhood, no one has the right to that expectation.

You might object, Is Samantha stuck forever with doing everything around the house? Is that fair? Samantha can certainly change her mind at any time. She's not a slave, nor has the Law of Choice been repealed here. But if Samantha is unhappy, she needs to talk to Adam about changing their agreement. Mind you, she does not need his *permission* to change it. She just needs to tell him if she's unwilling to continue fulfilling her original promise.

Healthy Promises and Expectations

In the case of a promise—other than for love or happiness—you are entitled to your expectations, but *having* an expectation and *demanding* that it be filled are quite different. Let me illustrate this concept with an activity most of us do every day: driving a car. Imagine that you pull up to a four-way stop at exactly the same moment that another driver pulls up to his sign on the road to your left. In every state I'm aware of, you have the *right of way* because you're on the *right* side of the other driver. You therefore have the *right* to expect that the other driver will remain stopped while you drive through the intersection. He's made a promise to that effect by accepting his driver's license, which requires compliance with all the driving rules of the state.

But just as you edge out into the intersection, the other driver also moves forward. You could insist on your *right* to proceed, but if you do that, you could be *dead* right. Being right about your expectations in relationships is similarly unproductive. You may be right, but if you insist on it, you won't like the results.

If you promise to meet me for lunch at 12:30, I can reasonably expect you to do that. After all, without that expectation I probably wouldn't show up. My *having* this expectation is healthy. If I become disappointed or angry, however, when you fail to appear at the appointed time, I am *demanding* that you keep your promise, and that never leads to happiness. Most of us have been demanding that other people keep their promises for so long, we don't realize that it's even possible to have an expectation without also making a demand. When people don't do as they've promised, we feel entirely justified as we indignantly declare, "But you promised!" Our anger proves that we're making an unreasonable demand instead of having a reasonable expectation.

A major reason to avoid expectations is that there is no gratitude in expectations. Imagine that you expect me to bring you a dozen roses every morning at 9:00. On the first morning I bring you a dozen roses at 9:05, but you're disappointed and angry, because you expected me to arrive at 9:00. You wonder why I don't care enough about you to do as you've asked. The next day I arrive at 8:55, but that's no good, either, because I've interrupted your day by arriving too early. The day after that I arrive at exactly 9:00 but with eleven flowers, so you have a fit that I haven't brought a dozen. Although I'm giving you a lot, you can't be truly grateful for what you're getting because of your expectations, and then you can't enjoy it. Without gratitude, everything we have becomes meaningless and can't contribute to our happiness.

Notice that I didn't say anything about you being grateful *to me*. You don't need to be grateful to me or anyone else in particular in order to be happy. Real joy comes from being grateful *for* what you receive, not from being grateful *to me*. In fact, if there's too much *me* in your gratitude, you'll only feel *obligated* to me, and that won't make you happy. I would only insist on you being grateful to me if I had some need for praise and power myself.

In a successful relationship, expectations always occur in an atmosphere of Real Love. If you unconditionally care about the happiness of your partner, you can still expect the promised performance of a task, but enforcing the letter of the law will never be more important to you than feeling and sharing love. And if you're focused on the happiness of others, they will actually tend to fill their promises with greater faithfulness, much better than if you make demands of them.

Requests

When I talk about the importance of the Law of Choice and the negative consequences of demands, someone invariably asks, "What about *me*? If I don't tell people what I expect—in fact, with most people, if I don't *demand* what I want—I won't get anything at all. Are you telling me I have to be satisfied with nothing, or just take whatever they volunteer to give?" Not at all. You can respect the right people have to make their own choices but still *ask* them to do what you want. When you ask for what you want, you're making a powerful choice within the larger decision to live with it and like it. We can see the effect of requests as I talk again with Adam and Samantha about their household responsibilities.

Samantha says she wants to change the arrangement they have, but Adam likes things the way they are. "So what am I supposed to do now?" she asks. "I don't want to keep doing all the work, but he won't help me do any of it."

> Adam: I work full time and you don't. You can't expect me to come home and help you with things when you've had all day to do them.

Samantha: You seem to forget that I do work part time, and you only get home three or four hours later than I do. In that time I have to cook, clean, pick up kids, and do all the shopping and other errands—including *your* errands, by the way. Sometimes I need help.

Me: Samantha, you can't make him do anything—you've proven that, haven't you?—but you can make a *request* for what you want.

Samantha: A *request*? You've got to be kidding! I've asked him a hundred times now to help me, and he's never done a thing.

Me: You're not making *requests*. When he doesn't do what you ask, you get angry. That proves you're making a *demand*, not a request. You don't have the right to control anyone to do anything, remember? That's the Law of Choice. Adam, do you feel like Samantha is demanding that you help her?

Adam: Duh.

Me: And it's obviously not working. In fact, it's hurting your relationship. So I suggest, Samantha, that you try making a real request. You could say, for example, "Adam, in the few hours I have before you get home, I'm having a hard time doing all the housework, the cooking, and the errands. I'm feeling stressed, and then I'm not in a very good mood when I spend time with you or the kids. You've probably noticed that. Would you be willing to help me with this?" Now, Adam, if Samantha were to make a request like that, without any impatience or irritation, would you consider helping her do the work around the house?

Adam: Probably.

We must understand the difference between demands and expectations. If we don't, we'll often deceive ourselves into believing that we're making healthy requests when we're really hurting ourselves and others with demands. Let me summarize the underlying characteristics and meaning of requests and demands:

Requests	**Demands**
I have enough Real Love in my life to be genuinely happy.	I feel empty and afraid, not loved and happy.
Since I have enough Real Love, I don't require that you do any particular thing to make me happy.	I need you to do something to temporarily dull the pain of my emptiness and fear.
I have no expectation that you'll agree to my request.	Because of my emptiness, I have an expectation that you'll agree to my request.
After you agree to my request, I'll expect you to keep your promise.	After you agree to my demand, I'll expect you to keep your promise.
If you refuse my request, I'll still be happy, just as I was before I made it.	If you refuse me, I'll be disappointed and/or angry.
If you agree to my request but fail to keep your promise, I will still be happy.	If you agree to my demand but fail to keep your promise, I'll be disappointed and/or angry.
If you agree to my request and keep your promise, I can still feel Real Love from you, because I haven't done anything to force you to comply, and what you give me will feel like a gift freely given.	If you agree to my demand and keep your promise, I can only assume—often unconsciously—that you've responded to me under pressure, and then I can't feel Real Love from you.
Healthy	Uniformly destructive

Not understanding these differences between requests and demands, Samantha unwittingly makes only demands, but she makes them in the *form* of requests. When she asks, for example, "Would you please help me?", she's really saying, "I do everything around here, and you do nothing. I'm sick and tired of this, and if you weren't such a lazy, worthless human being, I wouldn't have to *ask* you to help." And that's exactly what Adam hears.

It's ironic that when Samantha makes demands of Adam, she virtually ensures two unpleasant consequences:

- She won't get the help she's looking for. When she attacks him, he feels even more empty and afraid, and he automatically reacts with the Protecting Behaviors he's familiar with: lying (exaggerating his contribution to the family and minimizing Samantha's), attacking (anger), acting like a victim ("You just don't appreciate all I do around here"), and running (leaving the room when the argument becomes too intense). He can't respond to the issue she's trying to discuss, only to the emptiness and fear that are intensified by her attack.
- She can't feel loved. Occasionally, in order to avoid Samantha's anger, Adam does a few things to help her. But then he resents every minute of it, and she feels that. Although she does get some physical compliance as a result of her demands, she drives him farther away and feels more alone herself. On rare occasions, Adam helps out because he actually cares about her, but even then Samantha can't feel his unconditional love, only a manipulated response to her demands.

We make many demands in order to get what we want, but with our demands we actually make it far less likely that we'll be happy. Until we understand that, our demands will continue to destroy our happiness and relationships.

Making requests without anger is much more than a technique. Although I suggested to Samantha the words she could use in making a request of Adam, they'll be useless if she's irritated. He'll feel attacked and will still respond with Protecting Behaviors. Speaking without anger is possible only when we feel loved and loving, so I described to Samantha how she could take the steps—which we've discussed on many occasions—to acquire those qualities.

In addition to being loving, productive requests must also be clear and specific, and they must be associated with clear and specific follow-up. We'll talk more about this in Chapter Ten, but for now let's illustrate the principle as I continue talking to Samantha.

Samantha: So I just ask him to help me? That's it?

Me: Yes, but you also need to be clear and specific. You can't just drop hints that you need help, and you can't ask for help in a vague, general way. You could say things like this:

- "Adam, it would be great if you could talk to the kids about keeping the living room and their own bedrooms clean. And you'll need to check on them every day for a while to encourage them. I can't keep nagging them."
- "I need you to take out the garbage and help me clean up the kitchen before and after meals."
- "It would be nice if we could go out to eat once or twice a week, or you could bring something home with you after work. That would save me a lot of time."

After you describe each of those things you need, you could ask if he'd be willing to do them.

Samantha: What if he won't agree, or he agrees and then doesn't do anything?

We'll discuss the answer to that question shortly.

Helping People to Accept the Law of Expectations

We often have a hard time accepting the Law of Expectations. We really do think we have a right to demand what we want from other people. As a wise man, you'll have many occasions to help people see that they're violating this law. At the beginning of the chapter we talked about Diane, who was unhappy with her husband's behavior. She and I discussed that one afternoon.

"I'm trying this 'live with it and like it' thing," she said, "but I don't think it's going very well. I'm not trying to control him, but he still doesn't care about me."

As soon as Diane voiced dissatisfaction with her husband, she was expressing her expectations, a form of the controlling she'd just denied. Having expectations of other people is so accepted in our culture that we think it's normal.

Me: You still have huge expectations that Ken will love you.

Diane: Sure, he's my husband. He's supposed to love me.

Me: You don't have a right to expect anything from anyone—especially love. As soon as you have expectations, you start controlling people to get what you want, and you create nothing but disappointment and irritation for yourself.

Diane: If I can't expect my own husband to love me, where do I get loved?

Me: If you consistently tell the truth about yourself, eventually you'll get plenty of Real Love, but you don't get to choose *who* gives it to you. You'll get loved by people who are *capable* of loving you and who *choose* to offer it freely. But it all goes wrong when you demand love from a particular person. They may not have any love to give, and even if they do, you won't feel it as Real Love. Love only feels unconditional when it's freely offered. Haven't you've already proven that your expectations simply don't work?

When people see that their disappointment and anger are sure signs of their expectations, and when they see the selfishness of them, they can begin to let go of them and experience genuine acceptance. A few days after the above conversation, Diane called me.

Diane: I didn't agree with everything you said about expectations, but it really hit me when you said that doing things my way—expecting Ken to change—isn't working. It's really not, so I decided to try something different.

Me: What did you do?

Diane: Every time I'm feeling disappointed or annoyed with Ken, I'm repeating over and over in my head that I don't have a right to expect anything from anybody, including love from Ken.

Me: How's that working?

Diane: It's helped a lot. I don't feel as angry at him, but I still feel like something's missing. I still get disappointed and irritated sometimes.

Me: How often are you calling and spending time with people who can see you and accept you?

She wasn't doing that. It's helpful to *understand* a principle and repeat it in your head, but *feeling* loved always makes a much greater difference in our lives than intellectual understanding. As Diane felt more loved and combined that with her understanding of choice and expectations, her disappointment and anger toward her husband diminished dramatically.

WE ALWAYS HAVE THE RIGHT TO MAKE OUR OWN CHOICES

Remember that Samantha asked what she could do if Adam didn't help her even after she'd made her requests. When we're not getting what we want despite making repeated requests of the people around us, we often feel trapped and frustrated. But we're not trapped. After eliminating the "live with it and hate it" and "leave it" choices, we still have lots of choices within the larger choice of living with it and liking it. If Adam refuses to help Samantha, he's making *his choice* not to help her, but how is he *stopping* her from making any of her own choices? The only choice he's making impossible for Samantha is the choice to control him. She doesn't get that choice anyway, so he's not really limiting her choices. She can still do anything she wants. But isn't she stuck with cooking and cleaning? Not at all. Let's continue our conversation with Samantha.

Samantha: So what can I do if he doesn't help me?

Me: If he doesn't help, you'll feel stuck with all the cooking and cleaning, right?

Samantha: Of course. If I don't do it, who will?

Me: Maybe no one. He's not *making* you do anything. You're not under court order here. He's only making *his own choice* not to help. You can still choose what *you* will do.

Samantha: I don't think I understand.

Me: If he won't help you, you have several options.

- You can get your children to help you.
- You can continue to do all the cooking and cleaning, and offer it as a loving gift to Adam, instead of resenting it.
- You can choose to do *part* of the work around the house—the part you can do without feeling all stressed out—and leave the rest not done.

Samantha: I don't understand that last one. If I only do part of the work, who will do the rest?

Me: Probably no one. The Law of Choice states that you can choose what *you* do, but not what other people do. So make *your* choice. Make your request of Adam, and then choose how much of the work *you* will do. Adam can then choose what *he* will do. Whatever happens after that is a consequence of the choices you've both made. For a while, there might be some jobs that don't get done.

Samantha does make her request of Adam, specifying exactly what she'd like him to do, and he says he'll think about it. But then he doesn't do anything. Samantha chooses to continue doing the part she feels is reasonable, but that leaves many things undone, so the mess begins to pile up. Adam comes to me and bitterly complains about the condition of the house.

Adam: I can't live like this.

Me: Isn't this a result of *your* choices?

Adam: (angry) No, *she* won't clean it up.

Me: As I understand it, the part of the house she agreed to clean is spotless. It's the part she asked you to clean that's a mess.

Adam: I didn't *say* I'd do it. I said I'd think about it.

Me: Fine, but here are the facts: She's chosen to do part of the work. *You've* chosen to do nothing. I have no idea who's *right* here—it's not important to me—but the mess *is* a result of the choices both of you have made. You've caused the mess every bit as much as she has.

Adam: But *she*—

Me: You have three choices: Live with it and like it, live with it and hate it, or leave. Do you really want to keep being unhappy?

Adam: Well, no.

Me: That takes care of living with it and hating it. Do you want to divorce her over this?

Adam: I guess not.

Me: That leaves you with living with it and liking it.

Adam: But I *don't* like it and never will.

Me: If you don't like the way things are, you can't change *her*, only you.

Adam: I won't do the housework.

Me: Not a problem. You get to make that choice.

Adam: But then the house will be messy.

Me: Bingo. You can make any choice you want, but you have to live with the consequences. So if you continue to choose to do nothing, you have to live with a messy house, or you could work out with Samantha what part of the house you will help with, and then you could have a clean house. But you can't make the choice of having a clean house while you do nothing to help.

It could be argued that Samantha's refusal to do some of the housework is a manipulation to get Adam to help—blackmail, really. Indeed, if Samantha is leaving part of the work undone *so that* Adam will do it, that would be a manipulation. But Samantha isn't doing that. She's simply making *her own* choice about what she'll do and allowing Adam to do the same. The same behavior can therefore be manipulative or not, depending on the intent.

We also have the right to make our own choices in the workplace. In that environment, you may be given requests or even assignments, but you're still not forced to comply with them. You can choose to do whatever you want, but then you have to live with the consequences, as Adam did. Unfortunately, the consequence of doing what you want at work may be termination of your employment.

What Choice Do You Really Want To Make?

Although we can always make our own choices, they'll be consistently foolish if we don't keep long-term goals in mind. If I choose to stay home from work today, for example, I might have a great time playing around, but if I make that choice repeatedly, I may lose my job. Or I can choose to neglect the oil changes for my car, because I hate the inconvenience, but eventually the engine will be ruined, which will be a much bigger inconvenience.

We often forget that our highest goal is to find the genuine happiness that is a natural result of our feeling loved, loving other people, and being responsible. When we remember that goal, we take a giant step toward making wise choices about the details of our lives. Adam illustrates this principle as we continue our conversation from above.

> Adam: I don't know what to do. I want the house to be clean and a meal to be ready when I get home. Since I work longer hours, that's not unreasonable.

> Me: Actually, it might *not* be unreasonable—I really wouldn't know—but the fact remains that Samantha isn't willing to do it all anymore, so you can't choose the end result you want without helping her. Your decision gets a lot easier if you remember that you really want something more important than a clean house and a belly full of food.

Adam: Like what?

Me: What's the greatest goal in life?

Adam has read *Real Love*, so he knows the answer. "To be happy, I guess."

Me: And how do you get that?

Adam: From feeling loved, but I'm not getting that from her.

Me: She's not getting it from you, either. Before you two can be happy, you need to share Real Love with each other. *That's* what you really want, more than a clean kitchen and a hot meal. You insist on those things only because you're not feeling loved. Do you really want to be happy or not?

Adam: Yeah, sure.

Me: Then you can't ignore what really leads to happiness. You have to pay more attention to loving Samantha instead of just trying to get what you want. In every single interaction with her, you need to ask yourself whether *your* behavior is contributing to the Real Love you want for both of you. Is it your primary goal to come home from work, immediately sit on the couch in a clean living room, and eat a hot meal? Or do you want a loving and happy relationship with your wife? Right now you can't have both. You have to choose one or the other.

Adam: I hadn't thought of it quite like that.

After seeing his real choices—being genuinely happy or getting what he wants in the short term—Adam chooses to do some of the things Samantha has requested. He doesn't choose to do all of them, but they do work it out between themselves and the children in a way that everything gets done. In the end, Samantha chooses to do more housework than Adam, but knowing that Adam genuinely cares about her, she does it as a gift to her husband.

You may not always be able to work things out with a partner as Samantha and Adam did. You must be willing to make requests that are unsatisfied. To hope otherwise is selfish. But you *can* always make your own choices. You are not trapped.

We often think our choice is between doing a particular thing we want or what our partner (spouse, child, co-worker) wants, but the reality is that we're constantly making much bigger choices than that. With every decision, we're really choosing between love and selfishness, happiness and misery, freedom and bondage. That doesn't mean we always have to do what other people want, but if we make our decisions while caring about their happiness—while we're loving—we'll make choices that are far more productive for them and ourselves. And while we're loving, we can always be happy, no matter what other people decide to do.

There once was a man who owned a beautiful apple tree. Every day he picked the delicious fruit and was very happy. Although some of the fruit was high in the tree and inaccessible, he still enjoyed what he could reach. But his appetite grew, and the day came when he could no longer pick enough apples to satisfy himself, so in order to get the fruit high in the tree, he cut it down and gorged himself. Never again did he eat the fruit of the tree.

In every relationship, we make a choice. We can enjoy the love and happiness available to us, or we can insist on more than we're offered—we can cut down the tree. Adam chose to modify his demands instead of cutting down the tree, and as a result, he found a level of happiness he otherwise would have missed entirely. What will *you* choose to do? Will you choose to be loving or miserable? Truthful or right?

Once we see these choices clearly, making them becomes much easier. It can all start with choosing to tell the truth about ourselves and feel loved. The more loved we feel, the less blinded we are by emptiness and fear, and then we can begin to see our choices more clearly and make wiser ones.

A NEW UNDERSTANDING OF FAIRNESS

When people first learn about Real Love, telling the truth, the Law of Choice, and the Law of Expectations, it's a lot to digest. We'll leave Adam and Samantha now and turn back to Diane, who's feeling stressed by all the things she's learning.

"So I have to tell the truth about *me*," Diane said, "and *I* have to change my whole life, but I can't expect Ken to do anything? It's not *fair*."

It's not unfair when we don't get what we want, or when everybody else is doing less than we are, or when we're suffering more. Such occasions are just the natural consequences of the choices we make, the choices other people make, and the natural flow of events. As other people exercise the right to make their choices, and as they learn from their mistakes, they *will* eventually inconvenience and hurt us. There will be times when they do less and suffer less. The only way to avoid that is to repeal the Law of Choice, which would be far worse than any inconvenience we suffer as a result of the choices people make.

Most of us are very insistent about fairness, or justice, but our real concern is getting what *we* want in any given moment. We only want justice if it works in our favor. If people do more for us than we do for them, do we ever complain that it's just not fair? We insist on justice for the purpose of controlling people, which gives us only temporary feelings of satisfaction, safety, and power. With perfect justice—as determined by you—your life *might* be more convenient, but you would not have the genuine happiness that can come only from feeling unconditionally loved and from loving other people. In fact, we often learn more about loving people unconditionally when they *are* treating us "unfairly." It's no great trick to like people when they're giving us what we want. Unconditional love is caring about other people even when they're *not* making our lives easier.

Fairness doesn't come from controlling others, or requiring all our burdens and rewards to be equal with those of other people. What *is* fair is that we all have the ability to make our own choices and to find the Real Love that will make us happy.

HOW OUR BEHAVIOR OFTEN CAN BE EXPLAINED BY A FAILURE TO UNDERSTAND THE LAW OF CHOICE

The importance of understanding the Law of Choice becomes more apparent when we see the effects of *not* understanding it.

- Selfishness is a belief that my freedom to choose is more important than yours. When I truly understand and accept your right to choose, how could I ever manipulate you to give me what *I* want?
- Expectations come from a belief that I have the right to determine the choices made by others.
- I act like a victim when I believe other people have an obligation to make choices that will benefit me.
- Anger is the feeling I experience when I can't control your choices so you'll do what I want.
- Attacking is acting out the belief that I have a right to limit your freedom to choose.
- Laziness is giving up my opportunity to make choices and instead sitting back and selfishly hoping that others will choose to serve me.

As wise men we must understand and teach that until we accept the basic right of other people to make their own choices, we can never see or love them.

HOW OUR CHOICES ARE AFFECTED BY PAST EXPERIENCE

Although we all have the right and ability to make our own choices at any time, those choices *are* influenced by many other factors, including our many experiences and choices from the past. As we discuss here two ways to see the effect of past experience, you may find one or both of them useful in understanding your own behavior and in explaining to other people their feelings and behavior.

Event → Judgment → Feeling → Reaction (EJFR)

Diane called me one day and said, "I understand that my expectations are wrong, but sometimes Ken says these really unkind things, and I can't help it—I just blow up. Sometimes he just makes me so mad."

It's natural that we blame our Getting and Protecting Behaviors on other people. After all, we reason, if this person hadn't inconvenienced us, attacked us, or whatever, we wouldn't be responding by attacking, acting like a victim, and so on. But our responses have their origin far earlier than the behavior of any particular person, and the better we understand the cause of our behaviors, the more effectively we can change them. One way to achieve that understanding is to talk about the process of EJFR: Event → Judgment → Feeling → Reaction.

An **event** is just something that *happens*: it rains, the sun goes down, your husband says something unkind, your wife is sulking when you enter the room, and so on. Contrary to the belief of most people, however, events do not determine how we feel or behave. First we make a **judgment**—based on past events—which then determines how we **feel** and **react**.

I was raised in a neighborhood where the dogs were vicious. Whenever I saw a dog, or heard one bark, I was chased or bitten. From this consistent pattern of **events**, I learned the **judgment** that dogs were dangerous. After learning that judgment, I became afraid (a **feeling**) each time I heard a dog bark and **reacted** by running away or attacking the dog with a stick.

For many years as an adult, I continued to carry around that judgment about dogs, so I became afraid whenever I heard or saw one. If a particular dog was friendly, I still felt afraid—because of the old judgment—and reacted to protect myself. It was inappropriate to protect myself from a non-threatening dog, but with my old judgment and subsequent fear, I could do nothing else.

We all have judgments like that about everything, judgments formed in the past which still greatly affect—even determine—our feelings and behavior in the present. As a child Diane learned that when she made mistakes, they were followed by criticism, withdrawal of approval, and loneliness. From these *events*, she learned the *judgment*—correct, it turns out—that mistakes consistently result in painful withdrawal of affection. She then became *afraid* and learned to *react* with Getting and Protecting Behaviors. Without experiencing any significant exceptions to the judgment she learned, she carried it with her into adulthood—as we all do.

When Ken made a critical comment about something Diane had done, she became frightened that she wouldn't be loved, and then she reacted with anger, a Protecting Behavior that often made Ken back off. Like Diane, we all react to our judgments and fears, most of which come from the distant past. Understanding this changes how we see every interaction. Now we know that when we're angry at someone (a **reaction**), we first **feel** afraid that this person will hurt us in some way, a **judgment** formed from past **events**, almost all of which had nothing to do with him or her.

If we can recognize our judgments, we can change them. You can better recognize judgments if you carefully observe the *feelings* and *reactions* which follow them. Any time you react in an unproductive way to someone—anger, acting like a victim, lying, running, clinging—consider what feelings you're experiencing. Almost uniformly, the feelings that motivate such reactions are emptiness and fear. You can then ask yourself *why* you feel empty and afraid, and again, the answer is the same in almost all cases: You don't feel sufficiently loved and loving, and you're making a *judgment* that someone can add to your emptiness or hurt you by attacking you, or manipulating you, or simply not loving you.

Then you can remember that you do not have to repeat the same old judgment all your life. Sure, this person may have been inconsiderate—even extremely inconsiderate—but *you* can determine entirely how you feel and react. Let me illustrate further how feelings and reactions are not determined by events.

Let's suppose that I take a walk on a path in the woods. I'm preoccupied with my thoughts, so I'm not watching very carefully where I'm walking. As I walk, I bump into four men also walking on the path, one after the other, several minutes apart. I don't bump them hard, but enough to jostle them and alter their course a little. Although I bump into each of them exactly the same way, their reactions are quite different:

- The first man is deep in thought, much like myself, enjoying the beauty and peace of the outdoors. When I bump him, his thoughts are briefly interrupted, but he's delighted that someone else is also enjoying the beautiful surroundings, and he stops for a moment to wish me a good day and ask how I'm doing.
- The second man is talking to a friend. He's thoroughly enjoying the conversation and doesn't even notice when I bump him.
- The third man came to the park angry at the world. He feels like a victim at work, at home, everywhere. When I bump him, he falls back in an exaggerated, almost theatrical way. He jumps up and down and screams at me, and in the process he turns his ankle and sprains it. Cursing me, he's carried out on a stretcher.
- The fourth man is deeply discouraged and angry. In fact, he's come to the woods with a gun in his pocket, uncertain whether he wants to live any longer. When I bump him, he screams at me, saying, "Why don't you watch where you're going?" And then he pulls out the gun and shoots himself in the head. Wow.

The third man blamed me for spraining his ankle, as many people would, and the fourth man blamed me for his *death*. So what *am* I responsible for? In each of the four interactions, I'm responsible only for my behavior, which was the same each time: I carelessly bumped a man on the path. *That's all* I'm responsible for. I'm guilty of carelessness, but no more. I am *not* responsible for any of the *reactions* I got. I am not to blame for the sprained ankle of the third man, nor the death of the fourth. If I *were* responsible for their reactions, how could we explain the second man having no reaction at all to the same event? And could I then claim credit for *causing* the kindness of the first man? *We are not responsible for the reactions of anyone.* We're responsible only for what we do—even when other people blame us for their reactions, which they often do.

The people around you *will* make mistakes. They will bump you on the path. But they're not responsible for your behavior, nor are you responsible for theirs. You can determine whether you react with acceptance (like the first man I met on the path) or anger (like the man who broke his ankle) or other responses—lying, running, and excessive guilt, for example—that are harmful to you (like the man who pulled a gun and killed himself). Of course, your ability to make those choices is greatly affected by the amount of Real Love you have, and shortly we'll talk about the interaction between Real Love and self-control.

Now back to Diane and Ken. As Diane understood EJFR, she began to recognize that Ken didn't *make* her afraid or angry. She had a *choice* about how to judge his behavior. She began to *assume* that he was *not* attacking her—a new judgment—and then she experienced no fear (which is the primary feeling) and no anger or need to withdraw (which are reactions to fear). Even on the occasions when she determined that he *was* attacking her, she made the judgment that he was simply empty and afraid and using a Getting and Protecting Behavior that would fill his emptiness or protect him. When she made that accurate judgment, she again experienced no fear, but instead had a desire to give him what he needed—acceptance and love. This was especially easy to do when she found more Real Love in her own life.

Event → Judgment → Feeling → Reaction. As we carefully examine our feelings and behaviors, we can see that they don't just *happen* to us. They have a cause, and when we identify it and take the steps necessary to change the cause (the judgment), our entire lives can change.

Role Assignment

As Shakespeare said in *As You Like It*, "All the world's a stage, and all the men and women merely players." From the day of our birth, our parents and others teach us the role we will play on the stage of our lives, as we see in the life of Stan.

Stan's parents taught him the role of Good Son because they were happier when he played the part well. Stan's biological father played the role of Father, whose job it was to make sure Stan was obedient, responsible, and successful. When Stan failed to perform his role adequately, the Father punished him with disapproval and anger. Stan's stepmother played Mother, who complained and acted like a victim in order to manipulate Stan into loving and taking care of her.

Although Stan was not genuinely happy in his role, which required him to work constantly at pleasing people, it was the only role he'd ever learned; he didn't know any other way to live. Most of the time, he used the various Getting and Protecting Behaviors to earn the approval of the other characters in their family play or to protect himself from their demands, disappointment, and anger.

When Stan grew up and moved away, the cast of characters in his play was no longer complete. Even though his role had often been exhausting, irritating, and even frightening, it was still the only role he knew, and without it he was lost and alone, the worst condition of all. Of course, he couldn't play *his* role without the other characters in the play. How could he be the Good Son and please the Father and the Mother if they were no longer on stage with him? So he found new actors to fill those roles, and then he was able to return to the familiarity and comfort of the old play, even though his original family was no longer with him. For the rest of his life, Stan interacted with everyone as if they were the characters in the play he'd learned as a child.

His supervisor at work had some of the same character traits as his biological father. And so, with no conscious effort, Stan naturally assigned him the role of Father. Because he'd cast his supervisor in the Father role, Stan reacted to everything his boss said or did as if it were being done by his original father. So, even when his boss offered positive advice or was genuinely helpful, Stan could only hear the critical and angry voice of his father, and, as a result, he responded by lying, acting like a victim, and getting angry.

When Stan found someone to play the role of Mother, he married her. Stan's wife often *did* behave like his stepmother, which is why he'd chosen her to join the cast of his play in the first place, but she was obviously not his mother, and Stan often misjudged her behavior. He tried to make his wife happy—as he had done with his stepmother—but he also resented her for manipulating him, even when she wasn't doing that.

To varying degrees, *we all do what Stan did*. At an early age, we are compelled to learn a role, and most of us have continued to play that part for the rest of our lives, because it's all we know how to do.

Ironically, we do get some important benefits from playing our role:

- It minimizes our pain. When we play our part well, people hurt us less.
- It maximizes our pleasure. People smile at us more when we're "good"—i.e., when we perform the role they assign us.
- It gives us a place in the world. Our greatest fear is being alone. Even though our assigned role requires us to satisfy the expectations of other people, it also assures us of relatively predictable interactions with the other characters in our play—and then we feel less alone.

But all these benefits are only forms of Imitation Love. As we play our role, we're always trying to win the conditional approval of other people, and the minute we do anything to persuade someone else to like us, Real Love becomes impossible, which means we cannot be genuinely happy. The following vignette demonstrates how the assignment of roles can interfere with the healthy interaction between any two people.

Amanda had left her car to be repaired, and when she came to pick it up, she spoke to John, the manager of the service department.

"Is my car ready yet?" asked Amanda.

"We got it done as fast as we could, lady!!" John snapped.

Amanda burst into tears and stomped off.

What happened here? How could two people who had never met become so upset over such a minor event?

First, let's look at this event from Amanda's perspective. She'd been raised by a man who had never felt unconditionally loved. Empty and afraid, he protected himself by being critical and angry with everyone. He defined the role of Father in Amanda's play.

Although he didn't do it intentionally, when her father was critical and angry, he made Amanda afraid and taught her that she was the Stupid Child. Her filling that role allowed him to feel less powerless and afraid. Because he felt relatively weak and unimportant elsewhere in his life, he used his anger and criticism to feel big and strong. In the absence of Real Love, *many* parents unconsciously use their children in this way to get a feeling of power. Amanda learned that when she acted pathetic and tearful—like a victim—her father was often less angry. So playing the role of Victim minimized the pain in her life.

Even in adulthood Amanda assigned the role of Father to most of the men in her life. When they spoke to her critically, she became afraid and reacted by acting like a victim. But very often she reacted the same way even when they were *not* being critical or angry. In either case, her behavior had negative consequences:

- Although her acting like a victim often minimized the anger of the men who really *were* angry, the price she paid for that bit of safety was high: she always felt more alone. We can never protect ourselves from people and at the same time feel closer to them.

- When she played the role of victim with men who were *not* being critical or angry, she was blaming them for her unhappiness, and they naturally felt as if they were being unjustly accused and attacked. Then they in turn reacted by doing one of two things: Either they avoided her, which made her feel even more alone (and of course, the only reason she'd acted like a victim in the first place was to attract sympathy so that she *wouldn't* feel alone), or they became angry, which means that she'd *created* anger where none had existed before.

In either case, her Getting and Protecting Behavior had created the very situation she'd been trying to avoid.

So when Amanda approached the service manager, she assigned him the role of Father, and she reacted to that *role*, rather than responding to the person as an individual.

Now let's examine this event from John's perspective. His mother had constantly manipulated people by acting like a victim in order to get Imitation Love. She'd taught him to feel guilty whenever he didn't give her what she wanted, and although he didn't enjoy his role, he avoided her disappointment and anger when he played it well. His role also gave him a defined place in the world, which made him feel less alone. With time, however, he became increasingly angry as a way to protect himself from the helpless feeling of being controlled by his mother.

For the rest of his life, John assigned the Mother role to most of the women he knew. Whenever a woman spoke to him, he heard the whining and accusation of the Mother, and he reacted with anger, as if these women *were* his real mother. He often did this whether they were actually whining and manipulating him or not. That role assignment had negative consequences:

- When women really *were* manipulating John, his anger usually frightened them and reduced their complaints, but it also kept him alone and unhappy.
- When women were *not* being manipulative, they responded to his anger in one of three ways: They avoided him *or* they became afraid and did what he wanted in order to make his anger go away *or* they reacted with anger of their own. In any of these situations, his Getting and Protecting Behavior made a real relationship impossible, and he was left more alone than ever.

So when Amanda approached John at the service counter, he saw her as the Mother before she'd even said a word. When she asked, "Is my car ready *yet?*" he heard the same accusatory tone he'd heard all his life from the Mother, and he responded with anger: "We got it done as fast as we could, lady!!" It would have been more accurate if he'd said, "I got it done as fast as I could, *Mother!*" All his life, John reacted to women as though they were the Mother, and that reaction kept him angry and alone.

Amanda and John were not aware they'd each assigned the other a role from their past. But that's exactly what they were doing, and, as a result, neither one of them could react to the person who was actually standing there in the moment. In effect, John's mother and Amanda's father were at the counter in the service department confronting each other.

Because most of us were assigned similar roles as children, what happened to Amanda and John occurs over and over again when we interact with people, even though we're largely unaware of it.

How many times have you said something you thought was perfectly innocent, only to have people react as if you'd attacked them? Or have you wondered why you feel defensive around certain people, even when they've done little or nothing to hurt you? That happens because we assign each other roles from our past, and we react to those roles without truly seeing the person who's standing in front of us. When your spouse says something inoffensive, for example, and you become mortally wounded, it's likely that you hear the criticism and anger of your parent—or some other character from the past—who *did* say many critical and angry things to you. Regrettably, in that moment you're reacting to all those past events—quite an accumulated assault—instead of hearing what your spouse really said. This pattern of role assignment makes loving relationships impossible.

As we find unconditional love, however, we're no longer blinded by emptiness and fear; only then are we able to see people as they really are, and, seeing them clearly, we can accept and love them.

The Interacting Effects of Real Love and Self-Control

Imagine that you're hungry, and you're preparing to go out and get some bread with your last two dollars. Suddenly, I dash into the room, snatch the two dollars off the table, and run away before you can stop me. You'd almost certainly be angry at me.

Now imagine that the next day I do exactly the same thing—steal two dollars off the table as you're getting ready to go out and buy some bread—but this time you have twenty *million* dollars in the bank. How do you feel this time? Probably not concerned—the loss of two dollars matters very little when you have twenty million.

Having sufficient Real Love really is like having twenty million dollars all the time. And then, when people are inconsiderate, when they fail to do what we want, and even when they attack us, they're only taking two dollars, which we can easily afford to lose. When we feel unconditionally loved, everything else becomes relatively insignificant.

How we react to other people is largely determined by how unconditionally loved we feel and not by their behavior. Without Real Love, we're starving to death and down to our last two dollars. In that condition, we're limited in our ability to remain happy and loving when a thief steals our money. Children who are raised without unconditional love can only be *severely* affected as they attempt to find happiness in the absence of the most essential ingredient for emotional and spiritual health. If that lack of Real Love is not corrected, a child will then become an adult who feels empty and afraid, and who will respond to others with Getting and Protecting Behaviors.

But is there more to us than our past experience? If you've received no Real Love as a child, does that mean you are absolutely doomed to use nothing but Getting and Protecting Behaviors as you interact with other people all your life? No. We're not sticks and stones, which can only be acted upon. We have a measure of self-control we can always choose to exercise. I talk about that in several places in *Real Love*. Even when we don't feel sufficiently loved, *to some extent* we can still choose to withhold our Getting and Protecting Behaviors and make efforts to be loving. I re-emphasize, however, that our ability to choose is greatly affected by the Real Love we have. Most people raised without Real Love simply cannot choose to be as loving as those who *have* been loved unconditionally, anymore than a starving man can choose to run as fast as a healthy one.

As I say in Chapter Two of *Real Love*, for years I found it very difficult to split oak logs with an ax. And then I discovered a maul, a tool that enabled me to split oak quite easily. I initially made a *choice* to split logs with an ax—no one *made* me use it. It was the best choice *I could see* at the time—better than a shovel or my bare hands. A maul would have worked much better, but I didn't know it existed. After learning about it, I was able to make a better choice.

In a similar way, we always have choices about how we feel and behave, but if we don't have experience with Real Love, Getting and Protecting Behaviors may be the only choices *we can see* in a given situation. And even after Real Love has been described to us, we may *see* it as a choice but still be incapable of *making* the loving choice, because we don't actually have the love to give. As we find Real Love and feel it, we're better able to make new choices—loving, happy choices.

Although I stress that a lack of Real Love causes the emptiness and fear that lead to our Getting and Protecting Behaviors, I intend that to be an *explanation* for our behaviors, not an *excuse* for continuing them. Even when we feel unloved and unhappy, it is always *our* responsibility to learn what we can do to change our choices, and as we make wiser choices we will find the love and happiness we seek.

At this point, many people ask, With each decision we make, what is the relative influence of self-control compared with the amount of Real Love we feel? Exactly how strong is our ability to simply *choose* a loving behavior even when we've experienced relatively little Real Love? To what degree can our will power overcome the obviously crippling effects of insufficient Real Love? I don't know anyone who can answer these questions with any certainty, and even if they could, the answer wouldn't change the fact that we can—and must—do all we can to increase *both* our self-control and the Real Love we have. Both factors operate in a synergistic way—they support and nourish one another and create an effect much greater than either could do alone. We can exercise self-control and make a conscious choice to tell the truth about ourselves instead of using our familiar Getting and Protecting Behaviors. That choice creates the opportunity for us to feel more unconditionally loved. With Real Love, in turn, we have less *need* to use Getting and Protecting Behaviors and can more easily make conscious decisions to be more loving instead. As we make decisions (self-control) to love other people even when our bucket is not full (Chapter One), we experience the miracle of feeling more Real Love ourselves.

Other than Real Love and self-control, there are other factors that contribute to our behavior. Certainly genetics plays a role, but how much? And what is the effect of other inborn qualities we don't fully understand—in the spiritual realm, for example? I haven't addressed these issues simply because they make no practical difference to us. Although the questions are fascinating and provide stimulating conversation, the answers wouldn't change the fact that at this point we can't alter our genetic structure, nor can we control what other characteristics we'll be born with. So regardless of the answers to all these interesting questions, our approach to altering our feelings and behavior remains the same: tell the truth about ourselves, find Real Love, share it with others, and exercise self-control as we make decisions to be loving instead of using Getting and Protecting Behaviors.

OTHER PEOPLE NEVER MAKE US ANGRY

Perhaps the most destructive choice we make on a regular basis is anger, which instantly makes our own happiness impossible and causes incalculable damage to our relationships. We've been blaming other people for our anger for so long—and seen other people do the same—that we sincerely believe it when we say, "He/she makes me so mad." As long as we believe that lie, we cannot give up our anger.

We need to see not only that anger is a choice, but that it's a uniformly bad one. In *Real Love*, I define *right* as anything that contributes to being genuinely happy: feeling loved, being loving, and being responsible. Anything, therefore, which interferes with those goals is *wrong*. Using that criterion, we can see that anger is always wrong. When we're angry, we're unloving, blind, trying to control other people, and making our own happiness impossible.

Many people will challenge you as a wise man to explain how anger is not caused by their partners, so let's discuss several ways to demonstrate this truth. We know that anger is not caused by other people

(1) when we understand that anger is a response to a lifetime of insufficient Real Love.
(2) when we see how our anger changes toward the same event from one time to another, and when we see how people respond differently to the same event.
(3) when Imitation Love eliminates anger.
(4) when Real Love eliminates anger.

1. When We Understand That Anger Is a Response to a Lifetime of Insufficient Real Love

I've already explained how Real Love affects our happiness more than anything else, and how a lack of it leads to Getting and Protecting Behaviors, including anger. It's this long-term lack of love in our own lives that leads to anger, not any individual behavior—or many behaviors—of a partner. The concepts of EJFR and role assignment also help us to understand the effect of the past on our present decisions.

2. When We See How Our Anger Changes Toward the Same Event from One Time to Another, and When We See How People Respond Differently to the Same Event

Have you ever noticed that when people behave a certain way, you become irritated on some occasions but not on others? That proves your anger is a *choice*. If it were not, you'd respond the same way on all occasions to that behavior.

Similarly, anger is proven to be a choice if any two people respond differently to the same event. In World War II, millions of people were imprisoned and killed in concentration camps. We have many oral and written accounts from survivors of those camps, and we've learned that many of them understandably became angry and bitter because of the unspeakably hateful treatment they received at the hands of their captors. But some of the inmates chose not to become angry. They forgave their tormentors and even learned to love them. They saw the terrible effects of anger and hate, and they refused to give in to them. Victor Frankl spoke of such people in *Man's Search for Meaning*, as did Corrie ten Boom in *The Hiding Place*.

Some people get angry when people do terrible things to them, and others do not. Clearly, the problem is *not* the people who do the terrible things. If that were so, *everyone* would become angry when they were treated badly, and that doesn't happen. In fact, if you get angry when I do something, and we can find even one person in the world who *doesn't* get angry when I do that same thing, then I did not *make* you angry. Apparently, some people *choose* to become angry and others do not. Anger is a choice.

3. When Imitation Love Eliminates Anger

Several times in this chapter we've discussed Diane's relationship with her husband. On one occasion when she blamed her husband for making her angry, I said, "If I gave you a million dollars in cash right now—and a new car—would you be less irritated with him?"

Diane: (laughing) Yes, I suppose so.

Me: Then your husband didn't make you angry.

Diane: I don't understand.

Me: If a million dollars would make your anger go away, then it's obvious that the real cause of your anger is the lack of a million dollars, not your husband—right?

What we often call *happy* is really the sensation of a sufficient supply of Imitation Love, which does temporarily make us feel good in the absence of Real Love. But if we're running low on praise, power, pleasure, and safety, watch out! Without enough Real or Imitation Love, we become irritated at people—not because of the individual things they do, but because of our own lack of love. We prove that when a new supply of Imitation Love in any form makes our anger go away. Because we lose our anger in that case without any change in the people we claimed were the cause of it, we know they didn't really cause it.

4. When Real Love Eliminates Anger

I met Sandra for the first time in my office. She was quite angry at her husband, and we talked for some time about the Real Love she'd never felt in her life. As I explained her anger without any hint of blaming, it was obvious that she was beginning to relax and feel less irritated.

Me: How are you feeling right now?

Sandra: I don't know how to describe it. I've never talked about myself like this. I've talked about my husband a lot, but not really about *me*.

Me: Do you feel angry?

Sandra: (smiling) Not really—almost peaceful.

Although it's obvious that her husband's behavior didn't miraculously change during our conversation, Sandra's anger nonetheless went away, proving that *he* wasn't the primary cause of her anger. Her anger disappeared when she got the acceptance she really needed. As a wise man you'll have many opportunities to point out to people that with Real Love from anyone—even for moments—anger can be eliminated, which proves that individual people don't cause our anger.

The effect of Real Love on anger can be seen even better over longer periods of time. For months after our conversation, Sandra told the truth about her anger and her other Getting and Protecting Behaviors with several wise men and women, and as she began to feel accepted and loved, she slowly lost much of her need to use those unproductive behaviors, including her anger. One day we talked about that.

Me: Do you remember how angry you were when we first met?

Sandra: Sure, and I still get mad sometimes, but not like before. I can see now that I was angry at everybody, not just my husband—I was mad at the kids, at the people I work with, even drivers on the road I don't know. I was angry all the time, and I didn't realize it.

Me: So what's changed?

Sandra: I'm just happier now. It's like you said it would be—I started telling the truth about myself, and I did find people who loved me. Now there's no *reason* to be mad.

I've observed the effect of Real Love in the lives of uncounted people. People certainly don't lose their anger all at once as they feel loved, but it does go away, and then they learn beyond doubt that their anger was not caused by other people. It was a reaction to the emptiness and fear caused by the lack of love in their lives.

HOW LOVING IS THE NATURAL RESULT OF UNDERSTANDING THE LAW OF CHOICE

When we understand the Law of Choice, how could we ever interfere with the right of another person to do anything? We'd never want to control them. We'd understand that people must make their own choices in order to learn, and that they must make mistakes in the process. We'd never become angry as people exercised their right to choose. The natural result of understanding the Law of Choice is complete acceptance and love.

WE ARE RESPONSIBLE FOR OUR CHOICES

We treasure our right to make our own choices—the Law of Choice—but we're not nearly as excited about the Law of Responsibility, which states that we are all *responsible* for the choices we make. Most of us want to separate choice from responsibility. We act as we wish but want to avoid the consequences of our actions. We get angry but blame other people for our choice. We like to say whatever we want but don't like being held accountable for our words. We like to put off the assignments we're given, but then we hate the last-minute rush that results from those decisions. But there are enormous benefits that result from being responsible, as illustrated by my experience with Brian.

Brian was furious about an argument he'd had with his roommate, Eric, the previous day, in which they'd both said a lot of angry and blaming things to one another.

> Brian: I'm really mad about this. In fact, I'm thinking about having Eric evicted. I can do that because I have the primary lease on the apartment. Do you see anything else I can do?
>
> Me: Sure. Tell the truth about it.
>
> Brian: I did that. I told him what a selfish (expletive) he is.
>
> Me: (laughing) No, I mean tell the truth about *you.*
>
> Brian: But this isn't my fault. He—
>
> Me: You asked me for advice. You've already tried this *your* way—telling the truth about *him.* How did that work?
>
> Brian: Not too well. We were friends, but now we'll probably never speak again.

Me: So you have nothing to lose by trying something different here. In your conversation with Eric, were *you* loving?

Brian: *Me?*! *He* was the one yelling, and—

Me: Like I said, you've already proven that telling the truth about Eric doesn't work, so why not try telling the truth about you? Remember, I accept you no matter what you did with him. Were *you* loving when you talked to him?

Brian: (pause) Not really. I was pretty mad.

We talked until he saw that he'd been angry because of his own emptiness and fear, which had little to do with Eric. He admitted that he'd been pretty selfish as he'd protected himself and not thought of Eric's happiness at all.

Me: Way to go. That was honest. Now go and tell Eric what you just said to me.

Brian: No way. That'd be way too hard.

Me: Really? Look at what you have now, doing it your way. You've just lost a friend, and until you complete the eviction proceedings—couple of months, at least—you'll be living in a war zone. You think all that is harder than telling the truth?

Brian: I see what you mean, but I still don't think I can do it.

Me: Telling Eric the truth about yourself will probably be uncomfortable—because you're not used to doing it—but it couldn't be as hard as what you've got now. And it *might* make a difference in your relationship. I can't promise that, but you'll never learn what it's like to be truthful and responsible for your own behavior until you *do* it. Why not try it?

Brian did it. He talked to Eric and took complete responsibility for how selfish, afraid, and angry he'd been in their conversation. Eric was stunned and immediately apologized for the things he'd said. In minutes they were friends again. Imagine the confidence Brian acquired to be truthful in the next similar situation—with anyone.

Avoiding responsibility, as Brian initially did, appears to have its rewards. It *seems* to be easier. If you believe you're not responsible, you don't have to admit you're wrong, nor do you have to change. But there's a terrible price to be paid for that. If you claim something's not your fault, you'll see no reason to change anything about yourself and will therefore be almost certain to repeat your mistake. You're now stuck with your mistakes and their unpleasant consequences. In addition, name the last time you blamed someone for your mistake and then felt more loved by them or more loving toward them. Impossible.

Irresponsible people cannot feel loved and are doomed to repeat their mistakes. With every event in our lives, we choose whether we'll be responsible, and our choice determines whether we'll experience freedom and life or captivity and death. When we're responsible, we create the opportunity to look wrong and foolish, but we also create the opportunity to learn and be happy. We have a hard time admitting that we're wrong only because we haven't experienced the joy of doing it.

Some people can't seem to stop talking about their partners. This attempt to shift blame is a longstanding and destructive habit that they cannot overcome without help. To such people, you could say, "For the rest of our conversation, try speaking without uttering the word *he/she/him/her* or the name of the person you're mad at." We simply can't be happy while we're irresponsible, and wise men need to help people see when they're headed in that direction.

Fear of Responsibility

Accepting responsibility for our choices is obviously frightening to us—look at how vigorously we avoid it. We make excuses, blame people, rationalize our behavior, and lie about our part in mistakes, all to avoid responsibility for our flaws, our happiness, and our misery.

Our fear is understandable. We've learned from an abundance of past experience that mistakes lead to criticism, ridicule, and painful withdrawal of approval and love. When we discover a mistake, we hunt down the person responsible so we can blame or punish him.

When the company's profits are down, we find someone to fire. When the football team is on a losing streak, we publicly flog the coach. When milk is spilled at the table, we say something unkind to the child who spilled it—instead of just cleaning up the milk. Being responsible is a frightening thing.

All our Getting and Protecting Behaviors, in fact, are usually just attempts to avoid responsibility:

- We don't lie because we're bad; we lie, blame, rationalize, and make excuses in order to avoid responsibility for our mistakes.
- When we attack people—with anger, for example—we're blaming them for how we feel instead of taking responsibility for our own choices.
- Avoiding responsibility is the primary motivation for people to act like victims. If victims can convince you that everyone else is responsible for their problems and unhappiness, they escape all possibility of being responsible themselves.
- Running is an obvious avoidance of responsibility. Whenever things are difficult, we can flee the whole situation—leave the relationship, quit the job, get a little drunk. How can I feel responsible if I'm not even there?

We avoid responsibility more than we like to admit. As we identify those times, we can make more responsible, happier choices.

We Have a Limited Responsibility for Our Mistakes

While it is important that people take responsibility for their choices, many of us have a tendency to carry that activity too far. In the following sub-sections, we'll discuss what happens when we exaggerate the responsibility we place on ourselves and other people for the choices and mistakes we all make.

Punishment—Requiring Other People to Suffer
for Their Mistakes

As I've said, mistakes are unavoidable in the process of learning. How else could we learn except by making choices with imperfect knowledge, making mistakes, and trying again? To succeed, we must have the freedom to fail. Frequently, our mistakes will inconvenience other people. As we learn, we all get in each other's way. It could not be otherwise. To keep from hurting them, we'd have to make no choices at all, and then we'd be nothing.

Unfortunately, most of us tend to make a big production out of the mistakes other people make. When they inconvenience or hurt *us*, we want them to *pay*. We want them to apologize, suffer, be humiliated, be restricted, and never commit a similarly grievous offense again.

Most mistakes are small and unintentional. People don't usually intend to harm us. They're simply empty and afraid, and they inconvenience and hurt us only as they try to get love and protect themselves—as was the case with the man drowning in the pool in Chapter One. But in our society, we don't see mistakes as part of learning, or as Getting and Protecting Behaviors. Instead, we tend to label unproductive behavior—and those who use them—as bad or evil. And we measure the seriousness of mistakes according to their *effect* or *consequences*. That can be quite unfair. If someone makes a huge mistake that affects no one else, we call that a "small" mistake. If the same mistake happens to inconvenience or hurt many people, it suddenly becomes a "big" mistake.

I read in the newspaper, for example, that a man drunkenly drove into a ditch, knocking down some garbage cans. The police found him in the morning and took him home. The same evening, another drunk driver swerved off the road and killed a child riding a bicycle. He was charged with manslaughter and put in jail.

Both men did the *exact same thing*. They were lonely and unhappy. They inappropriately treated their pain with alcohol and then selfishly chose to drive home. Both became sleepy and disoriented and were unable to stay on the road, but one man hit a ditch, while the other man hit a child. The actions of the two men were the same, but we tend to view them quite differently, and we then impose vastly different consequences.

The death of the child was certainly tragic, but so is our blindness to the pain of people who make awful mistakes as they use Getting and Protecting Behaviors. I am *not* saying we should ignore the behavior of drunk drivers; I *am* saying that we inappropriately judge people according to the *consequences* of their behavior instead of looking at their *behavior* and seeing it as a sign of their emptiness and fear. We punish people for their mistakes instead of seeing their mistakes as an opportunity to help them.

People do need to be responsible for their mistakes. Occasionally they even need to be jailed or otherwise restricted—removing the driver's licenses of people who drink and drive, for example—so they can't make mistakes that endanger the property and health of others. But they don't need to be *punished*, which never serves the superior goal of helping them see their mistakes and learn from them. Wise men love people and tell them the truth, and as they do that, people learn and grow. Punishment doesn't accomplish anything but the administration of pain, which only makes people more empty and afraid and *more* likely to use Getting and Protecting Behaviors—more anger, violence, lying, and so on.

Guilt and Shame: Requiring Ourselves to Suffer for Our Mistakes

Most of us feel a need not only to punish *others* for their mistakes, but also to punish ourselves for ours. We've been taught to hate our mistakes. We feel ashamed of them. We carry them around like hot coals, never to be cooled.

Guilt is a feeling of regret about a *thing* we've done. Shame is a feeling of regret about who we *are*. We feel guilty about a *mistake*. We feel ashamed about *ourselves*. Some guilt is good—it motivates us to learn from our mistakes and avoid them—but shame and excessive guilt are needlessly painful and deadly.

We don't begin life ashamed of ourselves. Shame is learned. It's a judgment that who we are with our warts is unacceptable, even disgusting, to other people, and then we suffer the deadly fear that we'll be unloved and alone, as was the case with a man named Sheldon.

Sheldon's father wanted a son who was strong and accomplished. His mother wanted a son who was sensitive and caring, in addition to brilliant and handsome. As a baby, Sheldon did many cute and attractive things, but as he grew he was inevitably clumsy on occasion and inconvenienced people with his mistakes—as all children do. He often failed to do what his parents expected of him, and when that happened, they did what virtually all parents do: They sighed. They frowned. They stopped hugging him and smiling at him. They encouraged him with their words and behavior never to make those mistakes again. They behaved quite differently toward him than they did when he was a "good boy." From this Sheldon learned an awful lesson: "When I make mistakes something is seriously wrong with me," which is the central belief of anyone who is ashamed. Although we don't mean to do it, we teach this to our children at an early age.

Shame is crippling. When people feel ashamed, they can't feel loved. They can't see clearly. They can't learn or grow. Wise men help people eliminate shame from their lives with love and the truth—the same tools we use to overcome fear, anger, and all the Getting and Protecting Behaviors.

First, the truth. People feel ashamed because they judge that their mistakes make them defective and unlovable. A wise man can often make a big difference simply by showing people that this judgment is not true, as one wise man did with his friend Richard, who described some unkind things he'd said to his son the night before, adding that he felt ashamed of his behavior.

Wise man: Why are you ashamed?

Richard: What I did was terrible. I remember how I felt when my father talked to me like that.

Wise man: You think you *should* have behaved differently, don't you?

Richard: Of course.

Wise man: Do you know how to play golf?

Richard: No.

Wise man: Do you feel ashamed that you don't know how to play golf?

Richard: No.

Wise man: Why not?

Richard: Nobody ever taught me.

Wise man: And nobody ever taught you how to be a loving father, either. Why should you feel ashamed about making mistakes while you're *learning* how to do something? You only need to *see* your mistakes and *learn* from them.

Until we see a better way, we tend to do what we're familiar with, even if it's not right or effective. We do what we know. Although there were many times I knew I wasn't doing the right thing with my children, for example, it was all I could do until I learned something better. It's foolish to keep blaming ourselves for behaving in the ways we were taught all our lives.

None of this is to say that we're not responsible for our mistakes. Of course we are. I'm responsible for all my choices, and when I see that I'm wrong, I have the responsibility to tell the truth and choose differently. Shame, however, has no productive place in any of this. When we make mistakes, the correct response is to tell the truth about them and learn from them. But that's the end of it in most cases. Sometimes we can repair the damage caused by our mistakes, but we don't have to be punished for them.

Although the truth has an important role in the elimination of shame, intellectual understanding of shame is rarely enough. We still need to *feel* loved, and when we have that feeling, joy overwhelms fear, anger, loneliness, and shame.

I have a good friend who was sentenced to a long prison term for some serious mistakes he'd made. We've exchanged many letters, including this one from him:

> I've been so ashamed in this place. I've wanted to die as I realized what I've done with my life. I've been a complete failure as a father. I've betrayed everyone who ever trusted me. And now I'll probably spend the rest of my life here. But you and some others reached out and loved me without wanting anything from me in return. I've never had that before. I never

imagined what it would feel like. I feel like I have a well of love to draw from now, so I don't feel ashamed and discouraged anymore.

As a wise man it's useful to *explain* to people why shame is foolish, but it's even more powerful to simply accept and *love* them.

People feel ashamed about more than just their mistakes. They feel ashamed of their physical appearance, their race, their sex, and other things they did not choose. Again, they need the opportunity to talk about these things and feel accepted.

We Have a Responsibility to *Make* Choices

We not only have a responsibility *for* the choices we make; we have a responsibility to *make* choices. Making choices is more than a *right*—it's a responsibility. Without making them, we can't learn or grow or love others or be happy.

Carl complained that his wife, Paula, spent money irresponsibly, whined at him constantly, didn't take care of the house, never had sex with him, and was a lousy mother. I knew one of Paula's friends, and apparently all those things were true. Carl and I had talked about his situation before.

Carl: I'm sick of this. How can I keep putting up with it?

Me: I wouldn't. I'd *do* something about it. But so far, you haven't.

Carl was surprised at my answer. "What do you mean? What can *I* do? She won't change, and I can't make her—you told me that."

"Right," I said. "You can't make *her* change. That's not one of your choices. But you still have the three choices we've talked about, and they don't involve her. You can live with it and like it, live with it and hate it, or leave it. So far, you've made the second choice—live with it and hate it—but that's really a non-choice. There's no effort involved in that. You're just sitting around complaining and waiting for Paula to do something different. That's pretty lazy, really."

Carl's eyes opened wide as he looked wounded. He'd decided to act like a victim to get some sympathy.

Me: Hey, I'm your friend. I care enough about you to tell you something that will help. If I just tell you what a rotten deal you're getting at home, what will that do? Will that make your life any better? No. Do you want to be happy or not?

Carl: Sure.

Me: Then *do* something different. Make some decisions and act on them. Make the first choice or the third: Live with it and like it, or leave it. Which will it be? Are you ready to divorce your wife and keep being a loser at relationships? Are you willing to bounce your children between two parents? Are you ready to do that?

Carl: I don't know. I sure want to sometimes.

Me: The biggest reason you're unhappy right now is that *you* haven't felt loved all your life, not because of anything *Paula's* doing. If you divorce her, you'll still be unhappy. At this point, you're still learning how to be loving, so in my opinion you'd be crazy to divorce her, because you'd still have almost all the same problems you have now—and then some. So don't even *think* about divorce. First make a decision that you'll finally tell the truth about yourself and get the love you've been missing all your life, and then see what happens to your relationship with your wife.

Carl: I've been doing that a little.

Me: How many times in the last two weeks have you talked about yourself and felt unconditionally loved?

Carl paused, and I said, "Exactly. You've been piddling around with this. You haven't taken it seriously. You have a lifetime of feeling unloved, and you can't change that pattern by approaching this casually. If you really want to change your life, it will take a more consistent effort than you've been making. You have to make decisions every day to get what you need. As you do that, your relationship with your wife and children can begin to change. You can begin talking about yourself to Paula, too. Until then, you're just being lazy and hoping that things will magically work out for you. It doesn't work that way."

We find greater happiness only as we make choices, and the more choices we make, the faster we find it. It's true that as we make more choices, we make more mistakes, but we can also learn more and grow faster. With greater risks come greater rewards. It's worth it. Wise men need to encourage people to get off their backsides and *make choices*.

We Are Not Responsible for the Happiness of Other People

All our lives, we've been taught that we're responsible for the happiness of other people. When we made mistakes, they said things like this to us:

"I'm disappointed (in you)."
"You make me so angry."
"I think you owe me an apology."
"How could you do this (to me)?"

When we did what other people wanted, however, the feedback was quite different:

"Oh, I'm so proud of you."
"It makes me so happy when you do that. You're a good boy (or girl)."

These latter messages—although quite positive on the surface—were still not healthy in most cases, because we heard them only when we *earned* them with our behavior, and they placed a burden on us to make other people happy.

We *are* responsible for loving other people. That's always the right thing to do and the best and happiest way to live. It *is* my responsibility to learn how to love you and everyone else around me, but it's not *your* job to judge whether I'm fulfilling that responsibility. And if you're not happy, that's not *my* responsibility. Your happiness depends on the choices *you* make: telling the truth, exercising faith, using self-control not to use Getting and Protecting Behaviors, and loving other people.

When we understand that we're not responsible for making other people happy, two things disappear from our lives: guilt and anger.

Guilt

In Chapter Six of *Real Love* we talked about the role of apologies in relationships. People demand apologies from us because they believe we *make* them unhappy—and after years of hearing it, we *believe* them and feel guilty. But of course we know that's not true, because people who feel unconditionally loved *don't* feel injured when we inconvenience them, nor do they require apologies. People demand apologies because they feel unloved and are acting like victims. It *is* often appropriate, however, to offer apologies when you know it will help other people feel more loved. But you should not feel motivated by guilt. They felt unhappy and unloved long before you "offended" them.

You're responsible only for the mistakes you make, not for the unhappiness in the lives of other people. You do not have a responsibility to remove their anger or make them happy, despite their vigorous and repeated claims to the contrary. If you took money, return it. If you broke a window, fix it. If you were unkind, see your mistake and apologize. But unloved, victimized, and unhappy people demand that their emptiness be filled with the apologies and suffering of those they believe have offended them— and that is not possible.

Anger

If you're not responsible for the happiness of other people, is it not obvious that *they* are not responsible for *yours*, either? But when the guy ahead of us in heavy traffic does something stupid, don't we tend to get annoyed? And if so, what are we really saying? With astonishing arrogance, we're saying that he has failed in his responsibility—however minor—to make us happy. Every time we get angry, we're telling someone that they have some responsibility to make us happy, and we don't have the right to do that. It's *my* responsibility to tell the truth about myself and to learn how to love other people. When I do *that*, I will be happy. I will never become happier as I remind other people of their responsibility to love *me*.

The wise man's responsibility for the happiness of others

For some time Anne had been feeling loved and had been practicing loving other people.

> Anne: I have a friend whose life is a wreck. She hates her husband. She's depressed and drinking more than she should. I've talked to her a little about Real Love, and she seems to understand that she needs it, but then she withdraws and never calls. What can I do?

> Me: How long do you think she's felt unloved?

> Anne: Probably all her life.

> Me: You're not going to change that in a big hurry, and if *she* doesn't have a sufficient desire to change, you probably won't be able to help her at all. Remember that having a desire to change is the first step to finding love and happiness (Chapter Four of *Real Love*).

> Anne: But she *needs* this. She's miserable. Her whole family's falling apart.

> Me: It's not your responsibility to make her happy, and if you push her to accept something she doesn't want, it's actually intrusive—even though you mean well.

> Anne: So what can I do?

> Me: Keep being her friend. Keep accepting her. Be available to her. When she acts like a victim, you can remind her that *she* can make different choices, and that she's not helpless. But don't feel responsible for the choices she makes.

As wise men, we have a powerful *opportunity* to contribute to the happiness of other people, but we are not *responsible* for their happiness. When we understand that, we won't stumble as often on either of two stones which can be quite a distraction for any wise man: pride and discouragement.

Pride and Discouragement in the Role of Wise Man

When we unconditionally love people, it can make great changes in their lives. If we inappropriately take credit for that, the selfish pride we feel can make it quite difficult for us to continue seeing people clearly. When we feel proud of ourselves for helping people, we tend to work for more of that feeling. Unconsciously, we manipulate them for more praise and more of the feeling of power that comes when we get them to do what we want. That doesn't happen when we see that we're not responsible for the happiness of others.

Some wise men blame themselves when other people are unhappy, but that's just as foolish as being proud when they're happy. Pride and discouragement are two sides of a counterfeit coin. *Children* are happy as a result of how much their parents love them unconditionally. *Adults* are happy as a result of the love they've received *and* the choices they make—to tell the truth, exercise faith, give up their Getting and Protecting Behaviors, and love other people. *They* determine their happiness. You can only add to it, and then only if they allow you to do that.

In addition to explaining the Law of Choice to others, wise men must remember the Law of Choice for *themselves* as they interact with the people they're helping. The Wise Man told the Wart King the truth about his warts, but he did not force the king to accept the truth. He knew he didn't have that right. When the king ran down the mountain, the Wise Man followed the king and made himself *available* in case the king wanted to tell the truth about himself. He didn't force the king to do anything. If the king had insisted at any point that the Wise Man leave, he would have left.

Like the Wise Man, we make ourselves available to those who want to tell the truth about themselves. When they're not able to start the process on their own, we can even help them see the truth, but if they want to lie, get angry, act like victims, and run, we do not have the right to stop them. Although the Wart King eventually quit using his Protecting Behaviors and responded to the Wise Man, many of the people you talk to will not respond positively when you initially tell them the truth and love them. That's their choice to make. One purpose of this book is to describe some of the choices you can then make in response.

Chapter Summary

- The Law of Choice: Everyone has the right to choose what he or she says and does. The results of failure to understand this law are selfishness, expectations, acting like a victim, anger, attacking, and laziness.
- A relationship is the natural result of people making independent choices.
- In any situation or relationship we can make one of three choices: Live with it and like it, live with it and hate it, or leave it.
- The Law of Expectations: We never have the right to expect other people to do anything for us. Promises are an exception to this law, but it is still unproductive when we *insist* that other people fulfill their promises to us.
- Within the choice of "live with it and like it," we can still make requests of our partners, but demands—identified by disappointment and anger—are always harmful. Requests need to be clear and specific.
- Event → Judgment → Feeling → Reaction (EJFR). Events do not cause our behavior. Our behavior is usually a reaction to feelings that are determined by judgments that developed from past events.
- We tend to assign to other people the roles we learned in the play we originally learned as we interacted with our parents and others as children. We then treat people in the present as though they were the people we knew in the past, which causes much misunderstanding and unhappiness.

- Despite the powerful influences we feel from the past, we always have the ability and responsibility to exercise self-control, which acts in a synergistic way with Real Love to make us happy.
- Other people never make us angry.
- We are responsible for our own choices, but not for the effect of our choices on others.
- Making mistakes as we learn to make better choices is inevitable, and when we understand that, we see that it's unwise to feel either angry at others for their mistakes or excessively guilty about our own.
- No matter what choices other people make, we can always make our own choices. In fact, we have a responsibility to do that and learn to make better ones.
- No one—including wise men and women—is responsible for the happiness of other people.

Chapter Four

Starting with Good Principles

Telling the Truth —Why and When

Truth → Seen → Accepted → Loved. We've already established that we must tell the truth about ourselves before we can feel genuinely accepted and loved. But most of us have experienced the disappointment and irritation of other people when they've seen the truth about us, so we've put bags on our heads and used other Getting and Protecting Behaviors to get relief from the pain of our emptiness and fear.

THE PURPOSES OF TELLING THE TRUTH

Helping people tell the truth is usually the most difficult part of being a wise man. By comparison, holding their hands and being compassionate is easy. But love without the truth is useless. How can you feel loved if I love what you pretend to be? What if the Wise Man had never described the king's warts? Would the king have felt truly seen and accepted? Would his life have changed?

Carol came to talk to me about her daughter, Lindsey. After talking for several minutes, it was obvious that Carol had been trying to control her daughter, and, understandably, Lindsey fought against everything her mother did. With a chuckle, I finally said, "You're a pretty terrible mother, aren't you?"

Carol burst into tears and said, "Yes, I am!" After sobbing for a few moments, she said, "I've tried to tell my friends that, but they keep telling me it's all my daughter's fault. They tell me she's rebellious and needs more discipline. You're the only one who sees that *I* must be doing something wrong. I need to know how I can change and make things better."

We talked about some of the mistakes she'd been making with Lindsey, and Carol said it actually felt better to admit that *she* was the problem than to always be wondering what the problem was. She could feel that I wasn't criticizing her, just telling her the truth, and it was a huge relief to her. She'd already sensed that she was doing a terrible job as a mother, but she couldn't describe it—even to herself—because she was distracted by the praise of her friends as they told her she was doing fine. People had always told her what a great mother she was, and in the beginning, that praise felt good. But it had become obvious that something was wrong, and now she just wanted to know *what* was wrong so she could change it and help her daughter. She didn't want to cover up her mistakes any more.

This conversation with Carol illustrates the two principal reasons for helping people tell the truth about themselves

- to create an opportunity for them to feel loved. This requires the wise man to feel loved and loving. If I had been the least bit judgmental—in my tone, posture, or facial expression—when I said, "You're a pretty terrible mother," you can imagine how Carol would have responded. When we're loving, people will listen to almost anything we say.
- to create the possibility for them to make different choices. As long as we blame other people for our problems, we're helpless to solve them. We've placed our happiness in the hands of the people we blame, and then we can't become happier until other people decide to change. When we concentrate on telling the truth about *our* mistakes and failings, we can begin to make wiser choices, especially if we also feel loved.

Not everyone is as eager as Carol to hear the truth, but as a wise man you'll have many opportunities to help people start the process, however slow it might be for some.

Giving Up the Lies

We often can't give up our lies until we're convinced that (1) we *are* lying, (2) our lies are not working, and (3) we're safe and will be accepted when we tell the truth.

We *Are* Lying

Most of us have been lying for so long, we don't recognize that we're doing it. We need someone to show us that we're lying and help us tell the truth the first few times. The Wise Man, for example, simply told the Wart King, "You have warts on your face."

Some of the more common lies we tell—especially to ourselves—include the following:

- "I'm happy," or "I'm fine." We've all been taught that if we do the right things, happiness will be our reward. If we're *not* happy, therefore, we're faced with making one of three choices:

  A. We can admit that *we* are responsible for our own unhappiness and must, therefore, have done something wrong—or many things wrong—to cause it. We're not likely to make that choice, because we do *not* like to admit we're wrong—it would make us defective and unlovable.

  B. We can blame someone else for our unhappiness—a popular choice.

  C. We can pretend to be happy. Many of us do this, mostly unconsciously. No matter how empty and afraid we are, we tell people—even ourselves—that everything is all right. In our society, when people ask us, "How are you?" we're virtually obligated to respond with something positive. It's expected. In response to that question, when do people ever say, "You know, I've been feeling empty and afraid for the longest time"? As a wise man, you'll find that many people tend to strongly resist telling the truth about being unhappy, and we'll talk in Chapter Seven about helping people tell the truth about how they feel.

- Lies about our Getting and Protecting Behaviors. We hide these because they're embarrassing. We don't like to admit that we lie, attack people, act like victims, cling, and run, because somehow we know they're wrong. But until we do admit these behaviors, we can't feel seen, accepted, and loved. In Chapter Eight we'll discuss how to help people talk about these behaviors.

- Lies about our use of Imitation Love. Very few people see that they fill the emptiness in their lives with praise, power, pleasure, and safety. When they tell the truth about that, they can feel accepted and begin to find Real Love instead of using Imitation Love as a substitute.

Our Lies Don't Work

Vicki had just begun the process of telling the truth about herself, and it was not going well. She kept blaming her husband, Paul, for all her problems. I explained to her how other people never *make* us angry and pointed out that the lack of Real Love in her life had existed long before she met Paul.

Vicki was too angry to hear that. She'd acted like a victim all her life and was accustomed to blaming other people whenever anything went wrong. Most of the sentences she spoke began with the words *Paul* or *he*. She could see only this:

- Whenever she interacted with Paul, she was more angry after the experience than before.
- When she asked him to do the things that would make her happy, he refused.
- When she asked him to stop doing the things she disliked, he did them anyway, and then she felt irritated.
- After years of being married to Paul, she was more unhappy than the day they met.

To her all these facts proved that he must be the cause of her misery. She could not let go of this conclusion, and it was destroying her and their relationship. As long as she blamed him for her feelings, there was nothing she could do to change her life. She had unwittingly placed her happiness entirely in his hands and made herself his slave.

"How many times," I asked, "have you blamed Paul for how you feel and tried to change who he is?"

Vicki immediately leaped to defend herself. She began to carefully explain—once again—that everything *was* Paul's fault, and she insisted she wasn't trying to change him, just trying to help their marriage.

Vicki was lying—mostly unconsciously—as she denied her own selfishness and manipulation, but some people can't hear the truth in direct confrontation. Many of them, however, can begin to listen when they see how their lies simply *don't work*.

Me: Okay, how many times now have you been angry at Paul?

Vicki: For years, I guess, but he—

Me: I'm not talking about *him* here. I'm asking how many times *you* have been angry at him and blamed him for how you feel?

Vicki: I don't really know.

Me: You've blamed him at least a dozen times in the short time we've been talking, so you've probably done it thousands of times, wouldn't you say?

Vicki: (pause) I guess so.

Me: What do you do for a hobby?

Vicki: Gardening.

Me: Let's say I plant a particular kind of flower in one spot in my garden and it dies. But I don't give up. I'm positive that one of these flowers will grow there, so I get another one and plant it in the same spot. And it dies, too, but I'm persistent. I do this a hundred times in succession, and they all die. Would there be a word for this gardening technique?

Vicki was reluctant to answer, so I suggested, "Would you think it was stupid?

She smiled. "I wouldn't have chosen that word, but yes, that would describe it."

Me: After doing the same thing a hundred times, we know that what I'm doing is not working, don't we? I need to do something different—*even if I believe the old way is right.* That's why you need to do something different with Paul. Even if you believe you're right, it's simply not working. It's not making either of you happy.

Vicki: But he—

Me: (laughing) Do you really want to keep watching that plant die? Believe me, I understand that blaming Paul seems to make sense—I'm sure he does lots of things wrong, like the rest of us—but in all these years, has that ever made your relationship better or made you genuinely happy?

Vicki: No.

Me: Haven't you had enough? You just said it was *stupid* to keep doing something that doesn't work. You don't really need to understand *why* it doesn't. The plant just keeps dying. Do you want the plant to live or not?

Vicki didn't answer.

Me: I mean it. Do you want a loving and happy relationship with your husband or not?

Vicki: I do.

Me: Then *you'll* have to do something different.

I described the steps to finding Real Love, and Vicki followed them, even though it was hard in the beginning. As she tried something different and felt more loved, she could see how she'd been lying more than she realized. You will find, however, that some people get enough Imitation Love from their lies that they will not give them up. You often can't persuade them to abandon a pattern of behavior they've used for a lifetime. You can only give them an opportunity to tell the truth.

A comment here about the word *stupid*, which I used above. We tend to view that word as insulting—if we're stupid, we must be bad—but I intentionally use it to describe our destructive behaviors so we can learn not to take ourselves so seriously. If you can feel loved while you're admitting that your behavior is stupid, you'll feel much more loved than while you're minimizing that behavior.

We certainly do plenty of things that qualify as stupid. Getting and Protecting Behaviors are all stupid, because even though they lead to unhappiness in ourselves and misery in the people around us, we keep right on using them. Not smart. We need to learn to identify the futility of those behaviors, laugh at ourselves, feel loved despite our foolishness, and learn to behave differently. People who behave stupidly are not bad or unlovable. They're just feeling unloved and making mistakes.

Our Need for Safety Before We Can Tell the Truth

Let me use a fictitious story to illustrate the powerful need we have to feel safe before we can tell the truth.

After Billy's truck was hit by another truck, he sued the driver's trucking company for his injuries. In court, the company's lawyer confronted Billy: "But at the scene of the accident, didn't you say, 'I'm fine'"?

Billy responded, "Yep, I did, but you see, my mule Bessie—"

"Then you lied," roared the lawyer, and he moved that the case be dismissed.

Billy tried again: "But my mule Bessie, she—"

Again the lawyer interrupted, refusing to listen to a story about a mule. But the judge asked Billy to continue.

"I was drivin' down the road," Billy said, "with Bessie in the trailer. This big 'ol truck ran the stop sign and smacked into my truck. I was throwed into the ditch, and I laid there, hurtin' real bad. Pretty quick, a State Patrol came up. He heard Bessie moanin', so he went over to 'er an' saw she had two broke legs. He took out 'is gun and shot 'er between the eyes. Then he comes over to me with that gun in his hand and says, 'Your mule was in such bad shape, I had to shoot 'er. How are *you* feelin'?'"

When we're afraid, we immediately lie to protect ourselves. A wise man knows that and helps us feel safe enough to tell the truth about ourselves as he accepts, loves, and teaches us. Love is the most important ingredient in helping someone tell the truth—not logic or brilliance. You'll rarely get people to tell the truth about themselves by aggressively dazzling them with a list of their Getting and Protecting Behaviors. They only want to be certain that you unconditionally accept and love them. If they know that, they'll share the truth with you.

But Why the Negative Things?

After Jordan had participated one day in a discussion with myself and others about the need for telling the truth about ourselves, he was eager to ask a question: "I've heard many self-help and spiritual teachers say that we need to think more about the positive things in our lives, because we tend to become what we think about: 'As a man thinketh, so is he.' But you're saying we need to talk about our mistakes and fears and stuff like that. Isn't it better to just not think about those negative things? If we focus on them, won't we get more stuck and discouraged?"

There's no doubt, I told Jordan, that we can be inspired by positive goals and thoughts, but no meaningful growth can occur without a foundation of the *whole* truth, not just the positive qualities we hope for but also the great many "negative" characteristics we have that we have a strong tendency to hide. We don't usually tell the truth, for example, about *our* responsibility for the unhappiness in our lives. We blame others instead. Even when we do talk about our mistakes, we tend to dwell on guilt, pain, and being victims— not on responsibility and our need to change. Certainly, we don't want to *focus* on the negative, but we do need to talk about all of who we are before we can begin to grow from that place.

Imagine that you've lived in a garbage dump all your life. One day a traveler arrives and tells you he's seen a beautiful valley where there's no garbage and no foul odor. To reach this place, he says, you only have to leave the dump and start walking west. But because you can't imagine anything so different from what you've always known, you stay where you are. Every few months another traveler comes by and encourages you to visit the valley, so finally you strap everything you own on your back and start walking.

You arrive in a lovely valley and begin to set up camp, but you notice that this place stinks just like the dump, and within hours trucks come and dump garbage all around you. The next day, remembering the words of the travelers, you start walking west again, but the smell of the dump is still everywhere, and whenever you stop for the night, the trucks arrive. You repeat this process several times until one evening you meet an old woman on the road and tell her about your discouraging experiences. "I believed the travelers," you say, "and did exactly what they said. I left home and walked west toward the valley they promised, but everywhere I go, I wind up in a dump."

"My dear," she says, "You're in the valley right now."

"That's impossible," you say. "It stinks here just like it did at home."

"What's in your backpack?" she asks.

"Everything I own," you reply, and then you turn the bag upside down and empty out fifty pounds of smelly garbage.

"You've been carrying a dump around with you," says the old woman, "and you'll never escape it until you put it down and go on without it."

When you left home, you couldn't imagine going without all the garbage you'd spent a lifetime collecting, but now you realize that's why it smelled like a dump everywhere you went, and why the garbage trucks always came—each time you unpacked the garbage, everyone in the neighborhood assumed it was a new dump and sent their garbage to you. Now you have a choice: You can cling to your precious belongings, refusing to acknowledge that they're garbage, *or* you can admit the truth about what you have and leave it behind. What will you do?

Most of us have been raised in dumps of emptiness, fear, and Getting and Protecting Behaviors. Even when we're told there's a better place to live, we can't imagine anything so different from home, so we're content to stay right where we are. But occasionally we think positively and start walking. Of course, we carry with us the precious belongings we've spent a lifetime collecting—our fears, lies, anger—so everywhere we go, we're followed by that awful smell, which attracts everyone in the neighborhood looking for a place to dump their garbage.

Finally, a wise woman—or wise man—points out that we're carrying sacks of garbage on our backs. We could be offended and make her go away, or deny what we're carrying and keep hauling it around, but until we acknowledge that we *are* carrying sacks of garbage, the dump will follow us wherever we go. Identifying the garbage doesn't have to be a "negative" experience. We don't have to roll around in it after we recognize it. We don't have to hang it on the wall or create a shrine to it. But we do need to acknowledge it, because only then can we finally set it down and move on to a better place.

There's another important reason to tell the truth about our negative qualities. We rarely feel loved *unconditionally* when people accept us while we're being intelligent, handsome, beautiful, successful, and otherwise "good." When people accept us with those qualities, we tend to conclude—usually accurately—that they accept us only *because* of our doing something to earn it, which is conditional acceptance. We feel most loved when people accept us with our flaws. The life of the Wart King, for example, didn't change until he was accepted with his warts.

The Central Truth

The truths we help people see are not always painful and "negative," but are sometimes quite affirming, as we see in the case of Kevin, who is learning about Real Love from *you*, the wise man in this conversation.

> Kevin: Now that I've learned about Real Love, I don't feel any better. In fact, I feel worse. I see that I'm angry all the time.

I don't really love my wife. I'm frustrated with my children. I hate my job. I've made a mess of everything.

You: (smiling) Yes, you have, and that's not much fun to see in the beginning, but that's mostly because you're not seeing *all* the truth.

Kevin: What do you mean?

You: It's true that you haven't been loved and don't know how to love other people. It's true that you feel empty and afraid, and that you use Getting and Protecting Behaviors to fill your life with Imitation Love. *But* it's also true that without feeling loved, you could not have avoided most of that. I don't know many people who *haven't* made most of the mistakes you have—including me—but so what? It's also true that you're worth loving just like you are, with all those mistakes.

Kevin is clearly skeptical, which proves once again how rarely he's experienced unconditional love.

Kevin: That's hard to believe.

You: Have you ever held a newborn baby?

Kevin: Sure—my son.

You: Did you love him?

Kevin: Sure.

You: He was worthy of being loved right from the beginning, wasn't he? Without doing anything at all to prove himself to you?

Kevin: Of course.

You: *So were you* as a newborn. And if you were worthy of being loved as a baby, why would it be any different now that you're an adult?

Kevin: I've made a lot of mistakes since then. I've hurt a lot of people.

You: And why did you do that? Did you have plenty of Real Love in your life but simply made a conscious decision to withhold it from people?

Kevin: No, but—

You: There's no *but*, just *no*. Your Getting and Protecting Behaviors—your mistakes—were a reaction to your not feeling loved. That doesn't make you a victim here; it just explains much of your behavior. Sure, you've made mistakes, but who cares? You still deserve to be loved, and you can find that love as you learn to tell the truth about yourself and allow people to love you.

People everywhere require us to meet certain standards before we're acceptable. Our friends and acquaintances are always evaluating us—virtually a process of interrogation at times. At church people watch our behavior closely to assess our worthiness. Even in our own families, we see the love come and go, depending on what we say and do. As wise men, however, we know that we deserve to be loved as we are—even when we don't genuinely love others, when we fill our lives with Imitation Love, and when we use Getting and Protecting Behaviors every day—and we need to teach that to other people.

Although it was good that Kevin understood the *principle* the wise man explained, he was much more profoundly affected by the wise man's complete acceptance of him during that one conversation and in the following months. It's *unconditional love*, not words alone, that changes people's lives.

WHEN TO TELL THE TRUTH

After a lifetime of hiding and lying, telling the truth about ourselves can be quite uncomfortable, so most of us are hesitant in the beginning. But some of us are so excited at the feeling of being accepted that we go overboard and tell the truth to almost everyone. Many people are simply not prepared to hear all that, however, so we need to be somewhat discriminating and tell the truth to people we believe will be capable of accepting and loving us. But don't be *afraid* of telling the truth. Fear is deadly.

Usually, you can't know *beforehand* whether someone is capable of accepting you, but as you tell the truth, you will attract and create the wise men you seek. You don't have to expose your whole life—start with little things. If a friend at work, for example, says in the usual offhand way, "How are you?" you could take a small risk and consider saying one of the relatively easy things found on page 14 and in Chapter Four of *Real Love*. But don't feel pressured. Take your time and gradually take more risks with your truth-telling. Eventually, you'll learn that when you feel loved, people simply cannot hurt you, and you'll be able to tell the truth to anyone. *That* is real safety and power.

If the person speaking is generally critical and not accepting, however, you need to recognize that for them "How are you?" is just the usual social custom, and the appropriate reply may be to say, "Fine." Is that completely honest? No, but the purpose of telling the truth about yourself is to create opportunities for you to feel seen and loved, and if that purpose will not be served, being completely honest would be unproductive.

When to Help People Tell the Truth

Everyone *needs* to tell the truth, but most people are initially afraid, so they need the loving encouragement you can provide. If you push them too hard and too soon, however, you may add to their fear and contribute to their feeling even more unloved. Being a wise man is much like teaching people to swim when they're afraid of the water. You have to encourage them, perhaps even nudge them—emotionally speaking—to get in the water. But if you push them too hard and too fast, you can make them so afraid that they can't hear anything you say.

Just because someone needs to tell the truth does not give you the right to make them. On the other hand, many people are very grateful for the wise men in their lives who had the courage to speak up and tell them the truth even when they resisted it. The Wise Man told the Wart King about his warts even though he knew the king would not be pleased to hear it. Carol (pages 105-7) was grateful that I took the risk of telling her she was a terrible mother. We have to take risks as we help people see the truth about themselves, because only then can they feel seen and loved.

How do you know when you're pushing someone too hard? Mostly by making mistakes. Don't worry about that. Just be honest about your mistakes, and the more loving you become, the better you'll identify when your encouragement becomes pushing. As you become more loving, you'll also frighten people less.

As you consider whether to tell people what you think is true, don't be motivated only by what they *need* to hear, or by what you *want* to say. Also ask yourself, "*Can* this person hear what I'm about to say?" If you think he or she can't hear you—because of fear or anger—be quiet. If you keep talking—even when he or she badly needs to hear that pearl of wisdom you have—you're being selfish and foolish.

Helping People When *You* Are the Subject of Their Getting and Protecting Behaviors

Imagine that your spouse is angrily telling you about a mistake you've made. It's often unwise to say, "You're just angry because you haven't felt enough Real Love all your life. You're protecting yourself with anger and using it as a Getting Behavior to give you a sense of power." When *you* are the subject of their Getting and Protecting Behaviors, you often can't help people tell the truth about their behavior, because they'll perceive anything you say as defending yourself.

In such cases, it's usually best to tell the truth about *yourself.* To your spouse—or boss or anyone else—you could say, "My mistake. I wasn't being careful (or loving or whatever)." But what if it wasn't your fault? You can generally identify *something* about your behavior in that instance that was imperfect. Stick with the truth about yourself, and eventually some people will accept your attempts to help them tell the truth about themselves. One advantage of a group meeting is that when one person attacks you, another wise man in the group can help that person see the truth about himself.

When It's Just None of Your Business

It's exciting to share the truth with people and watch their lives change, so in an unconscious attempt to repeat that sensation, some wise men stick their noses inappropriately into other people's lives. My friend Virginia asked me for advice about such an experience.

> Virginia: Yesterday I was in the grocery store with my sister, and her son was fussing about something he wanted. All he needed was a little of her attention, but she was getting more angry and telling him to be quiet. So I said, "I've learned that when I'm angry, I'm wrong. Your son just needs some attention from you." I was only trying to help her see what she was doing, but she was furious. She told me she could take care of her own son just fine, thank you very much, and then she didn't talk to me all the way home. I thought I said what she needed to hear. How could I have handled that differently?

> Me: I know you were trying to help her—and her son—but your sister didn't ask for your help. Her anger proved she was already feeling empty and afraid, and in that condition she could only see your comment as an attack. You probably couldn't have said anything that would have helped, and it was pretty much none of your business to say anything. You just have to accept that there are billions of people out there that you can't help.

Remember that people have the right to make their own choices—and mistakes. You don't have a right to interfere just because you think they need to hear what you have to say. So when *should* you offer what you feel is the truth? Although I can't offer rigid rules on the subject, I will suggest that on the whole it's wise to wait until you have some kind of invitation. Following are some situations where you have an implied or direct invitation:

- When you're a spouse. In marriage you've agreed to care for one another's happiness. You can't genuinely care about your partner if you consistently stand by and say nothing while he or she is using Getting and Protecting Behaviors and feeling unloved. Telling the truth about your spouse must, of course, be done in a loving way.

- When you're a parent. It's the *responsibility* of parents to speak the truth to their children as they unconditionally love them.
- When you're asked. If someone actually asks you for your opinion, you have a *right* to give it, but that doesn't always mean you *should*. Many times I've been asked for my opinion by someone who could not hear the answer, and then I give only a partial answer.
- When you're in a group of wise men. People who come to group meetings or otherwise participate in a group—with phone calls or other contacts—are declaring a willingness to hear the truth. You then have a right to lovingly tell them what you see—if you believe they can hear it.

Too Much or Too Little

There are some people who will become frightened no matter what you do. All your attempts to speak to them will be either "too much" or "too little."

For several weeks, I was in a group with Ann and Joyce. Ann came to me privately and voiced her concern that I was being too soft and didn't sufficiently challenge the women in the group to tell the truth. The next day Joyce told me I was confronting people too much and loving them too little. The same approach will be too frightening and confrontational to some people but too mild and slow to others.

Similarly, as you vary your approach with a single person, you'll often find that you can only do either too much or too little. Some people learn nothing as you tell them the truth in a gentle or indirect way, and then when you speak more directly, they suddenly become offended. In a moment, you've moved from too soft to too hard. Sometimes there is simply no "just right." Do your best to speak lovingly and remember that you're dealing with years of emptiness and fear. You can't help everyone. We can illustrate the principle of too much or too little with the story of Earl, who is curious about Real Love and beginning to attend meetings of wise men.

Earl uniformly resists hearing the truth about himself and reacts by lying, attacking, and running. After several weeks of silence, he's invited to say something during a group meeting, but he declines this invitation and others for several more weeks. Finally, he responds.

Earl: I've had a good week. I'm happy.

Wise man: You don't look happy.

Earl: (irritated) Well, I am.

Wise man: When you came in the room tonight, you sat by yourself and spoke to no one. You didn't look happy at all.

Earl: I just felt like sitting by myself.

Wise man: Earl, I accept you whether you talk about your fear and anger or not. But you won't feel seen and loved until you do.

Earl: I know how I feel, and I'm sick of you pushing me to say something you want to hear!

Notice that for several weeks the group gradually offered Earl opportunities to be seen, but every approach was too little. When the wise man made an observation about Earl's behavior, that was too much. His fear made it impossible to approach him just right. I can't tell you how much effort you should put into helping someone tell the truth, but I can tell you that if you're not willing on occasion to do "too much" and take the risk that people might be angry at you, you probably won't be able to help anyone. As you're fearlessly trying to say the best thing, you *will* sometimes push too hard.

If you attempt to help someone tell the truth, and he or she reacts by running or attacking, for example, you haven't necessarily made a mistake. Even if you *are* wrong in your approach, the other person's Protecting Behavior isn't *caused* by you—they're reacting to the judgments and feelings of a lifetime (EJFR). Try to be as loving and effective as possible, but don't be either flattered or discouraged by the reactions of other people.

The Wise Man Telling the Truth About Himself

Not only did the Wise Man point out the warts of the king, but he also talked about his own warts. The king had never seen another man tell the truth about himself and not be ashamed, so the Wise Man's example was illuminating. As you tell the truth about yourself, people will see that you're not embarrassed by your warts but instead feel loved while you talk about them. Your example will give them faith and courage. Earlier in the chapter, for example, I told Carol she was not being a good mother to her rebellious daughter. That's a tough pill for most people to swallow, so then I described to her some of the many mistakes *I* had made as a father. As we laughed together about my mistakes, she felt much more comfortable admitting hers.

When you use examples from your own life as you talk with people who are in the process of telling you the truth about themselves, remember that you're helping *them* to be truthful, not giving them an opportunity to accept *you*. Don't take over the position of speaker (First Rule of Seeing from Chapter Four of *Real Love*).

Chapter Summary

- We need to tell the truth about ourselves both to create opportunities to feel accepted and loved, and to create the possibility of making wiser choices.
- We can give up our lies more easily when people help us see that we *are* lying, when we see that our lies aren't working, and when we're confident we'll feel safe telling the truth.
- We need to tell the truth about our "negative" characteristics, because that's when we feel most loved unconditionally.
- We need to help people see the truth about themselves only when we're being loving, and when they're capable of hearing what we have to say.
- With many people, there simply is no right way to help them see the truth. You can't help everyone.

Where the Rubber Meets the Road

How To Tell The Truth

Marie had read *Real Love* and finally understood why she and her husband, Frank, had been having a hard time in their relationship. She was eager to share this with Frank, so the next time he was angry, she said, "You only get angry at me because *you're* not feeling loved, not because of anything *I* did. When you tell the truth about that, you can feel accepted, and then you won't be angry anymore." Everything Marie said was true, but Frank only heard her telling him that *he* needed to shape up. Because Marie was still empty and afraid, her unconscious intent was to communicate exactly what Frank heard. She was protecting herself, and Frank *felt* that. In her defense, she also had *some* interest in actually helping him.

When Frank talked to me later that day, I said almost the same words to him that Marie had, but this time he nodded his head thoughtfully as he admitted that it was all true. It's not *words* that change people; it's a combination of knowledge and love that makes the difference. The function of wise men is to love and teach, and then to love and teach some more.

If you attempt to help people tell the truth about themselves when they don't feel loved, they *will* use Getting and Protecting Behaviors. If you don't feel sufficiently loved yourself, you'll become confused and afraid, and despite knowing the right words to say, you'll feel inclined to use your own Getting and Protecting Behaviors and then will not be able to help them. That doesn't make you bad, but in those moments you'll be useless as a wise man. Seeing people clearly and loving them is not a technique. It's a natural result of wise men feeling loved enough to share what they have.

THE FOURTH RULE OF SEEING

What can you do if you don't feel loved, and you're presented with a situation where people need you to see and accept them? Remember the Fourth Rule of Seeing in Chapter Four of *Real Love*: If you can't be a wise man, get one, which includes offering one to the person you're talking to *and* finding one for yourself. You may, for example, get a call from someone in the group at a time when you're not feeling loving. You could decide to make an attempt to see and accept him or her. As we discussed in Chapter One, sharing the love you have can sometimes miraculously multiply the love you feel. But if you continue to feel empty, you won't help the person you're talking to, and you could say something like, "I apologize. I'm trying to listen, but I'm not doing very well. I have some other things on my mind right now, and I just can't give you what you need—much as I want to. This has nothing to do with you. Can you call someone else, or call me back tomorrow?" As you do this, you're helping that person find a wise man. Additionally, you can get a wise man for yourself by calling someone who can accept you. With that, you'll be better prepared to be a wise man again.

If people speak to you *outside a group*, people who wouldn't understand the language of truth-telling—as above—you might excuse yourself from the conversation. But we can't avoid all conversations where we don't feel loving—we'd become hermits—so in those situations, simply do your best to listen, admit to yourself that you're not able to unconditionally accept your partner, and watch for any tendency on your part to use Getting and Protecting Behaviors.

After Marie's conversation with Frank, she asked me what she could have said that would have been more effective.

> Me: Words alone don't heal. If you want to be a wise man, you need to *love* and teach, and you can't do that if you don't feel loved yourself.

> Marie: But when Frank's angry, I have to say *something*. He needs to see what he's doing, or he'll just keep on doing it forever.

> Me: You can't give what you don't have, so if you're feeling the least bit defensive, or afraid, or annoyed, don't try to be a wise man.

> Marie: So what can I do when he's mad and I'm defensive?

> Me: If he's not actually speaking to you, say *nothing*. You couldn't help him anyway. If he *is* talking to you, you could say, "Frank, I really want to listen to everything you're saying, but I just can't hear it all right now. That's not your fault. Can we talk about this later today?" And then remember the Fourth Rule of Seeing. When you can't be a wise man, get one—in this instance, for yourself, not for him.

THE FIRST AND SECOND RULES OF SEEING

Although being a wise man is not a technique, it *is* useful for wise men to remember the First and Second Rules of Seeing. Let's watch Susan learn about these rules as she talks to you about her husband, Jeff. Because of her recent association with several wise women, she understands intellectually that her husband is not to blame for her unhappiness, but there are still occasions when she gets angry at him. "Two days ago," she says, "I got a note from the school that our son Jeremy is having trouble with two of his subjects. Yesterday, when Jeff got home from work, I told him we had to talk about it. He said he didn't want to and walked into the next room."

"*Before* you talked about Jeremy," you say, "did Jeff say anything?"

Susan thinks for a moment. "I guess I did ask him how work went that day, and he mumbled something about how it didn't go very well."

You: So after he told you his day went badly, you didn't ask him anything more about it—instead you charged right into the discussion about Jeremy's school, right?

Susan: I guess so.

You: I know you didn't mean to do this, but when Jeff told you he'd had a bad day, he was trying to communicate with you—even if he didn't realize it himself. But you ignored him and tried to get him to listen to *you*. It's no wonder he didn't want to talk to you anymore. It never works to have two people competing to be seen. There can only be one speaker at a time—that's the First Rule of Seeing.

Susan: But we *have* to talk about Jeremy.

You: No doubt, but you both can't talk at the same time, so you have to pick someone to be first. You could argue about it, or you could follow the Second Rule of Seeing: Whoever speaks first is the speaker. You asked him how work was. That made him the speaker. Then it was your job to listen.

Susan: But he's *always* complaining about work.

You: (laughing) So what? If somebody's *always* hungry, does that make their hunger less real? I'm *not* criticizing you, just suggesting that if you follow the First and Second Rules, you'll begin to hear each other. You can both say everything you want, but not at the same time. Right now neither of you feels seen. You're both too busy trying to get one another's attention.

Susan still looks skeptical, so you ask, "How do you feel when *I* listen to you?"

A look of understanding passes across her face. "I love it," she says.

You: So will Jeff, when you listen to *him*. And don't listen to him just so he'll listen to *you*. If you genuinely listen to him, it's very likely that he'll feel more accepted by you and will listen better when you do have something to say—about your son's school problem, for example.

Susan: But what can I do with the school thing right now?

You: Ask Jeff again to talk about it—when he's not stressed and you're not irritated—and accept that he still might not want to. If he doesn't, you might have to handle it on your own.

THE THIRD RULE OF SEEING

When Susan brings up the same subject the next day, Jeff still doesn't want to deal with it, so she handles the matter herself. But now Susan is armed with the Rules of Seeing for subsequent conversations, and a month later she asks Jeff to go with her to a parent-teacher meeting at school. He says he doesn't really want to go.

Who is the speaker here? Susan could argue that *she's* the speaker because she spoke first about the meeting. Jeff could argue that *he's* the speaker because Susan is asking him a question and therefore inviting him to be the speaker. Sometimes you have to be flexible with the Second Rule. If one partner is *unable* to listen, it's wise to let that person be the speaker *even if he or she didn't speak first.* When you're in doubt about who the speaker is, let your partner speak. If neither of you can listen, it's usually best if no one speaks.

Susan thinks of a dozen critical things to say to Jeff, but she remembers the Third Rule of Seeing: Whatever the details, the speaker is really talking about himself. When Jeff said he didn't want to go to the *meeting*, he was really talking about *himself*—mostly about his emptiness and fear—and with that in mind, Susan decides to really listen.

Susan: You don't like those meetings, do you?

Jeff: No, I really don't.

Susan: Don't worry about it, then. I'll go by myself and see you when I get back.

Susan is not surrendering or losing here. She wisely understands that application of the Rules will allow her to be loving instead of having another of those hurtful interactions where she struggles to speak and listen at the same time. The Rules simply make conversations more productive. They don't prevent you from saying anything you wish; they just give you guidance about when and how to speak and listen.

We all have a right to make our own choices, even when they seem selfish. Jeff is not being a supportive husband or parent, but Susan doesn't have a right to change that. The most important thing Susan can do is listen, and she's doing that. Jeff is pleased, of course, and as she takes this approach more often, their relationship improves and they're soon able to talk about their son and other subjects they've been avoiding.

By the way, why *didn't* Jeff want to go to the parent-teacher meeting? Because he unconsciously knew that he'd be told negative things about his son, and then he'd feel guilty about his performance as a father. Already empty and unloved, he was afraid of hearing about yet another mistake he'd made, and he reacted with the Protecting Behavior of running. But Susan didn't need to go through all that analysis—she just needed to realize he was talking about himself and give him an opportunity to do so more openly.

Remembering the Third Rule is sometimes more difficult when the subject of someone's words is *you*, not just a school meeting. One Friday evening, as Susan went out to run some errands, Jeff asked her to bring back some sausage for lunch the next day. When she returned, he went through the groceries, held up the package of sausage, and said with considerable irritation, "I can't believe you got this. You know this isn't the brand I like."

Susan couldn't understand Jeff's anger and immediately felt threatened and defensive. After all she'd done for him, how could he be so ungrateful and complain about such an insignificant thing? This is how countless arguments begin, and we don't usually understand why. How could two people let a package of meat affect something as important as their marriage?

Remember the Third Rule of Seeing. Jeff was talking about *himself*, not a brand of sausage. When Susan came back from the store without the brand Jeff he'd requested, Jeff heard her say with her behavior, "I don't care about you"—and in *that* situation, she *was* saying that. If her primary concern had been for him, she would have known that this sausage business was important to him, even though it seemed silly to her. She easily could have called from the store on her cell phone and said, "They don't have your favorite brand. Do you want me to get another kind while I'm here or just forget the sausage for now? Maybe tomorrow we could check another store." The call would have been a minor inconvenience compared with the conflict that actually occurred.

When Jeff said, "I can't believe you got these," he was really saying, "You didn't listen to me—again! For the hundredth time, you're telling me you don't care about me." Susan naturally felt attacked, so immediately she began to feel threatened and defensive. Jeff saw the initial look of anger on her face and braced for an argument, but then Susan remembered the Third Rule and made a decision to listen to what Jeff was saying about *himself*, not her. She correctly heard that he was feeling empty and unloved, so she said, "I knew this wasn't your favorite brand. I could have called and asked if you wanted something else instead, but I was in a hurry and wanted to get home. My mistake."

Jeff was astonished. After Susan listened to him and told the truth about herself, the argument was over. Please understand that I'm not suggesting that Jeff's behavior was acceptable. I'm only describing how Susan was able to listen to him more effectively.

When people speak, are they *always* talking about themselves? No. If you feel unconditionally loved, you won't have a need to get something for *yourself* or protect yourself when you speak, and then your communication isn't about filling your needs and protecting yourself. You can simply convey information to others and listen to them.

Using the Rules in a Group Meeting

In a group meeting Evan is talking about one of the men who isn't there. With obvious irritation, Matt interrupts, "I don't think we should talk about people who aren't here. It's a waste of time, and it's not fair to the person we're talking about."

Evan defends himself, saying he's not attacking the absent man, only trying to better understand the man's behavior and relate it to his own. But Matt persists in his original stand, and the discussion is going nowhere as they both become more agitated.

Finally, Evan realizes he's not being an effective wise man, and he remembers the Fourth Rule: If you can't be a wise man, get one. Turning to the other men in the room, he says, "Can you help me here? I'm not handling this well." When Getting and Protecting Behaviors are escalating between two people, it's not likely that either of them is functioning as a wise man.

One man in the group says, "I think the conversation would go better if we used the Rules of Seeing. There can only be one speaker, and Evan was speaking first."

Matt: But he was talking about somebody who's not here to defend himself.

Wise man: We can always talk about that issue after Evan is finished. You may not *like* it that he's talking about somebody who's not here, but if we start telling Evan what he can or can't talk about, we violate the Law of Choice, and soon nobody can talk about anything. We need to listen to him until he's done, and then we can listen to a new speaker.

There's silence in the room, so the wise man says, "I'm also not trying to force anyone to do what *I* want. There are no Rules Police here. Is it all right if Evan finishes talking?"

No one objects, but Evan says he was pretty much finished anyway.

Wise man: So if Evan is finished, Matt, you could choose to be the speaker

Matt: I still think it's wrong to talk about people when they're not here.

Fortunately, the wise man understands the Third Rule of Seeing. He knows that when Matt objects to Evan speaking about other people, he's really talking about himself, not just a principle. "Have there been times in *your* life," asks the wise man, "when people talked about you behind your back?"

"Yes," Matt says, "and I hated it. I don't think we should do it here." Matt isn't angry primarily about some other man being talked about. His anger is a reaction to his fear that somebody might talk about *him.*

"You're worried," says the wise man, "that somebody will be hurt by it, and that's understandable, but you're only worried—and angry—because you feel empty, and that's not caused by anything Evan said. You've been empty for a long time. The solution is not to control Evan, but to feel more loved yourself."

Several men point out that Matt was attacking Evan to protect himself, and they each talk about occasions when they've behaved in similar ways. As Matt feels their outpouring of acceptance, his fear and anger diminish considerably, and he sees that his fear and anger come from a need to feel safe and loved. Matt agrees that what he really wants is to feel accepted, and now his objection to Evan's behavior becomes unimportant to him.

Parenthetically, *is* it acceptable to talk in a group meeting about people who aren't there? I suggest that you not try to control a meeting with a rule like that. We really do get to make our own choices. Talking about someone not in attendance can actually be quite useful if the person speaking is trying only to illustrate a principle, or draw a comparison to himself, or help the group see another member more clearly. If the speaker is angry or otherwise attacking the absent person, the wise men in the meeting need to present the speaker with an opportunity to see the truth about his behavior, but they don't need to stop him from speaking.

There Are No Sides

At one point in the conversation, Matt accused the wise man of taking Evan's side. That's common. As a wise man, you'll inevitably be accused of taking sides, or you'll be *encouraged* to take sides so that one party will be *right*. You need to make it clear that there are no *sides* in a loving conversation. There's only the truth and an interest in people feeling genuinely happy. People who recruit others to their side are acting like victims.

WHEN THE SPEAKER'S NOT SPEAKING

We usually apply the first three Rules of Seeing only when people are actually opening their mouths, but people often speak loudly without uttering a word. Some studies suggest that as much as 93% of human communication is non-verbal. At least half of that is transmitted by way of facial expression, while other modes include tone of voice, arm and leg position, foot and hand movement, and overall body posture and motion. If we really want to see and accept people, we must not wait for them to use words before we recognize that they occupy the position of speaker.

Doug had been Blaine's supervisor for two years, and he believed they had a pretty good relationship. Then Doug learned more about Real Love and discovered that he was using attacking and running as Getting and Protecting Behaviors much more than he'd suspected. He also noticed that whenever he and Blaine were in the same room, Blaine's tone of voice lost all its natural energy and became more controlled, flat, and strained. Blaine rarely looked directly at him or smiled at him.

Doug had never consciously noticed these behaviors before, partly due to a lack of experience and partly because he didn't *want* to see them. He preferred to believe everything was fine and thereby avoid any interaction that could be unpleasant. But he began to understand that Blaine was telling him in many non-verbal ways that he was quite unhappy with their relationship. He met with Blaine and said, "I appreciate your taking this time to talk with me. We've been working together for a couple of years now, and I apologize for being slow to notice something I believe you've been trying to tell me. I could be wrong, but you don't seem comfortable when I'm around. With other people in the office you seem relaxed, but around me you become formal and tense. You do not have to talk about this if you don't want, but if you're willing, I really want to listen. If there's something I can do to help you do your job better, or even just to feel happier here, I'd like to know what it is."

Blaine couldn't believe what he was hearing, and he was still somewhat skeptical, but after additional reassurances, he said, "I've wanted to talk to you for a long time, but I didn't think you'd listen . . . I work pretty hard here, and I do a good job, but you don't seem to appreciate what I do. Like when I finished that big Appleton project last month, it was completed early and under budget, and the client was very happy. You didn't say anything, but you have a lot to say when I make a mistake. And you often tell me how you want every little thing done on a job, instead of letting me figure out my own way."

This would have been a great opportunity for Doug to defend himself—he could certainly think of exceptions to what Blaine had said—but he didn't do that. He realized that Blaine was the speaker (Rules 1 and 2) and was talking about *himself* (Rule 3), not just specific events. Doug acknowledged the truth of what Blaine had said, and they talked for several more minutes to exchange specific ideas about how Blaine could more effectively report his progress to Doug without feeling micro-managed. Their working and personal relationships improved significantly.

We have opportunities every day to notice that people are speaking to us without words. As we see these communications, people will share themselves even more, and we'll learn better to love them. In a healthy relationship it should be the goal of both partners to look for every opportunity to make the other person the speaker.

LISTENING

While we're listening to a news report on the radio, we can listen intermittently while we read a magazine or daydream. We can change stations or even shout at the radio as we disagree with what we're hearing, and the radio will continue to broadcast its message without any regard for our reactions. But human beings are not radios. We all have a powerful need to feel accepted, and if we attempt to listen to one another without attending to that need, our communications will suffer badly. This is true even in the apparently sterile exchanges of information we might see in a business or educational setting. If you give any indication of not accepting the message or the speaker, the speaker's need to feel accepted will *strongly* affect what he or she says, as emptiness and fear lead to the Getting and Protecting Behaviors that make any communication unproductive.

Truth → Seen → Accepted → Loved. While it is important that people tell the truth about themselves in order to *be* seen and accepted, they must also *feel* seen, and that can only happen when we really listen. How, then, can we listen to people in a way that's accepting and productive?

Silence

As many people listen, they're only looking for an opportunity to speak themselves, and they frequently jump into the conversation without the slightest regard for their partners. Although we often do need to make responses, one of the most powerful indications we give that we're listening is that our upper and lower lips are sealed together.

Non-Verbal Signs

As I indicated earlier, people use many non-verbal forms of communication. They use those same signs to determine whether *we* are really listening to them and accepting them. As we raise our brows, shift our eyes, furrow our foreheads, sigh, shuffle our feet, cross our arms, and change our tone of voice, other people can easily recognize our lack of acceptance and/or interest. If they notice any of these signs, they will usually change what they're saying either to protect themselves or to get something they want—acceptance, cooperation, and so on. When they do that, we're no longer listening to the truth about *them*; we're listening to a defensive posture or a manipulation. We're hearing what they think we want them to be. Our conversation becomes a worthless lie or contest of some kind.

You won't long be able to fake these non-verbal signs of acceptance. If you don't feel accepting toward others, you *will* communicate that feeling, and the consequences are always serious. Real acceptance naturally springs from the Real Love you have and wish to share.

Verbal Criticism

In the early 1980s Saddam Hussein once surprised his cabinet ministers by encouraging them to freely voice their opinions on an issue troubling the country. One of the ministers offered a view contrary to the course Hussein had been advocating, and after the meeting the minister was sent home to his wife, in pieces, in a black canvas bag. Hussein asked for opinions only to get support for what he already believed, and when he didn't get it, he viciously attacked the offending speaker.

Although most of us don't go to such extremes, many of us still attack people in a similar way. We claim to have an interest in listening to other people, but then when they speak, we reveal that our real interest is to trap them in their words, argue with them, and even beat them down with the evidence they've provided with their own mouths. When they speak, for example, the first word out of our mouths often is *but*. Now it's true that we may have something brilliant to add to the conversation, but when we say the word *but*, we might as well say, "I didn't really want to listen to you. I just wanted to be right." When we criticize and contradict people, we feel powerful or look good by comparison.

Certainly there are times when we need to suggest a course different than the speaker has offered, or when we actually need to correct a piece of misinformation, but (there's that word again) we can usually do that without detracting from the speaker's message and contributing to his or her feeling unaccepted.

Re-State What You Hear—"Eight"

If people don't get a feeling of general acceptance as they speak to us, our communication with them can become quite unproductive. Indeed, in many conversations, the *entire* goal is acceptance. Many times each week I speak on the phone with my children—who live in widely separated areas of the country—about what they're doing and how they're feeling. I do not fully understand all the details they describe—about the advanced mathematics of economics, or the construction of a house, or the management of pension funds—but that's not the primary reason they tell me those things. They don't need me to take action on their words, nor, in most cases, to offer technical advice about the subject of the discussion. They tell their stories because they enjoy the acceptance and love they feel when I demonstrate my genuine interest in every word they say.

Although the need for acceptance must never be forgotten, many people will need you to actually understand and respond to the *content* of what they're saying. When I tell you how I want you to paint my house, for example, I need more from you than a warm, fuzzy acceptance. I need you to indicate that you understand *what* I'm saying, so I'll have a glimmer of hope that the job will be done as I've described.

While it's obvious that understanding the content of a speaker's message is important when *tasks* are being accomplished—at work, home, and elsewhere—that understanding is also important as a way of communicating *acceptance*. As you tell me about the mistakes you've made and difficult experiences you've had, you'll likely enjoy the conversation if I listen intently, avoid criticism, and give you non-verbal indications of my acceptance. If in addition I also demonstrate that I actually understand what you've experienced, you'll feel a greater level of acceptance, because you know that I see you even more clearly. The more I'm able to communicate my understanding of exactly who you are, the more completely you can feel accepted. It's not enough that I do see and accept you; you need evidence of it so you can *feel* seen.

One way to demonstrate to the speaker that we understand what he or she is saying is to re-state what we hear, as demonstrated by Andrew and his wife, Lynn.

"I feel so mad right now," says Lynn. "I've asked you a million times to put food back in the fridge after you eat, but today I found a jug of milk you left downstairs when you were watching television. It was warm and spoiled, and now I can't use it for something I was planning to cook."

In the past, when Lynn talked about this subject, Andrew made excuses, frowned, grunted, made critical comments about *her* behavior, or walked out of the room, which you might imagine had a less than soothing effect on Lynn. But he's been learning about Real Love and how to listen, so this time he looks right at her, nods his head as she speaks, and says, "I'm sorry."

Of course, Lynn is pleased that he's not lying, attacking, acting like a victim, and running, but still his response is less than completely satisfying, because she's heard him apologize before with no subsequent change in his behavior. Wisely, however, she doesn't press her point, having learned a bit about Real Love herself.

In a few weeks Lynn again makes a comment about Andrew's carelessness about food, and this time he's armed with even greater understanding and compassion. "I know I didn't cover that meat before I put it in the fridge," he says, "and I can see you're angry at me. I'm sorry." This is an example of what many people call active listening. Andrew has repeated back to Lynn what she said—including the emotion she expressed—and he's done it in his own words. This is certainly better than just an apology—and far superior to responding with Getting and Protecting Behaviors—but so far Andrew has only demonstrated an ability to *repeat* her message, which is not the same as expressing a real *understanding* of it.

With more time and experience, Andrew begins to understand what acceptance and listening really are. The next time Lynn says something about him leaving something out of the fridge—with an edge in her voice—he goes a significant step farther than he has before. "Yes, I did that," he says. "I wasn't thinking about you when I left the milk downstairs. I've done that kind of thing a lot of times, actually—like yesterday when I used your cellphone and didn't put it back in your purse. I know you had to look around for quite a while before you found it. And sometimes I leave my clothes on the floor and hope you'll pick them up. When I do all that, you must feel like I don't care about you much."

Lynn immediately feels thoroughly seen, because Andrew has not only heard what she was saying about the food but has given more examples of his overall carelessness and then addressed her real concern—that he doesn't care about *her*. She was really talking about herself, not a container of milk (the Third Rule). The effect on Lynn was profound.

Andrew provides an example of a principle I call "Eight." Suppose I say to you, "Two, four, six . . ." and then I wait to see if you understand what I'm saying. You respond, "Two, four, six." Certainly you've demonstrated an ability to *repeat* what I said, but you do not show that you *understand* what I'm really saying. On the other hand, if you simply respond, "Eight," I know you understand what I said. When other people speak, they're almost always saying, "Two, four, six," and it's quite fulfilling for them when we can say, "Eight."

"Eight" is also a useful concept for us as wise men when we're trying to confirm that other people have heard what we're trying to teach. Suppose you talk to a woman about Real Love and Getting and Protecting Behaviors, and she says, "That's interesting. I hadn't thought about that before." You still don't have the slightest idea whether she understands a word you've said, and you won't know that until she says something like, "I realize I've never felt unconditionally loved in my life, and that finally explains the emptiness I've always felt. And I use Getting and Protecting Behaviors all the time. I get angry at lots of people, and when that doesn't work, I just withdraw from them, which is running." Until we get confirmation from people that they understand what we're saying as wise men—until they can say "Eight"—it's usually unproductive to keep introducing new principles.

Ask Questions

My asking questions as you speak serves not only to bring out additional information, but is a strong indication that I'm interested in understanding what you're saying, which will help you feel accepted. We often ask questions, however, that are only intended to express our doubts and objections. We ask, "Yes, but what about . . .?" Or "Can't you see that . . .?" The latter questions indicate that we're not really listening, just looking to convince the speaker that we're right.

Agree Where Possible

I'm not much of a carpenter, but that doesn't stop me from doing most of the building and repair around the house. On one occasion I had built a large playhouse for my children, and I was proud of it. I showed it to a friend, and with my words, facial expression, and body language I was saying, "Tell me what a fantastic job I've done." He said, "Are you going to paint the floor there or just leave it like that?"

Identifying flaws is so easy and natural. Although thousands of items may be perfectly lined up in columns and rows, for example, our eyes are immediately drawn to the single one that's out of alignment. We similarly notice anything that's out of alignment with what we believe or want, and that's understandable, but it's rarely productive to point out those exceptions first. So much more can be accomplished if we point out what's right, or what we agree with.

When Lynn said Andrew had left the food out a *million* times, he could have pointed out that she couldn't possibly be right about that. Instead he learned to *agree* that he had indeed been inconsiderate on many occasions, and then their conversations became quite productive. When a co-worker proposes a plan to increase sales, don't pick apart what you see as the flaws. Don't say, "Yes, but." Instead say, "Yes, and . . ." Of course avoiding the word *but* won't be effective if you can't communicate sincere acceptance of the speaker. Identify and agree with the elements of the plan that will work. Go the extra mile and do "Eight" as you describe benefits of the plan that he or she didn't even describe. Then add what you think might make the plan even better.

Be Quiet When it Doesn't Matter

I have a friend, Ross, who loves to share what he knows—about everything. He's a bright and knowledgeable man, but he never seems to know when to be quiet. If someone says, "That's a long drive you're planning. New York to Los Angeles is 2500 miles," Ross absolutely cannot leave that alone. He'll retort, "Actually, it's 2462 miles." I've no doubt that he's right most of the time, but people hate to talk to him, because he doesn't really listen to them.

Often people will state facts and express opinions that vary from what you know or believe. If that difference will result in emotional or physical harm to someone, or the demise of the company, it may be wise to speak up. But if it doesn't really matter, be quiet.

What If You Still Disagree?

But what if you're talking to someone who is just completely *wrong*—there's not a redeeming feature in a single word he's saying—and his course of action could be unproductive or harmful. I suggest two criteria here for speaking up: *your* responsibility for the matter and *their* ability to listen. If it's not your clear responsibility to say something—as a parent, spouse, co-worker, supervisor—it's usually best to be quiet. And even when it is your responsibility, a correction from you is usually unproductive if the speaker obviously can't hear what you plan to say because of their fear of being wrong and need to be right.

In many situations, however, it *is* your responsibility to speak up even when the speaker is not interested in listening. First, remember that the most important thing you can do is accept the speaker—with your words and non-verbal communication. When people *know* you accept them, you can say almost anything, and your disagreement will dissolve as you mutually decide what to do.

On some occasions, other people are incapable—because of their own emptiness, fear, and lack of faith—of feeling the genuine acceptance you offer. In those cases, a conflict will almost always arise. We'll talk more about conflicts in Chapter Nine.

THREE APPROACHES FOR ASSISTING
OTHERS TO TELL THE TRUTH

Even with the Rules of Seeing and an understanding of listening, most of us need more suggestions about how to help people tell the truth. As I discuss some possible approaches, I intend only to give you some ideas, not to prescribe what you should say to anyone. Don't get bogged down in any of the details. As always, it's far more important to *love* people than to say the *right thing*. Love and teach. Although I'm sure there are dozens of ways to help people tell the truth, I'll talk about three:

- Tell the truth directly
- Ask questions
- Propose words to say

Tell the Truth Directly

When people are unhappy, they're often completely distracted and confused by their emptiness, fear, and Getting and Protecting Behaviors. They have no idea how to get out of the quagmire that's sucking the life out of them, and they need you to just tell them what you see. You've seen other wise men do this in many examples in this book and in *Real Love*:

- "You're angry because you're reacting to your own emptiness and fear. You've never felt unconditionally loved, and that is not the fault of your partner. Until you see that, you'll stay angry forever."
- "Other people are not obligated to change who they are whenever you want something from them. They really do get to make their own choices."
- "You're constantly manipulating people to like you. That's understandable, but as long as you keep doing that, you can't feel accepted unconditionally, and you'll feel empty and alone."
- "You can't expect your parents to give you the Real Love they never got themselves. As long as you keep resenting them for not loving you, you'll be miserable."

- "I know it's scary, but until you tell the truth about your mistakes and your Getting and Protecting Behaviors, nobody can really see who you are, and you'll stay as alone and unhappy as you are now."

Many people will not see the truth until you tell them directly, as the Wise Man did for the Wart King.

Ask Questions

Some people actually respond quite positively when you make the direct statements above, but many people are understandably threatened by that approach. They prefer to be asked questions and realize the truth at least partially on their own.

- "When you were a child, what happened when you made mistakes and inconvenienced your parents?"
- "Did you feel unconditionally loved and profoundly happy *before* you met your spouse? What does that tell you?"
- "Right now, as we're talking about your mistakes, how do you feel?"
- "How have you felt all your life when people have wanted something from you before they'd like you?"
- "I can see you've been angry and blaming him/her for a long time, but I have a question: has that ever made you happy, or improved your relationship with him/her?"
- "What do you really want, to be happy or right?"

When you ask people questions, they often feel more involved than when you tell them what they're doing and how they're feeling. Questions are especially effective for attackers. People only use anger when they're afraid, and to them the direct approach of truth-telling can sometimes seem additionally threatening. Then they will almost certainly defend themselves. If you ask them questions instead of telling them the truth directly, they may feel less threatened.

Questions are also a good way to learn whether people understand what you've been teaching. From time to time, simply ask them to tell you what they're learning or feeling. With that information, you can make better decisions about what to say or do next.

Although questions are effective, they're usually not enough. When people have been immersed in their emptiness and fear long enough, they really can't see another way to live, and questions alone won't give them the guidance they need. There are other disadvantages to asking questions. Some people will be eager to please you and will answer your questions by telling you what they think you want to hear. Other people handle questions poorly because they feel like you're prying or threatening or challenging, and they respond by lying, attacking, or acting like victims. Still others freeze up when they're asked a question, as though they were on stage with a spotlight trained on them.

Propose Words to Say

Many people really don't know how they feel, or what they're thinking and doing, and they might need you to help them find the words to describe themselves.

- "You say you're frustrated, but I think it would be closer to the truth to say you're *angry*. Would you agree with that?"
- "I do not want to put words in your mouth here, but it seems like you have a hard time talking about how you feel. It might help if I suggest how you might be feeling. I'll do that, and if what I say isn't right, you tell me, okay?"
- "You've talked about a lot of things you don't like about your marriage. Would it be accurate to say that you just don't feel like your husband loves you?"
- "You look much more relaxed now than when we first started talking. Do you feel more accepted?"
- "You seem very reluctant to say anything negative, about yourself or anyone else, but it looks to me like you're angry, and you're just afraid to say that."

I use this method only when people can't express how they feel after I've tried the other two approaches. You may feel uncomfortable using this technique, as though you're trying to read someone else's mind. I have seen, however, many people dissolve in tears or light up like a Christmas tree when they finally hear the words they've wanted to say for years.

Some people will agree with almost anything you say, which helps no one. Relax. We risk influencing people in the wrong direction every time we open our mouths. If you propose words that are not what someone would say, you should be able to see that easily enough. He or she will frown, squint, stare blankly at you, or otherwise look confused. No harm done—remember, you're just trying to help people express their feelings when they're unable to do it themselves. Try again with some other words. When you do say the words people are looking for, they'll show it.

Which Method?

A combination of approaches is usually necessary. You can't just ask questions, for example. As someone is learning how to be truthful, there are some things they just won't know, so you'll have to teach them. Some people will unintentionally lie in response to your questions. When you ask, for example, how someone is feeling, he or she might say, "Fine," when that's obviously not true. On those occasions, you could say, "You don't look like you're doing fine. You look pretty angry." In this case, you're both proposing words to say and directly telling them the truth.

As you feel increasingly loved and experienced, you won't be aware of using a *technique* at all. If you remember nothing else, just *accept* people and you'll do fine. Play around and have fun as you learn. Be patient. Learning about the truth, unconditional love, and Getting and Protecting Behaviors requires that most people change the way they see the whole world. That takes time and effort.

Chapter Summary

- To function as a wise man, you must feel loved yourself.
- If you can't be a wise man, get one for those who need one and find one for yourself (the Fourth Rule of Seeing).
- There can be only one speaker at a time, and the first person to speak is the speaker (the First and Second Rules of Seeing).
- Whenever people speak—regardless of the details of the content—they are speaking about themselves.
- We need to recognize that people often communicate non-verbally, using facial expression, tone of voice, arm and leg position, foot and hand movement, and so on.
- As people tell the truth about themselves, they must sense that we are actually *listening*, which we demonstrate with:
- Our silence (not interrupting)
- Non-verbal signs of our acceptance
- Absence of verbal criticism
- Re-stating what we hear, including our understanding of "Eight"
- Asking questions
- Agreeing where possible
- Being quiet when it doesn't matter
- As you assist others to tell the truth, you can use many approaches, among which are telling the truth directly, asking questions, and proposing words for the speaker to say.

The Power That Makes It All Happen

Faith

Helen and Laura are attending their first group meeting. They've read *Real Love*, and because they both know someone whose life has changed after finding Real Love, they're eager to begin the same process.

The two women are fascinated as they watch several interactions where people allow themselves to be seen and accepted. Helen decides to jump in and participate, and the wise men and women in the group—including you—accept and love her as they help her see the truth about her anger. Although Laura doesn't speak, she does share the truth about herself in a meeting the following week. You suggest that she call people in the group during the week.

> Laura: I wouldn't know what to say. I don't know the people here.
>
> You: What do you need to know? *They care about you*, and they understand your need to be loved. What else is there? Just call and say you don't know what to say. Anyone in this room can take it from there.

Later that week, Laura is still nervous about calling, but she remembers how it felt to be accepted in the meeting and how happy some of the people in the group were, even though they'd once been as empty and afraid as she is now. So despite her fear, she picks up the phone and tells you that even though she doesn't know what to say, she's calling because you suggested it.

The conversation is easy after that. You ask her how she felt at the last group meeting, and she says she felt accepted and peaceful. As a result, for several days she's felt less impatient with her husband and children. You talk about her job, her family, and other things. Laura feels like she's been re-united with an old friend.

At the third group meeting, Laura can't wait to talk more about herself. In the following weeks, she attends every meeting and calls someone from the group almost every day. Although she's anxious at times, she takes responsibility for her feelings and behavior, and begins to radiate a deep contentment. As she feels loved herself, she acquires the ability to accept and love other people. It's like watching a butterfly emerge from a cocoon.

Helen, on the other hand, has quite a different experience from Laura's. Although Helen spoke at the first group meeting, she makes no phone calls. At the second meeting, when someone asks her if she's contacted anyone during the week, she says she's been too busy. When something comes up at the last minute, she misses the third meeting and never goes to another one.

IT'S ALL ABOUT FAITH

Many people *say* they will do anything to fill the emptiness in their lives in a healthy way and find happiness. But when the time comes to actually *do* something, most people's hands and feet turn to stone. A single word describes the difference between those who talk about changing their lives and those who do it: faith.

Faith is so much more than passive belief. Faith is a *choice* we make to believe and then act on our belief. Talk is cheap. If we intend to learn and become more than we are now, we have to take action, in spite of the fear that often seizes our tongues and limbs. When you express your intellectual confidence in the strength of silk, that's belief. When you weave silk into cloth, make a parachute, and jump out of an airplane, that's faith. It's only faith when you actually take a step forward, which means take risks.

Both Helen and Laura were unhappy in the beginning. Both *needed* to tell the truth and feel the acceptance and love of wise men. Both *understood* what they needed to do, and both expressed a *desire* to do it. Helen even tried it once, but only Laura had the faith to keep telling the truth. I talked to Laura about that on one occasion:

> You: You look so much happier than you did a couple of months ago.
>
> Laura: I *am* happier. I don't feel that gnawing emptiness all the time. And I don't get angry at my husband nearly as easily as I used to. I still get irritated occasionally, but I understand that it's not his fault, and it doesn't last as long.
>
> You: So what do you think has made the difference?
>
> Laura: That's easy. It's all of you in the group. I've never had people care about me like this. Now when something difficult happens, like when my husband gets mad or does something else I don't like, it doesn't bother me like it used to, because I feel loved by you guys. It makes a big difference.
>
> You: Don't skip the part *you've* played in all this. I can't begin to tell you how many people I've talked to about Real Love who are still miserable. They had the same wise men and women available to them that you've had, but *you* chose to make the phone calls, come to the meetings, and tell the truth about yourself. Most people don't do that.
>
> Laura: I don't understand why they don't.
>
> You: They want to be loved, but they're not willing to do what it takes. Were you comfortable the first time you came to a group meeting?
>
> Laura: (laughing) No, I was pretty nervous. I almost didn't walk in the door.
>
> You: So why did you come?

Laura: I hoped I could find something that would make a difference in my life.

You: So you came even though you were afraid.

Laura: Yes.

You: That's called faith. You took action even though you didn't understand what you were doing and even though you were nervous about it. You didn't tell the truth about yourself at that first meeting, did you?

Laura: No, I was too scared.

You: But you came back the second time, and the third.

Laura: Uh-huh. I could see that you all had something I wanted. I heard your stories. Some people had been pretty miserable, but they changed. They were happy, and I wanted that.

You: And you made a decision that if you did what they had done, you could find the same kind of happiness they did. That's what faith is. It's not a feeling. It's a decision we make to take action. You did that. Do you remember those first few phone calls you made to people in the group?

Laura: (smiling) Sure—I called you, and I felt like a child. All I could say was that I didn't know what to say, but you made it easy after that.

You: And *you* kept calling people. All these changes you're experiencing have only been possible because you had faith that they could happen.

Not long after this conversation with Laura, you get a call from Helen, who hasn't spoken to anyone since that second meeting. She's having an especially difficult time with her husband, Arthur, and she wants some advice about how to handle him. She's angry.

"Arthur is not your problem," you say. "The problem is that you don't feel loved. When you're unhappy, anything he does seems overwhelming and threatening, and then you react with anger."

Helen said, "But he . . ." and then she launched into a list of her husband's offensive behaviors.

After a few seconds, you interrupt. "I'm sure he does all those things and more. No doubt he's selfish, thoughtless, and inconsiderate. He probably deserves to be shot, but he's still not the real problem. You are. You're the one who doesn't feel loved, and *that* is why you're not happy. *You* can do something about that, whether your husband changes or not. You need to focus all your energy on your own happiness. Has all your nagging and complaining ever changed him one bit?"

Helen: Well, no, but—

You: There's no *but*. It just hasn't worked, so after all these years, why do you keep doing it?

Helen: What are you suggesting, that I just let him keep acting like this?

You: Yes, exactly. You can't control him anyway, so stop trying. But you *can* make huge changes in the way you feel. Do you want to be happy or don't you?

Helen: I just don't see how that's possible.

You: Sure you do. You've read *Real Love*, and you came to two group meetings. You've met people who've completely changed their lives without changing the people around them at all, so you know it can be done. You have to tell the truth about *you* and allow yourself to feel unconditionally loved. It makes all the difference in the world. As you feel loved and happy, it will matter less and less what other people do, and eventually you'll be able to stay happy no matter what anyone does. You'll actually be able to accept and love people, even when they're inconsiderate, even when they get angry and attack you.

Helen: But I did tell the truth about myself, and I didn't see any big difference.

You: I remember that. You told the truth about yourself at *one* meeting, and then you quit. You can't expect that one experience like that would change your whole life. Why did you stop?

Helen: I just don't see how just telling the truth about myself is going to change everything. It can't be that simple.

You: No amount of explanation will ever prove it to you. You won't really understand it until you actually *do* it and experience the love you're looking for. Faith means doing something *before* you completely understand it, but you want proof that this will work before you put in the effort or take the risks. Most worthwhile things in life require faith. What if you called a stockbroker and asked him to pay you a return on a stock before you actually purchased it? What would he say?

Helen: He'd probably laugh in my face.

You: But that's what you're doing here. You want to see your life change *before* you've made the required effort, but it doesn't work like that. The only way you'll see how telling the truth and getting loved make a difference is to do it. You want to *understand* it, but you don't need understanding. You need *faith*. You need to simply decide to do it and see what happens.

Helen: I don't know . . .

You: What have you got to lose? Do you like the way your life is going now? Isn't that why you called in the first place, because you *don't* like how it's going?

Helen: Well . . .

You: And you have more than just faith to go on here. You have hard evidence. You were there for two meetings. There was a room filled with people whose lives have changed because they learned how to tell the truth about themselves. They're proof that it works. Do you remember Laura from that meeting?

Helen: Yes.

You: No one has a life exactly like anyone else's, but you and she have many similar circumstances. Her husband does a lot of the same things yours does. You may remember that Laura was pretty miserable, but now she's feeling loved and happy most of the time. Even though her husband still does a lot of things she doesn't like, she doesn't get angry at him much anymore because she feels loved. And it all happened because she decided to start being truthful and responsible. She learned how to do that in the group and carried it into the rest of her life. Like you, she didn't quite understand how telling the truth would help—or even that it *would* help—but she tried it anyway. She had faith, and that's what you need.

Helen: Well, I'll have to think about it.

Helen was looking for happiness in a way that didn't involve any change on her part. She wanted to change her husband and everyone else around her. The last I heard, she was still unhappy.

We All Have Faith in Something

Helen appeared to have no faith, but she really did—faith that controlling her husband would eventually make her happy, and that anger and blaming would make her feel better, and she acted on that faith every day.

We all have faith in something. We just need to be careful what we choose to place our faith in. Most of us place our faith in the Getting and Protecting Behaviors and Imitation Love we're familiar with, but even though they make us feel better temporarily, they're always disappointing in the end and leave us feeling empty and alone. Why not choose instead to have faith in principles—love and the truth, for example—that are true and effective?

Without faith that we can tell the truth and find Real Love, we can only repeat the past. We continue to hide in the bags on our heads—empty, afraid, and alone. In that condition, we're certain to protect ourselves and use Getting Behaviors to buy the Imitation Love we hope will fill the emptiness in our lives.

WHY PEOPLE DON'T FEEL REAL LOVE EVEN WHEN IT'S GIVEN TO THEM

When Helen attended her first group meeting, she was surrounded by wise men and women, and when she told the truth about herself, she was seen, accepted, and loved: Truth → Seen → Accepted →

Loved. Everything in the process was there, so why didn't she feel loved and happy? Why didn't her life change like Laura's did? I've seen this happen countless times. We've already talked about the effect of faith in finding happiness, but we also need to understand that if people are sufficiently afraid and are using Getting and Protecting Behaviors, they may not feel any of the Real Love we give them.

Fear and Protecting Behaviors

Fear is crippling. When we're afraid, we can't see anything but our own need for immediate safety. Fear turns scholars into confused children, respected leaders into objects of ridicule. Our greatest fear grows out of our greatest need, which is for Real Love. I can't possibly overstate the pain that results from the emptiness we feel in the absence of sufficient love. We felt that stabbing pain as young children every time someone frowned at us, or raised their voice, or ignored us, or turned their back on us, or sighed with disappointment, or failed to smile when we came into the room. As adults, we may not even remember those moments, but the effects are still there. We'll do almost anything to diminish our pain. As Marcel Proust put it, "To kindness, to knowledge, we make promises only; pain we obey."

To prevent people from adding to our pain, we protect ourselves, even though it drives people away and keeps us alone. Even when we're offered Real Love, we're too busy protecting ourselves to feel it.

As a child, Helen had been accepted by her parents and others only when she did exactly what they wanted, and they continued to treat her that way as an adult. At some point in her life, she concluded—quite unconsciously—that unconditional love didn't exist. She became skeptical of the motives of other people and tended to find fault with them and criticize them rather than trust them. With that attitude, she felt very little of the Real Love she was offered—by the group at the two meetings she attended, for example, or anywhere else.

This is not a criticism of Helen, only an explanation of her feelings and behavior. Helen could not feel loved while she was afraid and pre-occupied with defending herself from injury. Even though she called you for advice on one occasion, she still protected herself, attacked her husband, and resisted everything you said: "I just don't see how that's possible," "I don't know..." and the oft-repeated *but.* She didn't call you to get genuine acceptance. She called to get *ammunition* to use against her husband, and with that approach, she couldn't possibly feel the Real Love you offered.

Laura was afraid also. Although she, like Helen, had a husband who was angry, she chose to lay her Protecting Behaviors aside for a few moments at a time and have faith in the process of finding Real Love. Helen and Laura both experienced the natural consequences that always come from making choices.

Emptiness and Getting Behaviors

As a child, Helen discovered that in the absence of Real Love, the conditional approval of other people felt pretty good. Over the years, she learned to earn that approval in many ways: She was intelligent and did well in school; she was pretty and enjoyed the flattery of both men and women; she worked hard at her job and got a great sense of accomplishment from the praise and power she earned there. Because she had a lot of talent and skills, she was quite successful at buying attention, praise, money, and power. Everywhere Helen went, she *bought* Imitation Love, and she was mostly unaware of doing it.

When Helen came to those two meetings, she did tell the truth about herself a little, but she also made her usual effort to get people to like her. Before the meetings, for example, she spent considerable time on her clothes, hair, and face so she'd be attractive. She also flattered people during the meeting in the hope that they'd like her (lying). When she said something that seemed to please people, she tried to say more such things so they'd like her even more. Almost all of us do that. When she talked about her husband's behavior, she consistently exaggerated the injurious effect on herself so she'd get sympathy from the group members (acting like a victim). And without being asked, she told the group about the successes in her career, thereby earning their praise and a feeling of power.

The people in the group offered Helen their unconditional acceptance, but with her manipulations she turned it into something quite different. She didn't *mean* to do that, but it still happened. All her life, any time someone had accepted Helen, it had been the result of Helen pleasing him or her in some way, so in the group meeting, when people accepted her, she could only conclude—without thinking about it consciously—that this was one more example of people accepting her because she'd been good, or clever, or attractive, *not* because they were simply loving her unconditionally. She enjoyed their approval, but she thought she was *earning* it—so she kept trying to earn it by doing the things that worked for her. Even though she was *getting* Real Love from the group, she was *feeling* the same Imitation Love she'd always earned.

When we use Getting Behaviors—when we do *anything* to manipulate someone for attention, approval, praise, sex, and so on—we can receive what we get only as Imitation Love. It takes faith to quit using Getting Behaviors and to tell the truth about ourselves instead. It takes faith to allow people to love us with our mistakes and flaws instead of trying to buy their attention.

HELPING PEOPLE FIND FAITH

As a wise man, you will know many people like Helen, and many of them will resist at least their first few experiences with Real Love. At times you may feel frustrated that these people you care about seem determined to be unhappy. You'll wonder how they could fail to take the relatively easy steps to eliminate the emptiness, fear, and anger in their lives. Why don't they just tell the truth about themselves and accept the love you offer?

Trying to love people who don't exercise faith is like trying to fill up a bucket with holes in the bottom. You can pour Real Love into their buckets in great quantities, but they never fill up. When you love them, they either push you away to protect themselves, or they interpret your attention as a reward for their latest manipulation. They also assume you are manipulating *them* for Imitation Love. They're trading Imitation Love with you even when you're offering the real thing. They don't know how to do anything else.

That's what Helen did with you and the other members of the group. She was accepted in the same way Laura was, but she didn't *believe* she was being unconditionally loved, so she didn't *feel* it. Her lack of faith entirely eliminated the effect of an experience that was life-changing for someone else. Laura made a choice to believe she was being loved and then exercised even more faith as she told the truth about herself and created additional opportunities to feel accepted.

We can continue to pour our love into buckets with holes in the bottom, but it's more effective to help people exercise faith, close up those holes, and feel the Real Love available to them. Faith is not a mysterious, indescribable quality. It's not just a feeling or belief. It's action. It's *moving* in an unknown direction, and some people need help making a decision to do that.

Desire

The first step toward faith is a desire to learn or change. If I'm entirely satisfied with the way I'm living, why would I bother to have faith in something I can't see? People who get enough enjoyment from praise, power, pleasure, and security see no reason to take the risks of telling the truth to find Real Love.

Before many of us will have faith in something different, we must be convinced that our way of living cannot bring us the genuine happiness we seek. We have to experience the total failure of Imitation Love before we'll listen to the truth. Before I was willing to change my own life, I had to experience the utter despair of drug addiction and near-suicide. Only then did I have sufficient motivation to *do* something different to change my life. Some people require the death of a loved one or the failure of a marriage before they'll make real changes in themselves. Sadly, until we clearly see that the way we're living isn't true happiness, we usually keep pursuing our present course.

As a wise man, you can *sometimes* help people acquire a desire to change. If someone is not happy and she argues with me about telling the truth and having faith in the process of finding Real Love,

I usually say something like this: "Do you like the way you're living now? Are you happy with your life? It's obvious from what you're saying and the way you behave that you're not. So what do you have to lose by trying something different? I'm not suggesting that you give up anything good in your life—only your unhappiness. If you keep living as you have been, you will continue to be exactly as unhappy as you are now, or worse. You've already proven that. There *is* a much happier way to live. Do you want that? Are you willing to try something different to get it?"

Once we believe that *our* way isn't sufficient to produce love and happiness, we become teachable. We can learn. If we have the smallest desire for something better, that is the beginning of faith.

Many people have known only the superficial satisfaction that comes from Imitation Love, so they believe that's all there is. Motivating such people to acquire a desire to change is very difficult, even though they're destroying their lives with Getting and Protecting Behaviors. Why should people want to change if they believe they're already happy?

A wise man offers people the example of his own life. It's more difficult for people to deny that it's possible to tell the truth and find love and happiness when you're standing in front of them as a living example of that process. Some people will be able to see that you possess the happiness they want, and they'll be willing to *do whatever you did* to get it. That willingness to do whatever it takes is faith, and by your example you can help inspire it. When I asked Laura why she had the faith to continue telling the truth about herself, she said she was motivated by what she saw in the lives of other people in the meetings.

A wise man introduces the possibility that truth can lead to love, and love to happiness. Faith is choosing to act on that possibility.

Increasing Faith with Evidence

Nyla is a single woman who has been convinced by her parents and others over a lifetime that she's worth very little. She's attended group meetings regularly for several months and has made intermittent phone calls to group members, but it's obvious that she's not genuinely happier. She still feels withdrawn, afraid, and resentful. She still becomes angry at the slightest inconvenience.

Imagine that you are with her in a group meeting. If you didn't care about her, you'd say nothing about the unhappiness you see in her, but you do care. "Nyla," you say, "I've been watching you for some time now. You've been coming to meetings and you've told the truth about yourself, but do you feel like you're happier?"

"Not really," she says. "I still feel alone. I get mad at people all the time. I never date."

Now what? She's telling the truth about her anger and loneliness, and she's not blaming other people for her feelings, but still she's not happy. Nyla is *getting* loved, but she's not *feeling* it, and without faith, she never will.

> You: In the past several months, you've spent quite a bit of time with the people in this room—here in meetings, on the phone, and in person. Have you noticed how they've treated you?
>
> Nyla: You've all been nice to me, but I still don't understand how that's supposed to help me.
>
> You: This isn't something you need to *understand*. It's something you need to *feel*. Real Love is not an intellectual exercise.

Nyla doesn't say anything. That's a good start. Many people use their minds to achieve most of the important things in their lives. With their intellect, they're accustomed to defending themselves and getting what they want. But understanding alone means nothing in the pursuit of the most important treasures of life.

> You: You've talked about yourself on a number of occasions here. How have people responded to you?
>
> Nyla: I don't know.
>
> You: This isn't complicated. Have they criticized you?
>
> Nyla: No.
>
> You: Laughed at you, looked down on you, been disgusted by you as you've talked about your mistakes and flaws and fears?
>
> Nyla: No.

You: Why? Why haven't they done any of those things?

Nyla: I'm not sure.

You: Then you've missed the entire point of being here. That's understandable, but it's also killing you. When I say that these people haven't criticized you or laughed at you, I'm saying that they accept you. Do you see that?

Nyla: I guess so.

You: Have you paid any of these people to accept you and be kind to you—here or in your phone calls and meetings with them?

Nyla: No.

You: Have they asked you to vote for them in an election? Or join a cult with them?

Nyla: No.

You: Then what explanation is left? If they're not trying to get something from you, why would they all accept you and keep spending time with you?

There's a long pause before Nyla says, "Because they care about me?" Most of us have a difficult time saying those words. We're too afraid it just won't be true. After a lifetime of people letting us down, we find it difficult to believe in the acceptance of others. We're distracted by the possibility that we'll be let down again.

You: After all this time, wouldn't you say that these people know quite a bit about you—good and bad?

Nyla: Yes, they do.

You: So these people really know who you are—warts and all—and still they accept you. You're not earning their affection in any way. So what's another word for their caring about you?

At this point, many people utterly choke on the next word, but Nyla says, "Love?"

You: Yes, love. In your whole life, you've never felt unconditionally loved, so you've learned to not trust that Real Love exists. You're always manipulating people to like you or protecting yourself from them. And here you're surrounded by people who *do* love you, but you don't feel it because you don't *believe* it. You're just not used to getting loved, but the more you *see* what you're getting, the more you'll *feel* it. This is not an exercise in positive thinking. I'm not suggesting that you simply *think* about feeling more loved if it's not true. I'm suggesting that you see something that's already there. So let's practice seeing it right now. Is there someone you spent some time with in the past week?

Nyla: Cynthia.

You: What did you do with her?

Nyla: We went for a walk.

You: What did Cynthia do while you walked?

Nyla: (pause) Mainly she just listened to me.

You: Were you friends with Cynthia before you started coming to these meetings?

Nyla: No.

You: Cynthia is twenty years older than you, and she wasn't your friend before this, but she gladly spends time with you. Is there some favor you do for her when you spend time together?

Nyla: No.

You: So again, why do you suppose she does that?

Nyla: Maybe because she cares about me.

You: You're avoiding the *L* word again. Try using it. You don't have to, but it will make a difference if you become more comfortable with it.

Nyla: Because she loves me.

You: Now, if you really want to feel loved, try saying to *Cynthia*, "I know that you love me." You don't have to do this, but if it's true, why not say it?

Nyla: Cynthia, I think you spend time with me because you love me, and that feels pretty good. Thank you.

Cynthia: That's true, I do love you, and I spend time with you because I like to.

You: Are there other people in this room who love you?

Nyla: Yes, but I don't think I saw it before.

Nyla is beginning to beam. She *has* been missing the point of all the meetings and the phone calls. Truth-telling and Real Love are useless unless the love is *felt*. Nyla needs to have faith that she's being loved, and you helped her exercise that faith by pointing out an example of her actually receiving love from others.

Make a decision

Sometimes this faith business is not easy. Although Nyla was touched by the meeting described above, the effect of such experiences often fades as it's eroded by the influence of a lifetime of past fears and doubts. You talk to Nyla a week later.

You: So what have you learned in the past week?

Nyla: Not much.

You: (laughing) Nyla, if you didn't learn much in the past week, you haven't paid attention. In the last group meeting, you began to understand and feel the love you've been getting, but now you say you haven't learned much?

It's clear from Nyla's face that she's still uncertain about being loved—understandable after a *lifetime* of living without it. People don't overcome this feeling overnight.

You: I can love you forever, and so can other people, but eventually—if you really want to change your life and be happy—you'll have to make a *decision* to believe that people are loving you unconditionally. Right now you doubt that, even with the evidence we discussed in the last meeting. You believe you *earn* my acceptance. You're smart and pretty and helpful, and without actually being conscious of it, you believe *that* is why I like you. All your life, people have liked you *because* of something. Everybody liked you when you were *good*. So you tried to always be good, and that got you lots of attention. But now you think that when people like you, it's *because* you did the right thing. You don't believe you're acceptable and lovable no matter what. Faith is a *decision* to believe that I care about you—and other people care about you—no matter what. Until you make that decision, it won't matter much that we love you. You'll stay unhappy.

Nyla: How do I make that decision?

You: Without realizing it, you've already made a decision to *doubt* that you're loved. In effect, you get up each morning and say, "Nobody will really love me, so I'll spend the day buying Imitation Love from everybody." All I'm suggesting is that you make a different decision. Every day say, "There are people who love me without my doing anything to earn it, and when I believe that, I'll see what they're giving me. When you make a decision to believe that, you'll immediately discover a greater level of happiness. I'm not suggesting that you believe something that's not true. From the behavior of the people in the group, you have lots of evidence that people *do* care about you. What have you got to lose?

Teaching about faith

Many people are simply unfamiliar with the concept of faith. They associate the term with religion and tend to avoid using it in everyday speech. As a wise man, use the term freely. We can't learn or grow without faith, so we need to talk about it. In the following story, Patrick learns to become comfortable with the concept of faith as he talks to his friend Tom.

Tom is talking about the kind of happiness he's found from feeling loved, but Patrick is cynical. Although he agrees that his life isn't wonderful, he's doing as well as anybody else he knows. How can there really be something out there that's a lot better than anything he knows?

Tom: It comes down to faith. If you'll believe there's something a lot better than what you know—and you actually *do* something about it—you'll find it.

Patrick: Faith? If I want a sermon on faith, I'll go to church, and I haven't been there since I was a kid.

Tom: (laughing) So forget the word faith. Just take a chance and try something different. Take a risk. Nothing works until you actually *do* it. I know you work out a lot. Why do you do that?

Patrick: That's how I stay in shape.

Tom: What if I wanted to become physically fit, how would I do that?

Patrick: You'd have to exercise. Maybe not the same way I do, but somehow.

Tom: Prove it.

Patrick: What do you mean?

Tom: Prove to me that exercise will make me physically fit.

Patrick: People prove that every day. All over the world. When they exercise, they become stronger and healthier. It's obvious.

Tom: I'm not so sure. Prove that it will work for *me*.

Patrick: I can't. You'd actually have to start exercising and see that it makes a difference.

Tom: But why should I *want* to start exercising?

Patrick: Because the result is a good thing. And you have nothing to lose.

Tom: And I'd have to *trust* what you just told me, wouldn't I?

Patrick: Yes.

Tom: Exactly my point about telling the truth and finding Real Love and happiness. You simply have to *trust* what I'm telling you about Real Love and take the steps before you can see what I'm talking about. You want me to prove to you that it works *before* you do it. I can't. I can tell you that many people have done it before you, and that it always works when they really follow the process—just like exercise does. But I can't prove that it will work for *you*. Only you can prove that—as you do it.

Faith is a difficult word for many, but everyone understands the concepts of taking a risk and investing something before you get a return. The opposite of faith is a combination of fear and laziness. People understand those words, too. We need to teach people that faith isn't a mysterious belief in the unknown. It's a choice we make. When I have faith, I *choose* to believe something is true and then *behave as though it were*. Anything short of that is not faith.

Men and women often say to me, "I really do want to change my life," and then they keep doing the same old things that made them unhappy. After learning that telling the truth about themselves could make a difference, they refuse to tell the truth. The truth is, they *don't* really want to change—not enough to do something about it. Imitation Love is sufficiently rewarding that they're not willing to give it up. When people say they want to change and then take no action toward that goal, what they're really saying is that they want the *rewards* of change but without the work and responsibility of it. They're saying they want to grow wheat, but what they really want is to eat bread. They don't want the plowing, sowing, weeding, harvesting, and baking that precede eating bread. Faith is in the farming.

Loving

Faith is promoted by simply receiving love. When I first felt the love of people who cared about my happiness without my doing anything to earn it, that turned my world upside down. I realized that unconditional love was possible and that my previous understanding of the world had to be wrong. I began to have faith that I could find happiness as I learned to live differently.

As you accept people, you give them an opportunity to feel the power of unconditional love. It is so much easier for them to have faith in telling the truth and in the possibility of changing their lives when they've actually had the experience of feeling loved.

Responding to Fear in a Group

The opposite of faith is fear, and sufficient fear can destroy the faith not only of the person who's afraid but also of those around him or her. Occasionally you'll see people who come to meetings only to sow doubts and prove that their skepticism is right. Certainly they have a right to do that, but don't allow fear and doubt to continue without addressing them. Without the effect of loving and teaching, the fear of only one person in a group can spread like a cancer to the other members.

I was recently in a group meeting where one person, Brad, repeatedly scoffed at the whole notion of Real Love. I also learned that he'd been calling group members between meetings to express his doubts even more vigorously.

Brad: None of this makes sense. You talk about Real Love and telling the truth and being happy, but I don't see how telling the truth about yourself can really make a difference.

You: Have you ever seen Real Love?

Brad: Of course not. It doesn't exist. If you think people can really love each other unconditionally, you're deluded.

You: Have you ever taken all the steps required to *find* Real Love? Have you had a sincere desire to change your life, exercised faith that Real Love exists, told the truth about yourself consistently, and given up your Getting and Protecting Behaviors?

Brad: Why would I? I don't believe it works.

You: As long as you make the *decision* to not believe in it, you're making a choice to not find Real Love, and you never will, nor will you ever see it when other people find it. All because of a *decision* you've made. You *really* do have the right to make that choice, but if you haven't done what it takes to find Real Love and see it, your opinion about its existence becomes rather, well, meaningless. If Real Love were something harmful, your skepticism might actually be helpful, but in this case, repeatedly voicing your doubts could only be for the purpose of making yourself right.

THE REWARDS OF FAITH

Steven trusted no one. In all his seventy years he had no memory of feeling unconditionally loved, so why should he trust that anyone could ever love him in that way? But he did recognize that he felt alone, and he wanted to do something about that. A friend introduced him to the ideas of Real Love and telling the truth. He was skeptical, but a wise friend suggested that he take a chance and apply the principles he was learning.

Steven had a desire to change, the first step toward faith. He made a decision not to run from what his friend was saying, nor from the acceptance his friend was offering. He chose to have faith—just a little, mind you—that things could be different. He began to tell the truth about himself, to his friend and to some other wise men—in group meetings and otherwise.

Although he didn't entirely understand the process intellectually, he knew he felt different as he was being accepted. "As I feel happier and less alone," he said, "my faith increases. Gradually, I'm seeing that I can be loved. I never understood what real happiness could be. I still don't understand it all, but I certainly can feel it around the edges."

That's how it is with faith. If you trust in things you can't entirely see or understand, miraculous things can happen, and you'll receive justification for the faith you blindly exercised. As Steven discovered, the more steps you take by faith, the farther ahead you can see. Living by faith is the only sensible way to live. Without it, we can't learn anything new. We can't grow or be happy. With faith, everything is possible. Faith simply works, and the more you exercise it, the easier it becomes.

THE FAITH OF A WISE MAN

I've spoken about the importance of people having faith as they tell the truth about themselves in the process of finding Real Love. It's also important that we as wise men have faith in the truth and in the power of love as we give people opportunities to feel accepted.

People's lives can seem very complicated. If you have no faith in the power of the truth and Real Love, the emptiness, fear, and anger you see in people can often seem overwhelming to you as a wise man. But unconditional love can heal all our wounds from the past, fill our emptiness, wipe away our fears, and eliminate our anger. That change of the human heart, from misery and despair to hope and joy, is the greatest miracle on earth, and we can see it only as we have faith that it's possible.

As you get involved in the details of an interaction with someone who is struggling with unhappiness, you'll have a tendency—if you're like most of us—to wonder what *you* should say and do. That's understandable, but at that point of anxiety, don't get confused about your role. Don't make the mistake of having faith in your own skill. You don't have the power to make people feel loved and happy. You're not smart enough for that.

When you realize that, it takes all the pressure off any situation, doesn't it? You don't have to figure everybody out or change anyone. You only present people with the opportunity to tell the truth about themselves as you unconditionally accept them. If *they* choose to tell the truth and have faith in the love you offer, they will feel it, and their lives will change. If you choose to have faith in that process, and not in your own power, you'll be much happier and more effective as a wise man.

Giving up

Some people have been hurt so many times in the past that they just can't seem to exercise faith in the possibility of Real Love. They're paralyzed by the fear born from past experience. That's understandable, but it's also deadly. When these people are loved by wise men, they keep doubting it and even find fault with those who love them. Don't be surprised when you're one of those they criticize and avoid.

Because some people just don't benefit from the love you offer, you may choose not to spend any more time with them. That doesn't mean you quit caring about them, but your time is not unlimited, and you can't spend it with everyone. Don't feel guilty about such a decision. You can't make someone exercise faith and accept what you offer. In addition, you don't know that they won't learn to tell the truth about themselves and find Real Love some time in the future.

Chapter Summary

- Without faith, we won't take the risk of telling the truth about ourselves, and then we can't feel unconditionally loved. Even when we're actually *getting* Real Love, we won't *feel* it.
- You can help people find faith in the truth and in love as you
  - ask them if the way they're living now is giving them the genuine happiness they're seeking, which can often give them the desire to look for something better.
  - give them evidence that they're being loved right now.
  - encourage them to simply make a decision to tell the truth, even thought they don't understand what will happen. Faith is a decision we make to move forward even when we don't understand the result.
  - teach them that faith is the principle which motivates us to invest in the future.
  - love them.
- As a wise man, have faith in the truth and in Real Love, rather than in your own abilities to make changes in people.
- Because of a lack of faith, some people will never tell the truth or feel loved, and you are not responsible for making them do that.

❧ Chapter Seven ❧

Sharing the Heart

Telling the Truth About Feelings

Watch what happens when a small child is happy and smiling as he plays around adults. They hold him, play with him, and talk to him in an endearing way. But how do they treat him when he's angry and throwing a fit? They frown at him, speak to him sharply, tell him to stop it, and often avoid him. Most of us experienced that lesson ourselves as children, that it was all right to express some feelings—happiness and gratitude, for example—but that other feelings were unacceptable.

When a child is angry, most parents feel threatened. They believe the child is *accusing* them of making him unhappy, and usually that's *exactly* what he's doing—although the accusation is often unconscious. An angry child is demanding that his parents do something to make him or her happy again, and parents don't like to hear that, especially when they feel incapable of doing something about it.

An angry child creates an instant crisis: First, there's an immediate problem to solve that didn't exist a moment before. It's an inconvenience, a bother, a disruption in the schedule of the parent. Second, an angry child makes us wonder if we've been good parents. Good parents, after all, raise happy children, so when we have an angry child stamping his feet in front of us, we have to wonder what we've done wrong. Most parents feel overwhelmed to start with. They don't welcome yet another reminder of their parental incompetence.

When faced with an angry child, most parents see two choices: They can give in to the child's demands and do what he wants in order to make him happy, or they can become angry and controlling and tell the child to stop it. If they choose the first response, the child learns to be demanding and manipulative. If they choose the latter, they re-establish peace and quiet for themselves, but they teach the child that anger is a "bad" feeling to have.

When a child is angry, what's really going on? Without sufficient Real Love, children are in pain, and then they reach out for whatever makes them feel good, even for a moment. With anger, they often feel a sense of power as they get parents and siblings to do things they wouldn't ordinarily do. Some children have fits of temper in order to portray themselves as victims and win the sympathy of others. Or they may use anger as a Protecting Behavior. With all these uses of anger, they get Imitation Love. It's not the Real Love they need, but each form of Imitation Love certainly feels better temporarily than getting nothing at all.

A child expressing anger is saying he doesn't feel unconditionally loved by his parents, and then his parents not only fail to love him, they also tell him it's unacceptable to be angry. It's an impossibly frustrating situation for a child, and that's how we learned to hide our anger. I am not criticizing parents here. They simply can't give what they don't have.

As adults, our expressions of anger have continued to result in negative experiences. Understandably, other people don't like it when we're mad—they feel afraid, guilty, and inconvenienced, much like our parents did—and to protect themselves, they respond by lying, attacking us, acting like victims, and running. All these behaviors leave us feeling more unloved and alone, so we feel punished for being angry, which makes it less likely that we'll express anger the next time—although the anger is still there, bottled up.

Many of us, however, did not learn to *hide* anger. When we were angry, we looked aggressive, strong-willed, and independent, and since those are actually qualities greatly admired among many adults, with our anger we often got praise, power, and safety. With those rewards, we learned to use anger often. We still do.

Why did some of us learn to hide our anger, while others learned to use it as a tool for getting Imitation Love? It comes down to what we were taught and what *worked*. If our parents often intimidated us with their anger—and if we saw them do that to others as well—we naturally imitated their example. Some of us have continued to use anger all our lives because it protects us and gets us Imitation Love in ways we saw our parents and others do. Others of us discovered that the penalties for expressing anger were greater than the rewards, so we hid our anger and learned to lie, or act like victims, or run instead. We do what works.

We learned to hide our fear in the same way we learned to hide our anger. When a child is afraid, some parents, siblings, and peers criticize or make fun of him or her—especially if he's a boy. How often have we heard people say to a child, "Oh, don't be afraid," or "Don't be such a baby," or "That's nothing to be afraid of." Sometimes these expressions are even intended to be helpful, but the child nonetheless learns that fear is a feeling he shouldn't express. This same pattern is true for other feelings: sadness, frustration, weakness, and so on. If a child learns that people love him less when he expresses these feelings, he will tend not to express them.

HOW WE LIE ABOUT FEELINGS

We hide our feelings in many ways, and we mostly do it without thinking. Although there are benefits from hiding, we also pay a high price—we're alone behind the bags on our heads. Truth → Seen → Accepted → Loved: We can't feel seen, accepted, and loved when we're hiding the truth about how we feel.

Minimizing Feelings

Michelle has waited outside for forty-five minutes to be picked up by her husband, Victor. She's cold, tired, and anxious to get home. He often makes her wait like this, and she's becoming increasingly angry.

By the time Victor finally arrives, Michelle is furious about the long wait and additionally angry that he's not apologizing. But she says nothing, and after several minutes of obvious silence in the car, Victor asks, "Are you okay?"

"Uh-huh," she says. "I was a little tired of waiting, but I'm all right."

Is Michelle "all right?" Is she a "little tired of waiting?" No. She's hiding her anger. She's lying because she learned as a child that when she told the truth about her anger, other people got angry in return and withdrew their affection from her. She was willing to do anything to prevent that loss of approval, so she stopped expressing her anger, as a child and later as an adult.

What Michelle really wants to say is, "I'm so angry I could push your head through the windshield. I married you because I thought you'd love me—you certainly *promised* to love me—but it's obvious you don't really care about me. Being late is just one of a million ways you tell me that. Now I'm becoming deathly afraid you never will love me, and I'm furious that you've betrayed me." But she knows Victor would be angry if she said that, so she lies, using words that make her feelings acceptable to him.

We all do that at times—instead of the truth, we say something less direct:

The lie (what we say)	The truth (how we often really feel)
I'm frustrated.	I'm angry at you, and I'm afraid you're never going to see me clearly or accept me.
I'm a little nervous about this meeting.	I'm afraid that when I open my mouth at this meeting, people will think I'm stupid and foolish, and then they'll laugh at me, and I'll feel alone and unloved. I'm even afraid to talk about my fear now, because then you'll think I'm weak.
I'm exhausted.	I feel empty and alone, and I'm afraid I always will.
It's annoying that . . .	I'm angry at *you*, but I'm afraid to tell you that because then you won't like me.
I'm disappointed that . . .	I can't believe you could be this thoughtless. I'm angry that you keep doing what you want and ignore everyone else, especially me.
I'm hurt that . . .	I have huge expectations that you'll do what I want, and when you don't, I feel like you don't care about me. And then I'm afraid.

We want to be liked, so we use language that will maximize our chances of being accepted and minimize negative reactions. "I'm frustrated" is much more socially acceptable than "I hate you" or "I want to slap your face for putting me in this position." So we lie.

Michelle doesn't like the way her marriage with Victor is going, so in an effort to do something about it, she begins associating with a group of wise women. But she's still afraid *they* will react to her anger in the same way other people always have, so she continues to protect herself by hiding her anger—she lies and puts a bag over her head. Because she doesn't talk about her anger, she makes herself invisible to the women in the group. Actually, some of the wise women *can* see her through the bag—they can see she's an angry woman—but Michelle can't *feel* seen and accepted as long as she's lying. She remains alone in the midst of women who are capable of loving her. What a tragedy.

Blaming other people for our feelings

Another way to lie about our feelings is to make someone else responsible for them. People commonly say, "He makes me so mad," or "I was scared because she . . ." but we've already discussed the fact that our feelings are never caused by other people.

Hiding our feelings completely

Sometimes we just hide our feelings completely, and often we don't realize we're doing this. We've been told that we're *supposed* to be happy and kind, not sad, or angry, or afraid. So we hide our real feelings for the purpose of pleasing other people. This is what Michelle did.

TELLING THE TRUTH ABOUT FEELINGS

Wise men help people tell the truth about how they feel, which creates opportunities for them to be seen and loved. As you help people tell the truth, however, remember how frightening that can be. In the beginning they may not be grateful to you for the opportunity you're giving them. They may defend themselves by lying, attacking, or running. Simply continue to tell them the truth and love them. Love and teach.

For several weeks Michelle continues to lie about her anger to the wise women in her group. She says she's hurt and disappointed, and she thinks her husband treats her unfairly. When she does that, her wise friends say things like, "Michelle, you're angry. Listen to your voice. Look at the tension in your face and neck and body. You're an angry woman." They don't justify her anger, and certainly don't blame her husband, but they know she needs to see how she feels before she can do something about it. Michelle sees other women in the group consistently tell the truth about their anger, and she sees that they're accepted and loved *with* their feelings. It's obvious that these women have become happier as they've accepted and loved each other. She's never seen such a thing before. The women in the group encourage Michelle to keep expressing her feelings, and she gradually begins to feel accepted and loved while she's angry. Of course, then her anger begins to disappear. When we consistently follow the steps that lead to Real Love, the results are predictably fruitful.

Michelle initially lied by using words that made anger more acceptable. One way to help people tell the truth about their feelings—all feelings, not just anger—is to eliminate minimizing words, like *frustrated, annoyed,* and *upset.* When you're telling the truth about your feelings, or helping someone else do the same, I suggest that the following words will serve you well in keeping your expressions plain and simple. Say:

- Angry—rather than irritated, frustrated, or annoyed.
- Afraid—not anxious, frustrated, or nervous.
- Empty—not confused, frustrated, anxious, or—sometimes—sad. Use *empty* when describing how you feel in the absence of Real Love. You could also use the words *alone* and *unloved* here.
- Sad. I recommend using this word only when referring to regret for the pain of *other people*: "I'm sad that John keeps choosing to lie and be alone instead of telling the truth about

himself and feeling loved. I feel sad that he's unhappy." When we're applying the word sad to *ourselves*, the real feelings are usually emptiness and fear. We're "sad" about events that interfere with the Real or Imitation Love in our lives. We'll talk more about expressing emptiness and true sadness later in the chapter.

- Happy, the feeling that naturally results from feeling loved, loving others, and being responsible.

I'm not suggesting that other words that could describe feelings are wrong, only that the words above make the expression of feelings clearer and more honest—they allow us to more thoroughly take the bags off our heads and feel more accepted. We use minimizing words because they're more socially acceptable and less likely to provoke an unpleasant reaction, and in many social situations we *should* use the more indirect words for expression of feelings. Remember that we tell the truth to create opportunities to feel seen, accepted, and loved. If people are incapable of accepting us, it may not be wise to tell the direct truth about how we feel.

TELLING THE TRUTH ABOUT FEAR

From the beginning of time, fear has motivated more human behavior than any other force in the world. Most people's lives are ruled by fear—fear of not being accepted, fear of not being loved, fear of pain, fear of being controlled, fear of hunger and physical pain and death. There are few men or women who aren't afraid much of the time. That's a sweeping thing to say, but look at the behavior of virtually any person you know:

- Does she lie in any of its forms? Does she exaggerate, minimize, or change a story to reduce her responsibility? Does she make excuses or spread blame? Does she pretend to be happy when she's not? Does she hide her mistakes?
- Does he attack people? Does he get irritated or angry? Does he belittle people who perform poorly or inconvenience him?

Does he enjoy making people look smaller than himself? Is he racist or sexist?

- Does she act like a victim? Does she say, "I couldn't help it," or "There was nothing I could do"? Does she often act like people are doing things *to* her? Does she whine that people should have done more things *for* her?
- Does he run? Does he avoid people? Does he quit jobs and relationships when they're difficult? Does he abuse alcohol or drugs?

Do you know anyone who *doesn't* do many of these things? Although lying, attacking, acting like a victim, and running are reactions to fear, we rarely recognize our fear. Unconsciously, we hide our feelings. A wise man will kindly point out Protecting Behaviors, and help other people see that they're afraid. And then he accepts and loves them, which helps to eliminate their fear and their need to protect themselves. All the Getting Behaviors are also rooted in fear. We use them only to eliminate our fear of feeling empty and alone.

A wise man sees the many signs of fear: A man who looks at the floor when he speaks; a woman who consistently sits by herself; people who argue, defend themselves, insist on being right, blame other people, and manipulate others to earn their approval. Even people who constantly intimidate others with their power and knowledge, and who appear to be so much in control of everything, are really driven by fear. A wise man understands that most people are motivated by fear much of the time, and he helps them see that, because that creates opportunities for them to feel genuinely seen and loved.

Larry has attended several group meetings, and as you discuss the subject of fear, he says, "I keep hearing you talk about how everybody is afraid all the time. But *I'm* not afraid of anything." Clearly, Larry thinks fear is an emotion reserved for weaklings.

Larry is a successful businessman, which he's only too eager to share with people. He likes to talk about how much money he makes and how he keeps a tight control on everything in his company. That approach extends to his family as well, which has led to two divorces. Although Larry doesn't show the obvious signs of fear—withdrawal, acting like a victim, and shyness—his life is nonetheless filled with it.

"Larry," you say, "you often tell people how much money you make. Why do you do that?"

Larry instantly acquires a defensive expression and leans forward in his chair.

Larry: What do you mean?

You: I never talk about how much money I make, and I rarely mention what I do for a living. But you've only been in these meetings a few times, and several times already you've told people about your position in your company and how much money you make. I'm asking if you know why you do that.

Larry: I still don't understand what you're getting at.

You: We don't do things for no reason. Without realizing it, most of us are *afraid* that other people won't accept us unless we give them a *reason* to do that. So we give them evidence that will *convince* them that we're worth accepting. I'm suggesting that you tell people about your money and career accomplishments because you hope people will think you're important and will like you. You're afraid that if you told them you were only a garbage collector—or unemployed—they might not be interested in you.

Larry: That's not true. I'm just making conversation, letting people get to know me.

Larry is becoming angry as he speaks, and you say, "I'm not picking on you. This is just an opportunity for you to see that you might be afraid, and to feel accepted *while* you're afraid. At various times, *everyone* is afraid of not feeling loved by other people.

"Well," Larry says, "that's just not true for me."

Despite being seen and accepted by you, Larry is becoming more angry. You can't force people to hear the truth. Don't try. "I didn't mean to make you uncomfortable," you say. "My mistake."

Despite his vigorous denials, you can see Larry's fear in almost everything he does. He works out every day, in part so he'll be physically fit, but mostly so he'll be attractive. He looks in the mirror a lot and brags about his exercise routine. All this is motivated by his fear that people won't like him if he doesn't look good. He's afraid of what people might say if he looks the least bit overweight. He's recently been in several shallow and unsuccessful relationships with women, looking for the happiness he didn't find in his two marriages. Among other reasons, those relationships failed because he was afraid to be honest about himself with his partners. He couldn't admit, for example, that emptiness and fear led to his need to tell people about his successes and his need to look attractive. He was afraid nobody would like him if he didn't supply them with plenty of justification to do so. In Larry's defense, he lied about his feelings and Getting and Protecting Behaviors mostly because he didn't *recognize* them.

Although Larry is terrified of being unloved and alone, he's more afraid of the solution—*admitting* his fear—even when you try to help him. You can't make someone see what they will not see.

Although people may be a little uncomfortable as you're trying to help them see the truth, you don't always have to stop trying. Some level of discomfort is unavoidable in the process of learning and growing. But when you decide that the person you're talking to *can't* hear what you're saying, it becomes foolish for you to continue. That's why you decide not to keep trying to get Larry to see the truth about his fear.

Fear is often harder for men to admit than for women. Men must be strong and manly in public, not afraid. Ask any man the last time a guy spoke up in the locker room and said, "I've been feeling afraid a lot lately. I'm afraid I'm just not good enough as a father and husband, and I'm afraid you guys won't accept and love me." That's exactly how most men feel, but you could probably live a hundred lifetimes before you heard anything even close to those words. When men express fear, other men tend to laugh at them and take advantage of them. If you doubt that, watch the boys in a sixth grade class on the playground at recess—and it gets worse with age.

Although Bob has attended group meetings for several weeks, he speaks today for the first time, during the check-in (described on page 41). "I'm Bob," he says. "I feel a little anxious, I guess."

After everyone has checked in, you speak up.

> You: Bob, during the check-in, you said you were anxious. Would you like to talk about that?
>
> Bob: I'm not sure.
>
> You: It's up to you, but isn't that why you're here?
>
> Bob: I guess it is—okay.
>
> You: You said you were anxious. What's another word for anxious?

Afraid is not an easy word for most people, especially for men, so Bob paused for a moment before saying, "Afraid?"

> You: I know that's a hard thing to say, but yes, if you're anxious, you're afraid. You look afraid. Almost all of us are afraid of many things most of our lives, but we rarely admit it. While we're afraid, we're paralyzed—we can't be happy, we can't love other people. It's easy to say you're *anxious*, because that's vague, but when you say you're *afraid*, you give people a chance to see who you really are. The next question is, what are you afraid of?
>
> Bob: (pause) I'm not sure.
>
> You: If you were at home on the couch, watching television, would you be afraid?
>
> Bob: No.
>
> You: Then your fear must have something to do with the people in this room.
>
> Bob: I guess so.
>
> You: What are you afraid these people will do to you? Is it likely they'll hit you? Or take your money? Or steal your car?

Bob shook his head after each question.

You: You're afraid of the same thing we're all afraid of as we interact with each other. What's the one thing in life we want more than anything else? What's the one thing we need to be happy?

Bob: To be loved.

You: So what is it you want the most from these people?

Bob: (pause) Love?

It's easy for us to talk about the need *other people* have for Real Love. It's a good deal more difficult for most of us to say, "*I* want *you* to love me."

"Of course," you say. "We all want to be loved by each other. Even though you may not have thought of it in these words, when you came here tonight, you hoped that the people here would give you what you need most—love. So if love is what you need most, guess what you're afraid of—it's pretty obvious, isn't it?"

Bob understands what you're saying, but he can't bring himself to say the words without more help.

"Look," you say," I know how difficult it is to talk about fear— fear nearly destroyed my life—but when you can talk about your fears and feel accepted by people *while* you're afraid, that feels great. So let me try something. I'll pretend to be you for a moment. I'll try to say what *you* might say if you weren't nervous, and if what I say is true, you tell me. If it's *not* what you might say, tell me that, too—I don't care if I'm wrong. I'm only interested in helping you express what you're afraid of. Are you willing to try this?"

"Sure, why not?" he says. Bob gets considerable confidence from the acceptance he senses from you and the other members of the group.

"If I were you," you suggest, "instead of saying, 'I'm anxious,' I'd say something like this: 'I'm kind of new here, and I'm afraid I'll look stupid, and then you'll think I'm not worth accepting. And then I'll be just as alone and unhappy as I've always been.' Now, would that be true for you?"

Bob lets out a long sigh, smiles, and says, "Yes."

You're not doing this to make Bob uncomfortable. You're only trying to create an opportunity for Bob to feel seen, accepted, and loved—and it does have that effect. Bob feels *some* discomfort as he talks about himself, but that's unavoidable. How can we grow without some stretching? We always feel a little awkward as we step into strange territory.

"So now *I've* talked about your fears," you say, "but I'm not the one who *has* the fear. You don't have to do this, but it will make a difference if *you* actually say the words instead of just agreeing with me after *I* say them. Try it. Keep it simple. Try saying to the people in the room, 'I'm not just *anxious*. I'm afraid you won't love me.'"

Bob looks uncomfortable as he shifts in his chair, but then he says, "When I came here tonight, I was afraid you wouldn't accept me—love me. All my life I've been afraid of that."

Several members of the group then talk about how afraid they'd always been—and sometimes still are—that people wouldn't accept them. That fear drives us to use Protecting Behaviors every day and keeps us feeling alone and miserable. The more people talk, the more Bob feels accepted and connected to people in the group. It's a wonderful experience for him, and it's all happened because he told the truth about his fear.

Notice that as you talked with Bob, you used all three approaches—from Chapter Five—to helping people tell the truth. You didn't think about doing it, but as you've gained more experience as a wise man, you just naturally use whatever method serves the occasion best.

TELLING THE TRUTH ABOUT ANGER

It's quite popular in many forms of therapy for people to "vent" their anger. People are encouraged to blow up at their parents, their spouses, their bosses, and so on—although not with those people present—and this supposedly makes them feel much better as it releases the toxic emotions. I've watched people do this many times—in therapy and out—and at first I thought it was a good thing. People really do seem to feel invigorated, empowered, and free immediately after expressing their anger. But then I noticed that the same people vented the same anger over and over again—spilling exactly the same toxins. Again and again.

It does *no good whatever* for people to simply vent their anger. They can do that forever—as many people have—but never be done with it if they believe their anger is justified. The reason they feel better temporarily is that they briefly get a shot of Imitation Love in the form of power. In most cases, they've always felt helpless and unable to express their real feelings around the person who's the object of their anger, and when they can finally say how they feel, they feel less helpless for a moment. We also get an emotional rush from anger, but the whole effect of venting is superficial and brief.

As a wise man you can help people see that their anger is a reaction to a lifetime of emptiness and fear and is not caused by a particular person's behavior. They need to see that anger is unwise, and then they can take responsibility for learning to feel loved and loving, thereby eliminating their need for anger. When people understand all that and express their anger in an atmosphere where they can be accepted and loved *while* they're angry, *that* can be a life-changing experience. Anger must be recognized, understood, and eliminated with Real Love, not simply expressed, encouraged, and indulged.

All his life, Darrell's mother has loved him conditionally. He comes to a group meeting looking irritated. "Darrell," you say, "you look angry."

"No, I just had a difficult conversation with my mother, and I'm a little upset."

Rather than contradict him when he's obviously angry, you just ask about the content of the conversation.

You: "What did you and your mother talk about?"

Darrell: "My job, mostly."

You: What did she say about it?

Darrell: She's always telling me I should get more education and find a better career. I get kind of tired of hearing that.

You: What else did she talk about?

Darrell: My girlfriend. Mother thinks Alana's not good enough for me. She's always trying to control me—been doing that all my life. She doesn't listen to a word I say, like I was twelve years old.

As Darrell speaks, his tone, posture, and expression demonstrate that he's angry.

You: Darrell, this is important. You have an opportunity here for people to really listen to you, and for you to learn something about yourself. You're not twelve anymore. Your mother keeps telling you what to do with your life even though you're *thirty-five years old*. There's something wrong with that picture. She tells you what job you should have. She tells you what women you should be seeing. You've talked about other conversations with her, so we know she tells you what food you should eat, what hours you should be sleeping, and how to spend your money . If she could tuck you into bed at night, she would. If *I* walked around with you all day, telling you what to do and what not do with your every move—barking commands and opinions at you like you were a mindless child—how would you feel toward me?

Darrell: I'd be mad.

You: Yes, you would. And *you're angry at your mother, too*, because that's just what she does with you all the time. But you don't talk about being angry at her, because you believe it would somehow make you a bad person to be angry at your own mother. Right?

Darrell: Well, yes, I guess I do. I never thought about it like that.

You: Although you do care about your mother, it's also a fact that you're angry at her. When you talk about her, you clench your jaw. Your tone of voice is angry. Everything about you radiates anger, but you're afraid to *say* you're angry. She's definitely trying to control your life. That doesn't make her bad, just controlling and unable to see you. And none of this *justifies* your anger. It just explains it.

Darrell: (smiling weakly) I guess I *am* angry. All these years I've just been calling it *upset*. Every time I'm on the phone with her, I break a pencil or bend a paper clip into a pretzel, but then I say I'm not really *mad*, just frustrated.

You: It's pretty natural that you're angry after all these years of being controlled and ignored. That doesn't make you bad, but it does make you unhappy, and you can't change that until you tell the truth about it. The real problem is not that she controls you. The real problem is that she's not giving you something you badly need. Instead of her giving you advice all the time, what would you *like* her to give you?

Darrell: I'd like her to just shut up! I hate hearing all her opinions! I don't want to hear what she says about my job and girlfriends. I don't want to hear any of it anymore.

You: I got that. You don't want any more advice. But what *positive* things would you like from her?

Darrell: I'm not sure.

That's a common answer. Darrell has never gotten anything but controlling and criticism from his mother, so he can't imagine getting anything else.

You: What do you see people in this group getting from each other?

Darrell: I didn't even think of that. I guess it would be nice to get a little acceptance from her.

You: What's the likelihood of you getting unconditional acceptance from your mother—judging from your past experience all these years?

Darrell: (laughing) Not likely.

You: Your mother is *not* a bad woman. She's just never felt unconditionally loved herself, so she doesn't know *how* to accept you. When she gives you advice and controls you, she feels needed and important. It's the only thing she knows to do. It would be nice if our parents could love us, but most of our parents *can't*. Fortunately, they don't have to. It turns out that it really doesn't matter *who* gives you the Real Love you need. You can get it from *anyone* who has it. You can get it here, for example. As you tell the truth about yourself and feel accepted—here or anywhere—you'll find the love you need, and eventually it just won't bother you when your mother talks to you like she does.

Over the next several weeks and months, Darrell continues to talk about himself to the members of the group, and as he feels accepted and loved by them, he becomes much less upset by his mother's advice.

Indirect Expressions of Anger

Like many of us, Marcia had not felt unconditionally loved since childhood, so she'd spent her life looking for people who could fill her emptiness with Real and Imitation Love. Her work supervisor, Emma, was one of those people she expected to see her and accept her. It was entirely natural and virtually unavoidable that Marcia did that. We *must* have Real Love to be happy, and we tend to assign the responsibility for loving us to anyone close by—spouses, teachers, bosses, and peers. Unfortunately, we don't choose people who are *qualified* for the position—people who have Real Love to give—and we therefore guarantee disappointment and frustration for ourselves. When we don't get what we need, we blame our unhappiness on the people we expected to love us. To us it doesn't matter that they were incapable of handling the job from the start. We just know that we had a need and they *failed* us.

Despite Marcia's expectations, Emma was no more capable of seeing her and loving her than the many other people in her life had been. When Emma failed to give Marcia what she wanted, Marcia was hurt and blamed Emma for her pain—an understandable reaction but completely unreasonable.

Although Marcia was angry, she'd been punished as a child for expressing anger directly, so she'd learned to attack people indirectly, which she did with Emma. She worked slowly on projects that had important deadlines, for example, which created problems for Emma. She didn't look Emma in the eye when they spoke or passed in the hall, because she had unconsciously noticed that Emma felt uncomfortable when she did that. She never spoke about Emma in an openly negative way, but her comments about her were always filled with reservations, and those comments created subtle doubts in the minds of others. Because Marcia was afraid of what would happen if she engaged Emma in open battle, she shot at her from the bushes. It made her feel less helpless and weak, but it also isolated her from the very person she wanted to feel close to.

Many of us play this game with people, and because indirect anger is harder to identify than the open variety, we often don't recognize it, and it continues to take its toll on us and our relationships. It keeps us unloved, alone, and unhappy. It even affects our health, contributing to high blood pressure, heart disease, ulcers, bowel dysfunction, and other disorders.

Eventually, wise men and women helped Marcia talk about her anger, and as she was accepted and loved by these people, she no longer had a *need* to feel angry—at her supervisor or other people.

What a Waste

Anger is not only a waste of time, but also a waste of joy. Any time I spend being angry is time I can't be happy. In every moment, I choose whether I see the love I do have or focus on what I don't have. As soon as I choose to think about my unfulfilled expectations, and feel the anger that goes with that, all the joy I could have had vanishes. It's gone.

TELLING THE TRUTH ABOUT SADNESS

Imagine you're meeting Allison, an old friend from your group, for lunch, and as soon as you greet her, you can tell something is wrong. "You look like something is on your mind," you say. "You want to talk about it?"

Allison says, "My son, Michael, has been doing worse in school over the past year or so. I don't understand it. He's always been such a good student, but now he's failing a couple of classes, and that's really going to hurt him when he starts applying to colleges in a few months. All his life, I've stood over him and made sure he did his homework and got good grades, but now he won't even talk about it. I'm really sad. I feel shut out and frustrated."

Allison appears to be telling the truth about her sadness, but is she really? Does the word *sad* really communicate how she's feeling? There are two feelings we commonly identify as *sad*, and although they're quite different, we use the same word for both. Our sadness is usually one of two of the following feelings, or a combination of them:

- A compassion for the pain of others. This is genuine sadness, as we mentioned earlier in the chapter.
- A regret for the lack of Real Love in our own lives. This is better called *emptiness*.

Our inability to identify this distinction can often obscure the motivation for our subsequent behavior, and can also keep us from feeling unconditionally loved.

You've known Allison for years, and you've seen her control her children on many occasions. She's made them take piano lessons when they didn't want them, she chooses the clothes they buy and wear, and she maintains a heavy hand in almost everything else they do. When they fail to do what she wants, she becomes angry.

When we're genuinely concerned for the happiness of other people, we want to help them change their behavior for *their* benefit. We love them and teach them. When we want to change their behavior to make *ourselves* feel better in any way, we use Getting Behaviors. Even if you hadn't known Allison for years, you would have seen that her sadness and frustration (her words) are in great part a result of her not getting what *she* wants from her son. She says she has stood over him all his life making him get good grades, and now *she* feels shut out and frustrated. She's trying to control him and only regrets that she can't, so she's really voicing a concern for *her* interests, not his.

You: It sounds like he's doing some things that could interfere with his happiness down the road. That is sad. I wonder, though, if you're feeling more than just sadness. I *know* you're concerned that he might be hurting himself, but I also know that all his life you've really needed him to do what *you* want, and that has not been entirely selfless. There's no disappointment or anger in Real Love, but when your kids don't do what you want, you're big-time disappointed and angry. That's a big part of what you're calling sadness.

Allison: I can't believe you'd say that. I love my son.

You: I have no doubt you care about him. I'm only concerned that there is also a part of you that *needs* him to do what you think is the right thing. When he doesn't, you lose control over him, which you don't like. You also look bad in the eyes of other people—you don't look like the perfect mother anymore.

Allison now looks thoughtful, instead of just hurt and irritated. "I never saw this before," she says. "So you're saying I'm being selfish, aren't you?"

You: Yes. That doesn't make you bad, Allison. It just means you don't feel sufficiently loved yourself, so you need to get Imitation Love from your son. That's very common. I've done it many times myself. When you control your children, you get a sense of power. When other people think you're a great mother, you feel approval, which is praise. Now that you're losing some of your power and praise, you say you're sad, but it's mostly for your own loss. Don't feel guilty about this, just do something about it. When you admit what your sadness really is, you can begin to change your behavior toward Michael. Right now he can *feel* your real motivation—your need to control him—and it's hurting him. When you can eliminate filling your own needs and care more about his, he'll feel the difference.

Allison: I'm embarrassed.

You: That wouldn't help. You'd only be embarrassed if you thought you wouldn't be loved as much while you're making this mistake. Do I look disgusted by you or critical of you?

Allison: No.

You: Remember that. If you tell the truth about what you're really doing with Michael, you can feel accepted by myself and others. That's Real Love, and with it you'll be able to love your son even better. But if you don't tell the truth about your own emptiness, and about your Getting and Protecting Behaviors, you won't feel loved. So you'll just keep hurting Michael as you try to get something from him.

If we distinguish genuine sadness from emptiness, we'll feel more accepted ourselves and will be able to change our selfish behavior.

True Sadness: Compassion for the Pain of Others

We feel genuine sadness when we respond to the suffering of others, in ways similar to the following:

- "For many years my good friend has had arthritis, and now she's in almost constant pain. I wish I could take that away from her."
- "I saw on the news today that there are 15,000 starving children in Somalia. I feel sad when I think about it."
- "While I was driving yesterday, I hit a dog. It broke my heart listening to him cry until his owner came out and took him to the vet."
- "Thousands of acres of forest are being destroyed every day. I'm sad that we're not taking better care of the planet."

Even when we're pre-occupied with our own emptiness, and our Getting and Protecting Behaviors, we still have an inclination to feel genuinely sad when we see suffering. This feeling is strong evidence of our innate, natural desire to love others.

The Sadness We Feel for Ourselves
When We Lack Sufficient Real Love

When Holly checks in at her second group meeting, she says, "I'm sad." Later in the meeting you give her a chance to talk more about that.

"Holly," you say, "when you checked in, you said you were sad. Sad about what?"

"My marriage," she says, and then she talks about her husband for several minutes. But instead of getting involved in all the details, you address what's most important. Knowing that she's read *Real Love* and understands those principles somewhat, you can ask her some direct questions.

You: What would you like most in all the world?

Holly: To feel loved.

You: If you did feel unconditionally loved, would you be unhappy?

Holly: No, I guess not.

You: Then clearly you *don't* feel loved, not by your husband or anyone else.

Holly: But my husband does love me.

You: You just said that if you felt loved, you wouldn't be unhappy, but you *are* unhappy. So there's no way you feel loved by him. You said, for example, that Blake gets angry at you pretty often, right?

Holly: Yes.

You: And he spends very little time with you?

Holly: True.

You: Except when he wants sex, and *then* he wants to spend time with you, doesn't he?"

Holly: Yes.

You: It doesn't sound to me like he loves you. It sounds like he mostly uses you and gets mad when you don't do what he wants.

Holly: No, he still loves me. He's not *always* angry. Sometimes he's nice.

You: So, in effect, when you *pay* him—by doing whatever he wants—he's nice to you, but when you don't pay him enough, he's angry and demanding. Would you call that unconditional love?

Holly has no answer for that.

You: I am not criticizing Blake. Many people have relationships like yours, where they just trade favors with each other: "I'll be nice to you if you'll be nice to me. And if you're not nice to me, I'll ignore you or be angry at you." That's often how it works. That's how it works with you two. Do you see that?"

Holly: I don't know what to say, but everything you've said sure does describe our marriage.

You: Blake is not doing any of this intentionally. He's loving you as well as he can, but what he's giving you is not Real Love. It's conditional love, but Real Love is the one thing we *must* have to be happy. Without it, we can only feel empty, alone, scared, and angry. That's the whole reason you feel unhappy much of the time. And then you can't be unconditionally loving toward other people—Blake, your children, anyone.

Holly: This makes a lot of sense.

You: So now you can see that when you checked in and said you were sad, you were really saying that you didn't feel loved.

TELLING THE TRUTH ABOUT HAPPINESS

At a meeting several weeks later, Holly bounds into the room with obvious enthusiasm.

You: What's up with you?

Holly: I'm amazed at the difference in my life over the last several weeks.

You: Like what?

Holly: Since I started coming to the group meetings and calling people, I feel happier. I don't get angry as easily at Blake or the kids. The things that used to bother me at work don't upset me as much, either.

You: Why do you think that is?

Holly: You know the answer to that. I feel more accepted by the people in the group. When I remember that, the things that used to bother me just don't matter as much as they used to. I'm free. You told me this would happen, and it did. Feeling loved really does make a difference.

Sometimes it must seem like I only encourage people to talk about "negative" feelings and experiences. That's because it's those things that tend to keep us unhappy—those are the warts we hide. But it's also important to talk about feeling happy, as Holly did. When we talk about our happiness and recognize the sources of it, that magnifies our faith in the process of finding Real Love and increases our connection to other people.

Chapter Summary

- In the past, we've been criticized and ridiculed when people have seen our feelings, so we've learned to hide them. We then feel safer momentarily but also unloved and alone.
- One way we hide our feelings is to minimize them with vague, socially acceptable words. We better create opportunities to feel seen and accepted when we use clear, direct words for our feelings: angry, afraid, empty, sad, and happy.

Chapter Eight

No More Hiding

Telling the Truth About Getting and Protecting Behaviors

The absence of Real Love is so intolerable that we use Getting and Protecting Behaviors without thought or hesitation. Most of us use them so commonly that they virtually fill our days. I realize that may seem like an exaggeration, but let's examine a day in the life of an "average" man. As we identify the Getting and Protecting Behaviors he uses, we'll get an idea of how often we all do these things. As wise men we need to see these behaviors in ourselves and help other people see them in *their* lives.

Jack is married, has a good job in a computer company, and is the father of two children, ages eight and ten. As he opens his eyes and lifts himself from the pillow this morning, he senses—from her breathing and movement—that his wife, Amy, is awake in bed. He knows she'd love to hear him say, "Good morning"—certainly she's complained on many occasions that he doesn't talk to her enough—but he can think of so many reasons *not* to say anything: She always has that look of disappointment and disapproval on her face; she never appreciates what I do and always wants more from me; and she has something critical to say every time I speak.

It's no surprise that Jack doesn't like how Amy behaves toward him, so his solution is to avoid her as much as possible. This morning, as he rolls over and gets out of bed without speaking, he's using his first Protecting Behavior of the day—*running*. He's also silently acting like a *victim*, because his justification for running is his belief that Amy is always doing something *to* him, the classic claim of the victim. This morning, he has an additional excuse to run: He knows if he speaks to Amy, she'll probably ask him about some jobs around the house he's been putting off for weeks, and he doesn't want to admit that he's been irresponsible. In addition to running and acting like a victim, Jack is also *attacking* Amy. He hates it that she nags him and criticizes him most of the time, and without thinking about it, part of the reason he rolls out of bed and withholds his greeting is to punish her.

During breakfast, Amy speaks to him several times, but he continues to run by responding with grunts and single words. Finally, she tells him that yesterday their 10-year-old son, Justin, let the family dog into the house without permission, whereupon the dog tore up one of the cushions in the living room couch. Jack responds by summoning Justin into the room and delivering an angry lecture about obedience and responsibility. When his children don't obey him, Jack feels helpless and out of control, so he's using his anger and position of authority with Justin to get some relief from those painful feelings. He's protecting himself and getting a sense of power as he controls his son's behavior. Although they do it unconsciously, most parents use anger with their children in this way.

Because the discussion with Justin takes longer than Jack anticipated, he's five minutes late for a meeting with an associate at work. When he arrives, he *lies* to prevent his co-worker from thinking less of him. "Sorry I'm late," he says. "The traffic was terrible."

At 9:38 a.m., Jack talks with someone in shipping about an order he placed two days earlier.

Jack: This is Jack, in sales. I sent you an order for several items to be shipped to Akron, Ohio, but I never received a confirmation that those items were actually sent. I want to know why.

Clerk: (pause) I'm sorry, but we had some delays yesterday, so those things didn't go out—but they'll be shipped first thing today.

Jack: (angrily) "You guys screw up my orders half the time. I'm the vice-president of sales, and I expect things to go out within twenty-four hours of my putting in the order. Do you understand me?

Jack is using anger and his position of authority to attack the shipping clerk and get what he wants. He's also lying again since he knows that the shipping department does not "screw up his orders *half* the time." He behaves like this with many other people during the day.

11:00 a.m. Jack gets a call from the purchasing department of another computer company. The caller wants to know why Jack hasn't e-mailed her the information she asked for several days ago. Jack blames his subordinates for not getting some necessary data to him, but the entire responsibility for the delay is really Jack's. Without hesitation Jack has *lied* and *attacked* to protect himself.

12:15 p.m. Jack goes to lunch with his boss, and several times during the conversation he laughs at light-hearted comments the boss makes. He does this so the boss will like him. Although we don't tend to think of an innocent behavior like this as lying, we are lying whenever we manipulate people without telling them what we're doing. In our defense, we're often not aware of our deception.

2:38 p.m. Someone in the office says, "Jack, that was a nice job you did with the Mitchell account."

"Thanks," he responds in a falsely humble way. "I just thought of a few ways they could use that new software we developed." And then he tells the whole self-congratulatory story about how he sold the account. This is *clinging*, squeezing every bit of attention and praise you can get out of other people.

5:00. Jack could go home to be with his family, but he doesn't. He's *running* from his responsibilities as a husband and father, because those roles constantly require him to give attention and love to others, and Jack isn't prepared for that. Whereas he can earn praise and power from his co-workers and superiors with relative predictability, he doesn't get that immediate and consistent reward from his efforts at home, so he often stays at work. Praise and power are not Real Love, but they are a welcome temporary distraction from the pain of feeling empty.

6:45. On the drive home the traffic is still heavy in places, and Jack drives aggressively, darting in and out of the congested lines of cars. When people get in his way, he impatiently curses at them and occasionally honks his horn. Jack is *attacking* the drivers around him. He's also acting like a *victim*, believing that other drivers are just trying to annoy *him*.

When Jack gets home, he again avoids conversation with Amy, and he doesn't go looking for his children to talk to them, either. Instead he sits in the living room and reads the newspaper while he drinks a beer, which helps him escape from the tension of the day—all running.

This is a small sampling of the ways Jack filled his entire day with Getting and Protecting Behaviors. When we don't have sufficient Real Love in our lives, it's very difficult for us to avoid doing as Jack did, and we need to tell the truth about our behavior in order to feel loved and change the ways we interfere with our happiness and our relationships.

TELLING THE TRUTH ABOUT LYING

We're lying any time we fail to tell people that we're manipulating them to get praise, power, pleasure, or safety. That includes a vast range of behaviors. We're lying when we

- act happier than we feel.
- act stronger than we are.
- exaggerate our successes.
- spend a lot of time on our physical appearance—hair, make-up, clothes, body.
- try to look tough to hide our fears.
- talk about our expensive cars and other toys.
- brag about the men or women we've had relationships with.
- minimize our faults.

We do these things so other people will think we're worth loving. And who doesn't tell many of these lies? A wise man helps people see how they lie and how their lies can only attract Imitation Love. He accepts them and gives them Real Love, which is what they really needed in the first place. With that love, their need to lie decreases and eventually vanishes.

TELLING THE TRUTH ABOUT ATTACKING

We attack people with criticism, physical intimidation, legal prosecution, withdrawal of approval, sarcasm, and especially anger. But as I explained in Chapter Three, when we're angry, we're wrong. When we remember that, and when we teach it to others, we can all avoid much more easily the destructive effect of that Getting and Protecting Behavior.

Robert, Rich, and Alex are attending a weekly group meeting.

Alex: Robert, when you checked in this evening, you said you were angry.

Robert: Yeah, I'm angry. I've just about had it with my wife. I work as hard as I can all day long, and when I get home, all she does is whine and complain. She says I smoke too much, eat too much, and leave my stuff all over the house. Then she says I don't spend enough time with her, but geez, why would I want to be around somebody who complains all the time? Then she spends all the money I make. I'm tired of it.

Alex: Robert, if you're angry, you're wrong.

Robert: You sound like my wife. I don't need any more of this.

Robert rises from his chair to leave the room. While it's true that Robert needs to tell the truth about his anger to feel accepted and loved, and to make different choices, people don't learn to feel loved, be loving, and be responsible all at once, or in the moment we think they should. Right now Robert isn't ready to take responsibility for his anger. He needs to feel more accepted first. I am not criticizing Alex. Many people *could* have accepted Alex's comment exactly as he made it. You'll always be discovering how much teaching to do—and what kind—while you're accepting people. If you tell them the truth too directly when they're empty or afraid, they won't be able to hear you.

Confused and afraid because of Robert's attack, Alex has no idea what to do next. But he does remember the Fourth Rule of Seeing—if you can't be a wise man, get one—and he looks over at Rich.

Rich understands that he's being asked for help, and he smiles as he says, "Robert, I don't think Alex was trying to criticize you. He was just trying to teach you something about anger—but that can wait. Right now you feel criticized and unappreciated by your wife, and you probably don't get a chance to talk about that very often. Would you be willing to sit down and talk about it some more? I'd like to listen.

Robert slowly sits down and says, "Look, I don't need anybody to tell me I'm wrong. I get enough of that from my wife. That witch whines at me all day, and I'm sick of it."

Rich: I understand that. She doesn't seem to accept you very well.

Robert: That's an understatement. She criticizes everything I do. Nothing is good enough.

Rich: That must be exhausting.

Robert: Yeah, it is. How would *you* like it?

Rich: I've felt like that many times in my life, and I didn't like it at all. But I learned to *do* something about it. I started spending time with people like this—the people in this room. As I felt accepted by them, it didn't matter as much when other people—like some of the people in my family or the people at work—didn't accept me.

Rich sees that Robert is not ready to talk about the selfishness of his anger, but he also understands that blaming is never healthy and can't continue. People use anger as a Getting or Protecting Behavior only when they don't feel loved. The solution is to get loved.

Rich: The awful thing about anger is that it always makes me unhappy. I've never felt angry and happy at the same time. Have you?

Robert: I've never thought about it, but no, I guess not.

Rich: I'm not suggesting that you *shouldn't* be angry—not at all. I'm only saying that it's exhausting and makes you miserable. If you spend time with people who accept you, you'll feel less angry. It just happens without thinking about it. In fact, right now as I'm talking to you, you look like you're feeling less angry.

Robert: Yeah, a little.

Rich: You only get angry to protect yourself and to feel less helpless. When you feel unconditionally loved, you don't have a *need* to be angry. Call me any time you want this week. You're not alone here. And I've no doubt that some of the other people here would love to spend time with you, too—on the phone or in person. If you get enough love here, that will stay with you when you go home. Then when your wife nags you, it won't bother you. That may not happen right away, like tonight, but it will happen eventually.

Robert: That would be nice.

TELLING THE TRUTH ABOUT ACTING LIKE A VICTIM

Victimhood is the belief that other people have an obligation to make us happy. A victim doesn't see other people as human beings with their own character and needs. He sees them as objects which will either serve him or hurt him. He sees everything being done *to* him or *for* him—there is no neutral. Following are three examples of how ordinary events are viewed by a victim and a non-victim.

Whine and Fine both wait in line for an hour to register their cars at the Department of Motor Vehicles. When they get home, their wives each ask them about the experience.

Fine says, "It wasn't bad. I had to wait in line for an hour, but I read a magazine I brought with me. There was a problem with the registration, too, but it's all done now."

Whine says, "Those stupid people made me wait in line all day. Nobody down there knows what they're doing—as usual. Idiots— all idiots." He rants like that for several minutes.

After lunch on Friday, Whine and Fine are each given difficult assignments at work that must be accomplished before the end of the day. When they get home late that evening, they talk to their wives.

"Long day," says Fine. "Sorry I'm late, but I had to finish that project. At least now I won't have any work to do over the weekend."

When Whine gets home, he's in a terrible temper: "They're always doing this to me. They never plan ahead, and then they dump stuff on *me* at the last minute. And did anybody offer to help me out on a Friday afternoon? Oh no, of course not. There I was in the office all by myself doing *their* work. Do you think they appreciate it? Hah!" Whine complains about his experience until he goes to bed—and for much of the next day.

Whine and Fine each arrive a few minutes late at their first business meeting of the day.

"I'm sorry I made you wait," says Fine. "I knew I should have left the house earlier."

Whine says, "The traffic was terrible. I don't know when they're finally going to do something about those roads."

These examples illustrate some of the favorite tools of the victim. The victim cries out, "Look what you did *to* me," "Look what you should have done *for* me," and—a real favorite—"It's not my fault." Victims behave as they do because it frees them from responsibility. As victims, we're never wrong—everyone else is responsible for our problems and our pain. Unfortunately, we're also irrevocably stuck with our problems—if we blame other people for our unhappiness, we cannot escape our misery until those people change.

I have come to believe that it's much easier to recover from cocaine addiction than it is to recover from victimhood. Once we believe that other people owe us something, that is a very difficult belief to unlearn.

Melinda is raising a four-year-old son, Cody, by herself. Her boyfriend abandoned her during the pregnancy, and now she's working full-time while going to school. She's been attending group meetings on and off for months and is always complaining about how difficult her life is: Nobody ever helps her enough, people are always treating her unfairly, and nothing is ever her fault. She's talking about this to you and others at a group meeting.

"My mother's always telling me how to raise my son," Melinda says. "She thinks I spoil him. And then she disciplines him right when I'm in the room—can you believe that? Things aren't easy at school, either. The other day I was only one day late with an assignment—because Cody was sick—and the teacher took ten points off my grade. I couldn't believe it! Nobody seems to understands how hard it is to go to school, work full-time, and try to raise a child."

You know you can't do Melinda's schoolwork for her, or go to work for her, or raise her son. We can't solve everyone's immediate problems, but we *can* give them what they need most to be happy— we can love them. When people feel loved, they approach every other problem with less emptiness and fear, and then they make better decisions. That's why you'll address Melinda's need for Real Love instead of talking about each of the problems she's mentioned. You also know she's read *Real Love*, so you can speak with the assumption that she understands the basic principles in it.

> You: Are you spending any time with people who can give you the love you need?
>
> Melinda: I don't have time for that. Like I said, I'm already too busy to do everything I'm supposed to do. How would I have time to call people?

Victims characteristically present long lists of problems that need to be fixed, but when a solution is presented that involves *their* doing something different, they invariably respond with reasons why the solution won't work. They're looking for an answer where *other people* will save them. They're not malicious about this, just lazy and irresponsible. They've learned from past experience that they can get other people to give them sympathy and support, so they continue to act like victims instead of telling the truth about their irresponsible choices and learning to make better ones.

It's especially useful with victims to remember the Laws of Choice and Responsibility. Victims need to be reminded that they always have a choice and are then responsible for the choices they make.

You: How long does it take to pick up a phone and call people who can see and accept you?

Melinda: I just don't have time to do *everything*.

You: In everything you do, you're making a *choice*, and so far you're making a choice not to feel loved. You're choosing to act like a victim instead of changing the way you live.

Melinda: I don't understand.

You: You act like all these problems were dumped on you, but *you* chose to go to school. You chose to have your job. You chose to have your son, and you chose to have your mother take care of him. As you choose to make no contact with people who could love you, you're also choosing to stay unhappy. And now you're complaining about the natural consequences of your choices. It doesn't make much sense.

Melinda: Are you saying I *chose* to be a single mother? I'm not the one that ran away. My *boyfriend* did that.

You: Did you have sex with the father of your son or not?

Melinda: Well, yes, but he left me to raise Cody by myself.

You: That was *his* choice, and you couldn't control that, but I'm trying to help you see how many choices *you* had in this. *You* chose to have sex with this man, and you chose to do that while you were single. I'm not judging the morality of what you did, only pointing out that *you* created the possibility that you would become a single mother. Were the two of you absolutely in agreement about raising a child together for his entire life?

Melinda: Well, not exactly.

You: So he *didn't* agree to raise a child with you. Knowing that, did you do everything possible to keep from getting pregnant?

Melinda: Well, no, I—

You: If you two hadn't agreed completely that you were going to raise a child together, and you weren't doing what it took to keep from getting pregnant, didn't you virtually guarantee that you'd be a single mother? In effect you made a *choice* to raise this baby alone.

Melinda: So what about my mother? Are you saying that's my fault, too?

You: You're not responsible for her behavior, but you *did* choose to be around it, and now you're complaining about the choice *you* made.

Melinda: I don't get it.

You: Don't you know exactly what kind of woman your mother is? Haven't you been around her all your life?"

Melinda: Well . . .

You: Hasn't she always given you advice—about everything—and tried to control you?

Melinda: Yes.

You: Then when you decided to leave your son with her to get the free babysitting, you *knew* her advice and controlling would be part of the package. You *chose* that.

Melinda: But what else can I do? I don't have the money for anybody else to take care of him.

You: So be grateful that she helps you out when you can't afford anything else, and quit expecting her to suddenly become a different person for your convenience.

Melinda: Well, I still don't have time to make those phone calls.

You: There's no doubt you have a lot of demands on your time, but you're ignoring the most important thing you need. You need to feel loved, and if you don't get that, everything else you do won't really matter. Is your son important to you?

Melinda: Of course.

You: You've often said that when you get busy with so many things, you get tired and grouchy. When you're like that, are you kind and loving toward him?

Melinda: (pause) I try to be, but no, I get impatient with him—and I hate that.

You: There's nothing in your life right now more important than being happy and raising your son to be happy. If you had to drop out of school for a semester to learn how to do that, it would be well worth it. That may not be necessary—I'm just making the point that you need to do whatever it takes to get what you really need. No amount of school or money will mean anything if you're unloving and miserable.

Melinda: (pause) I see what you mean.

You: Melinda, if I didn't care about you, I wouldn't say anything when you say you don't have time to make phone calls and do what it takes to change your life—but I really do care about you. If you want to change your life, you can. You are not helpless. You are not a victim.

Melinda slowly begins to see that she's always acted like a victim, and she begins to feel accepted by the members of the group. She's still a single mother and has to work to support herself and her son, but she's finding the happiness she's always wanted.

It often seems harsh to tell the truth to victims, but there's no other way to help them change their destructive course. They're frustrated by the apparent lack of a solution to their problems, but they also enjoy the sympathy they get from other people when they complain. Moreover, they enjoy the sense of irresponsibility that comes from being in a situation that has no solution, because then they can claim that the situation is not their fault. As a wise man, you can help victims see that almost all their problems are a result of the choices they've made, and that there's always a way they can find happiness, regardless of what their problems are.

Seeing Victimhood

You can recognize victimhood more easily when you understand that it lies at the root of the other Getting and Protecting Behaviors. Let's quickly review the Protecting Behaviors:

- Lying. People lie only because they're afraid of being *injured* if they tell the truth. That requires labeling someone else as the monster who will hurt them. Only victims label other people as monsters.
- Attacking. People attack to protect themselves from a perpetrator. Only victims see other people in that way.
- Running. People run from a perpetrator, again the view of a victim.

Victimhood also plays an important part in Getting Behaviors. Why would people have to manipulate others (lie, attack, cling) unless they thought the perpetrators of the world were withholding the love (Real and Imitation) that was rightfully theirs?

As a wise man you don't tell people they're acting like victims to criticize or condemn them. You describe what you see only so they can see themselves clearly and choose a happier course in life. It's not possible to tell the truth, or be loving, or make wise choices and be responsible while acting like a victim.

The Payoff For Acting Like a Victim

Victims portray themselves as always being treated unfairly, but they get a lot from their supposedly unfair situations.

Emily's husband, Dean, treats her like a child. He gives her an allowance, and she has to account for every dime. She can't go anywhere without his permission. If he doesn't like the clothes she's wearing, he says so and she changes into something else. He controls virtually every aspect of her life. Emily widely complains about this, and she gets a lot of sympathy for it. How could he treat you like that, her friends say, and how in the world do you put up with it? But a wise woman in Emily's group knows that no one can be happy until they tell the truth about *themselves*.

Wise woman: What do you *like* about your relationship with Dean?

Emily: Like? Not much. I don't know why I put up with it. I guess I just don't think people should get divorced.

Wise woman: Doesn't Dean completely take care of you financially?

Emily: Well, yes, but that doesn't give him the right to treat me like he does.

Wise woman: All right, for thirty seconds we'll talk about Dean. Dean doesn't feel unconditionally loved, and when he controls you, he gets a feeling of importance and power which temporarily makes him feel less empty and alone. That is not a loving way to live. It's wrong, but he has a right to choose to live that way. That's the Law of Choice. Now I'm done talking about Dean. He doesn't determine your happiness or your relationship. A relationship is the natural result of the choices two people make *independently*. Dean has made the choice to control your life. You can't change that, but you *can* make your own choice, and so far you've chosen to *let* him control you. That's why your relationship is like this. *He* didn't make it that way. The *two of you* did. You can be a victim here only if you *allow* yourself to be.

Emily: I don't understand. *He's* the one who treats me like a servant. What can *I* do about it?

Wise woman: You said he tells you what to wear, right?

Emily: Yes.

Wise woman: So if you put on something he doesn't like, what does he do?

Emily: He says he hates it.

Wise woman: And then . . .

Emily: I change.

Wise woman: (smiling) Does he grab you by the hair, drag you into the bedroom, tear your clothes off, and put new ones on you?

Emily: No.

Wise woman: Then you make a *choice* to change clothes, don't you?

Emily: (pause) Sort of. But if I didn't change, he'd get angry.

Wise woman: You're still making a choice. You make it out of fear, but it's still a choice. He can certainly *tell* you what to do—that's his choice to make—but then you can choose to say *no.* You're not a victim, or a child. You're a willing participant in this relationship, Emily. Do you see this?

Emily: I'm afraid of what he'll do if I tell him no.

Wise woman: Has he ever hit you?

Emily: No.

Wise woman: Then what do you really have to fear? You're already unhappy—it doesn't seem like you have much to lose. Do you want your relationship to change or not?

Emily: I do.

Wise woman: If you start making some of your own choices—about clothes, money, or whatever—you'll see changes in your relationship with Dean. It *has* to change, because *you* will be different. Don't be demanding or angry with him. That won't help your relationship, and you won't be happy. Just state what you want, and what you will or will not do. On some occasions, you may *want* to do things his way, just because you care about him, but then it's a loving choice, rather than something you do as a victim.

Emily: If I start doing this, I know he'll get angry. What do I do then?

Wise woman: Call people in the group and talk to them—not to complain, but to tell the truth about *you* being angry and acting like a victim. If you feel loved by other people, it won't bother you as much when Dean gets angry at you. And then keep talking to Dean—about money, how you feel, your mistakes, everything. If he cares about you at all, he'll work this out with you. Don't give up. A worthwhile relationship takes time to develop.

Victims get a lot from their behavior. Although Emily complained about her relationship with Dean, the rewards were considerable. She didn't have to work. She made no difficult decisions about insurance, investments, maintenance on the house, or anything else. She played tennis, painted, and worked in her garden. Dean even took her out to eat once or twice a week so she didn't have to cook. The overall experience was *positive*, which is why she stayed in the marriage. What she got out of it was more than she suffered from it, but then she chose to complain about the part she didn't like. She was angry that he would inconvenience her while he was completely taking care of her.

Most of us tend to do that. In a relationship we want only the positive characteristics of our partner, but that's not possible. When we make a choice to be with someone, we get the whole package. If you decide to buy a car so you can experience the convenience of driving at fifty-five miles per hour from here to there instead of walking, you also make the decision to experience all the inconveniences that go along with that—flat tires, car payments, oil changes, inconsiderate drivers, unexpected repairs, road hazards, terrible traffic, insurance payments, and so on.

We choose to have relationships with people because they have characteristics we like, and then we resent them—we act like victims—because they also have qualities we *don't* like. We view people as a restaurant menu from which we can pick and choose, but people are not menus. We get them as they are, all of it. As we've discussed before, we only have two choices in a relationship that ever lead to happiness: we can live with it and like it, or we can leave it. Trying to change our partners doesn't work, nor does living with the relationship and hating it.

As much as victims complain about their suffering, they're rarely in a situation they can't escape. They usually stay where they are because, overall, they enjoy the combination of sympathy and irresponsibility they earn. They use and abuse the people around them—though usually not intentionally—all the while appearing to be the injured and innocent objects of abuse and neglect. Victims are reluctant to walk away from this productive arrangement.

As I've discussed with people situations like Emily's, some of them have objected that it's wrong to tell a woman to disobey her husband. Notice that the wise woman did *not* tell Emily what to do. She told Emily that she had a *choice* in everything, and that if she chose to do as her husband demanded, it was foolish to complain about it. Wise men rarely tell people what to do, other than encouraging them to tell the truth about themselves and find the Real Love they need.

The Cost of Being a Victim

Despite the rewards of being a victim, the price is very high. Victims have to lie about their responsibility for the choices they make, and they have to lie about other people being perpetrators. These lies separate them from the truth and the possibility of feeling Real Love. Victims can buy sympathy and attention, but never Real Love, which is the only thing that will make them genuinely happy. They can only feel alone, and that's why wise men must help them tell the truth about their lies and their behavior.

What About Real Victims?

Some people suggest that there are *real* victims in life, not just people who *act* like victims. What about battered wives, for example? What about people who are falsely accused of crimes and imprisoned? What about slaves? I make no excuse for injustice, nor do I dismiss the pain that accompanies the cruelty of others, but just as other people cannot make us angry, they cannot *make* us victims. They can certainly hurt us and *treat us* like victims, but how we *react* to our circumstances is a choice. When we feel genuinely loved and loving, we have what matters most and are not devastated by the things that happen to us, which is not to say that we do not experience inconvenience and pain.

There is a group that qualifies as real victims: children. They're in a position where they can be injured and have little or no ability to choose to be happy while experiencing the wounds inflicted upon them. That puts parents in an awesome position of responsibility.

The Solution to Victimhood

People act like victims as a response to fear, and fear is destroyed by Real Love. The solution for victims is the same as for people who use any of the Getting and Protecting Behaviors. Victims need to hear the truth, tell the truth, and be seen by those capable of accepting and loving them. They need to see that they always have a choice and then take responsibility for the choices they make. Until they do that, they can never see themselves and others clearly. They can never feel accepted and loved.

Even though acting like a victim can only lead to unhappiness, the people who use this Getting and Protecting Behavior get a lot of Imitation Love from it—that's why they've been using it for a lifetime—and therefore will understandably resist you when you make attempts to point out the truth about it. Don't be surprised by their defensiveness and righteous indignation. Just love them and tell them as much truth as they can hear. Also remember that you're not responsible for changing anyone's life.

TELLING THE TRUTH ABOUT RUNNING

One way to protect ourselves from pain is simply to run away:

- Withdrawing from people is a form of running. When a conversation becomes difficult, many of us become silent as a way of avoiding the pain of conflict or rejection. Shyness is really a way to run from the pain that comes from exposing ourselves to the possibility of disapproval.
- Many of us run from relationships completely. We get divorced when our marriages become difficult, or bounce

from one relationship to another, unable to make a commitment in the first place.

- Alcohol and drugs provide an artificial way to run from the responsibilities of the world.

The primary interest of a runner—like anyone who uses Protecting Behaviors—is to get away from pain. A wise man helps people see when they're running so they can make different choices and create opportunities to feel loved—the usual reasons for telling the truth.

For several months Charles has been dating Kate. He's been coming to group meetings for three weeks.

> Charles: I don't think I'll stay in this relationship. I'm just not getting anything out of it.
>
> You: What do you want from it?
>
> Charles: I want to feel more accepted—like I get here—but I don't get that from her. She only accepts me when I give her what she wants. If I don't, she gets critical and angry.
>
> You: Kate may not be unconditionally accepting you—I don't really know that—but I suggest you ask yourself whether *you* are telling her the truth about yourself. Do you tell her about your fears? Have you talked about your Getting and Protecting Behaviors? Have you talked about your relationship like you're talking with us right now?
>
> Charles: Well, no, not really.
>
> You: Then how do you know whether you can have an honest relationship with her, or whether she's capable of really accepting you? If you leave this relationship before you've been honest with her, you're just running.

Charles has already started a relationship with Kate based on lies and Imitation Love, and now he doesn't like what he has and doesn't know how to change it. He's afraid she won't accept him for who he really is, so rather than risk being rejected, he's ready to run. The wise men and women of the group then talk with Charles about how to start telling the truth about himself to Kate. It proves to be a wonderful experience for both of them, and Kate eventually comes to the group meetings herself.

TELLING THE TRUTH ABOUT THE GETTING AND PROTECTING BEHAVIORS OF OTHERS

When Sylvia learned about Real Love, she was eager to share that with her husband, Miguel. She began to point out all his Getting and Protecting Behaviors, but after a couple of minutes, he said, "I'm not interested in this psychology stuff from you. Go sell it to somebody else."

Later that week, in a group meeting, Sylvia talked about her experience.

Sylvia: I was only trying to help. He needs to see what he's doing or he won't be able to change it.

Wise woman: Has Miguel recently invited you to help him see his behavior and change it?

Sylvia: Well, no.

Wise woman: In the past, has he enjoyed any efforts you've made to tell him what he's doing wrong, or when you've suggested how he could change?

Sylvia: No, actually, he hates it.

Wise woman: (smiling) So what were you thinking? What made you think that he'd enjoy you telling him about his behavior this time?

Sylvia: But how's he ever going to learn this if I don't tell him?

Wise woman: You can't change the fact that Miguel doesn't want to hear this from you right now, but you *can* tell him the truth about *yourself.* You can tell him that when you're angry, you're protecting yourself and manipulating him to give you what you want. You can tell him that when you're angry, you're wrong. He may not entirely accept you when you do this, but he'll certainly feel less threatened by you. And if you keep telling the truth and finding the Real Love you need from others, you'll be able to take that back to your marriage. As Miguel sees the difference in you, he just might be curious enough to ask you what you're learning. He might not, but he certainly never will while you're pushing him to listen.

We find Real Love when we tell the truth about *ourselves.* When we share that love with others, we make it possible to have great relationships. Don't be too eager to be a wise man to people who don't yet want one.

Keeping Score

Sylvia continues her conversation from above.

> Sylvia: Why should I tell him *I'm* wrong to be angry. He gets a lot madder than I do, and then he says some pretty terrible things. He's the one that needs to admit he's wrong.
>
> Wise woman: Sylvia, Miguel probably does all that, but are *you* willing to do what it takes to change your life? It won't do any good to talk about what *he* does wrong. Things will change only as *you* admit you're wrong.
>
> Sylvia: But he can really be hateful, and sometimes he yells at me. I never do that. And after he gets mad, sometimes he sulks for days.
>
> Wise woman: So you're saying that his Getting and Protecting Behaviors are *worse* than yours, right?
>
> Sylvia: Well, yes.
>
> Wise woman: Okay, on a scale of one to ten, let's rate how serious your Getting and Protecting Behaviors are. What would you say?
>
> Sylvia: Maybe a three.

Wise woman: And Miguel's?

Sylvia: Probably a six.

Wise woman: So let's assume you're right, that Miguel is twice as wrong as you. Now what? We could chain him to a post and whip him, but that wouldn't change *you*. Can *you* be loving and happy while *you're* angry or acting like a victim?

Sylvia: Well, no, I guess not.

It doesn't matter what your partner is doing wrong. It's always *your* emptiness and fear and your Getting and Protecting Behaviors that make you miserable. But we don't like to admit that, so we keep score with our partners, and when they do worse things than we do, we enjoy the sense of being *right*. Of course, it always turns out that our partners are "more bad"—they have a greater negative score—because we define *bad* as anything we don't do ourselves. If we really want to change our lives, we have to assume that we're 100% responsible for the unhappiness in our relationships—no matter how wrong our partners may actually be. With that assumption, we can finally begin to change.

THE TRUTH SHALL MAKE YOU FREE

When we're truthful about our Getting and Protecting Behaviors, we create the opportunity to be seen, accepted, and loved while being honest about our worst traits—our anger, hatred, selfishness, lies, jealousy, pettiness, whining, and so on. There's an inexpressible freedom that comes from feeling accepted by other people while we're at our worst. After people have accepted us with our least desirable qualities, what's left to hide?

The truth frees us from the chains of unhappiness that always result when we use Getting and Protecting Behaviors. When we tell the truth about ourselves and feel loved, we lose our emptiness and fear and no longer have a need to protect ourselves or manipulate other people for Imitation Love.

Chapter Summary

- We must see our Getting and Protecting Behaviors before we can talk about them, feel loved with them, and eventually give them up.
- We can only tell other people the truth about *their* Getting and Protecting Behaviors when we're loving, and even then they have to be willing to listen.

뎡 Chapter Nine ᏕᏬ

Grace Under Pressure

Eliminating Conflict and Resolving Differences

Seldom do we experience more confusion and pain than when we're trying unsuccessfully to resolve a conflict with a spouse, a child, another family member, a friend, or someone at work. But we must learn how to resolve these conflicts, because while we're learning the process of feeling loved and loving others, one significant conflict can wipe out the effect of a dozen occasions where we have felt loved.

By *conflict* I do not mean disagreement or differences. I mean any interaction that involves Getting and Protecting Behaviors—most often anger. Without those behaviors, I can disagree with you about many things without the slightest conflict.

THE ORIGIN OF CONFLICT

When I was a child, my mother occasionally baked pies—pumpkin, mince, apple, rhubarb, cherry—and to this day I can think of few things more appealing than a piece of pie with a generous dollop of whipped cream. After she cut the pie into "equal" wedges, I was determined to select the largest piece for myself. Of course, there was an immediate conflict with my brother, because there was only *one* largest piece and only one pie. Had my mother baked twelve pies and told us we could eat until we exploded, there would have been no argument over that one piece. It's the presence of scarcity—or the perception thereof—that leads to conflict; with abundance, conflict disappears. If there were an overflowing supply of everything—food, money, land, power, health, and so on—what would people argue, fight, and go to court about?

When we realize that it's Real Love which influences our happiness more than anything else, the lack of other things becomes far less significant. I fought with my brother over an extra quarter-ounce of pie only because I didn't have enough Real Love, the worst condition in the world for a child—or for an adult. Without Real Love, every bit of Imitation Love—in this case the pleasure of eating pie *and* the sense of power that came from seizing the largest portion—became very important. I believed that a piece of pie would make me happy, and for a moment it seemed to.

A piece of pie seems a trivial thing to create a moment of happiness—and to fight with a sibling over—but most of us fight with each other over similarly petty things to create brief moments of superficial happiness. In the absence of Real Love, we wrestle for whatever scraps of Imitation Love we can find. We rush to grab that parking space, for example, and then we say and do some pretty hateful things when people get in our way. Many of us devote our entire lives to the pursuit of money, and we're willing to neglect our families, break the law, and ignore deeply held moral values to get it. We step on each other's heads and bloody our souls to get those coveted promotions. We've proven throughout history that we're willing to kill each other—singly or by the millions—for moments of power. We'll lie, cheat, and steal to earn praise, credit, and glory. In an argument, we'll stomp the other guy into the ground, just for the sake of being right. It's not so different from grabbing a piece of pie.

The Obvious Illusion

There's an obvious problem with this constant struggle for Imitation Love: No matter how much we get, we can never be happy. But it does give us momentary relief from emptiness and pain, which feels great, and *that* is the greatest danger of Imitation Love, namely that it temporarily gives us the deadly illusion of happiness. We believe that if we can only get enough of this temporary satisfaction, we'll find the joy we've always wanted. And so we set off on a quest for more and more, pathetically searching the world for that happy combination of praise, power, pleasure, and safety we'll never find. In the process, we inevitably come into conflict with those who are on a similar quest.

THE ELIMINATION OF CONFLICT

We need to learn to tell the truth about ourselves and find the Real Love that will eliminate the emptiness and fear that lead to the Getting and Protecting Behaviors that fuel every conflict. That is the long-term solution, but what can be done to resolve the conflicts we're experiencing right now? We can use the following principles:

- Realize that it's always about Real Love
- Listen
- Never speak in anger
- Tell the truth about yourself
- Tell the truth about your partner
- Recognize what you really want
- Determine *how* you and your partner can get what you want
- Remember the Law of Choice
- Refuse to be in conflict

It's Always About Real Love

We often believe that if we can "get to the bottom" of things and determine the facts—if we share enough information—every conflict will resolve, but that is not true. For centuries, people have tried to resolve conflicts by gathering the best available information, but the conflicts have persisted, and that's because the people involved have neglected the critical role of Real Love. Real Love is essential to, and part of, every other subsequent principle or action that contributes to the elimination of conflict. It does not matter how much information we share if we are not loved and loving. With insufficient Real Love, people can't hear the truth about anything.

Listen

Perhaps the most powerful way you can communicate to people that you accept and care about them is to genuinely listen to them. Certainly, *not* listening immediately communicates an enormous lack of caring that will make resolution of conflict virtually impossible. See the discussion about listening on pages 133-40.

Never Speak in Anger

Although you may achieve some kind of strained agreement while you are angry, you will never truly resolve a conflict. When you're angry, therefore, I recommend the five steps to eliminating anger, which are discussed in greater detail in Chapter Nine of *Real Love*.

- Be quiet
- Be wrong
- Feel loved
- Get loved
- Be loving

Be Quiet

When you're angry, there is nothing you can say that will make you or your partner (spouse, co-worker, child) happy. Nothing. In the presence of accusations and misinformation, it may sometimes be necessary to point out inaccuracies and injustices, but if you're irritated, you will make the situation worse, no matter how cleverly you respond and how *right* you believe you are. I've tried hundreds of ways to express my anger at people in a productive way, and I've watched hundreds of others do the same. I can say with absolute certainty that when we're angry at people, we cannot communicate as effectively with them.

This does not mean you can't talk about your anger, but *while* you're angry at someone, do not express your anger *to that person*. You'll damage your relationship, your happiness, and the solution to any specific conflict. Instead, express your anger *to another person*, not to someone who will only sympathize with you and thereby perpetuate your anger, but to someone who can help you see the selfishness of your anger and accept you.

This also does not mean you have to agree with or "give in" to people when you're angry. Throughout the chapter we'll discuss many things you *can* do to resolve conflicts, but all these principles and actions are more effective when you're not expressing anger yourself.

When I say you need to be quiet when you're angry, I don't just mean that you need to stop *talking*. You also need to avoid the many non-verbal forms of communicating a lack of acceptance that we talked about on pages 134-5. Obviously, you can't avoid all these forms of expressing anger unless you're actually *not* angry. If you are angry, you *will* express it in some way. You won't be able to fake it for long, if at all. We'll now discuss how to go beyond being quiet and eliminate anger.

Be Wrong

It's easier to be quiet when you can see that every time you're angry, you're wrong. On page 84, I explain that when you're angry, you're trying to protect yourself and get what *you* want. You're unloving, blind, trying to control your partner, and expecting him or her to make you happy. Anger is always wrong, and once you admit that, it's much more difficult to stay angry or insist on whatever course of action you're pursuing.

In any interaction or relationship, we can always find something wrong with the behavior of our partner. That's easy. But it simply does not matter how wrong they are if *we* are angry. We cannot change the interaction or the relationship in a positive way until we admit the error of *our* anger.

Feel Loved (Remember That You're Loved)

Feeling unconditionally loved really is like having twenty million dollars (page 81). With Real Love nothing else matters; without it nothing else is enough. Sometimes, however, we do have a few million in the bank but *forget* we have it when confronted by a particularly stressful situation, like someone who's vigorously attacking us. On those occasions, we have the money, but we temporarily lose access to it. If we make a conscious decision to *remember* that there *are* people who genuinely love us, we can often gain immediate access to our millions, lose our emptiness and fear, and thereby lose our need to use anger as a Getting and Protecting Behavior. Of course, this step is only effective if we've previously told the truth about ourselves and actually felt Real Love.

Get Loved

Sometimes we take the three steps above, but we still don't have enough Real Love in the bank to handle a situation. On those occasions, we can tell the truth about ourselves to those who can accept and love us. We can take that additional Real Love back to the difficult situation and find that we're no longer overwhelmed by our emptiness and fear. We'll discuss this more in a few pages.

Be Loving

Doing something loving for someone we're angry at may be the last thing we want to do, but as we discussed on pages 8-9, sharing love with others can often have the miraculous effect of multiplying the Real Love we have, even if the people we love give us nothing in return. If, therefore, we make a conscious decision to behave in a loving way toward people when we're angry at them, we'll often find that the resulting love we feel will eliminate our anger.

Tell the Truth about Yourself

Most conflicts are characterized by multiple and often contradictory details that seem to weave an impossibly tangled web. Both participants offer undeniable evidence for every piece of information they offer, a justification for each feeling, and a vigorous rebuttal for each piece of evidence offered by their "opponent" in the struggle. It can all be quite confusing.

How can you keep from falling into this awful web and making everything worse as you struggle with all the threads? The answer: Tell the truth. But about what? When you're in a conflict, you tend to believe that every word you utter is the truth, but so does your partner, and since your views are contradictory, it's not possible that both of you are right.

We need to be careful about our claims that something is true. Following are a few examples of what you might believe to be facts:

- "You never do anything with me." Even if that's true, your partner will likely feel attacked, and conflict will then be guaranteed. But is it really true? Does your partner *never* do anything with you, or does it just *seem* like that when you have great expectations that are not being filled?
- "I've told you four times to do that." Maybe you did, or perhaps you told her once directly, hinted at it twice, and told her a fourth time only in your mind. And would it make any difference if you *were* right? What if you *did* tell her four times? Conflict is still guaranteed if either of two circumstances exists: First, she doesn't feel loved. In that condition, even if she does remember all four occasions, she'll deny them just to protect herself from your attack. Second, she simply doesn't remember the four instances. If you insist on being right in that situation, you'll worsen the conflict, because she will sincerely believe she's right and won't back down from that position.
- "But I did what you asked," which we often say when people criticize us for not doing something they asked us to do.

But is it a fact that we did what we were asked, or only our perception of what happened? Perhaps we did less than was asked, but because we were afraid of disapproval, we deluded ourselves into thinking we did more than we did. We tend to see things as we want them to be. Or maybe we did exactly what we were *asked*, but not what was *needed* or desired. In other words, we kept the letter of the law, but not the spirit. If, for example, we accomplished a specific task, but we did it with resentment, took a great deal longer than was reasonable, and produced an end result of less than superior quality, then "I did what you asked" is really a lie.

- "I was only trying to help." Perhaps you did have some desire to be helpful, but often that desire is partly driven by selfish motivations, like getting praise, power, and safety for ourselves. On those occasions, our "help" is tainted, and the consequences of our selfishness often outweigh the benefits of our assistance.

- "He doesn't like me." That may be a fact, but when you're empty and afraid, you can't clearly see the feelings and motivations of other people. It may be that you're simply demanding a certain amount of time and acceptance from him, and when he doesn't deliver, you say he doesn't like you so you can justify your fears and anger.

We can see from these examples that we often have difficulty identifying the truth about events, the feelings and behavior of others, and our own motivations. We're confused because we want to see these things in a way that makes us right.

So what *can* we productively tell the truth about? We can talk about our own emptiness and fear, our Getting and Protecting Behaviors, and our mistakes. We talked about how to do this in the previous two chapters. We can talk about what we *believe* to be true and what we want (more about that later in the chapter). We need to admit when we're *wrong*, sometimes to the people we're having a conflict with but on other occasions to a wise man. Sometimes we only need to admit to *ourselves* that we're wrong.

Tell the Truth about Yourself to the Person You're in Conflict With

Jennifer is talking to you about her husband, Daniel.

> Jennifer: Daniel and I were arguing about money, and it was the same old thing: He thinks I spend too much, but I disagree. We went round and round about it, and it was going nowhere.

> You: What started the argument?

> Jennifer: Daniel was paying the credit card statement for the month, and asked me about some things I bought.

You and Jennifer talk about the specific things she bought, and she agrees that none of them were really necessities. She also mentions that she and Daniel both agreed to discuss beforehand any large purchases they planned to make, and she admits that he does talk to her before he buys anything that could affect their budget.

"It sounds like Daniel's just afraid your family will get in trouble financially," you say. "When you spend money without telling him, he becomes more afraid and then gets angry, partly to feel less helpless and partly to motivate you to quit doing what scares him. Then when he tries to talk to you about it, you protect yourself by telling him you're right. That's an understandable reaction, but imagine how he feels. When you claim to be right, you're telling him that you're going to keep on doing the same thing, which frightens him even more. To protect himself, he reacts by becoming more angry. Without feeling unconditionally loved, what else could he do? And then your arguments are almost unavoidable. Do you see that?"

Jennifer lets out a sigh. "I do now," she says. "So how can I do this differently?"

> You: You can tell the truth about *yourself*. Go and tell him you've been wrong to be angry and also selfish as you've spent money without thinking of the consequences to the family finances. Tell him you'll be more thoughtful in the future. Can you imagine how Daniel will feel when you do that, and how it will affect your relationship?

Jennifer: I agree that I need to be more responsible about how I spend money, but he can be so demanding about this. After all the unkind things he's said to me, I don't see how I can tell him I was wrong.

You: I understand, but I've also learned from my own experience that being right is a pretty shallow pleasure compared with being happy. Decide which is more important to you, being right or having a happy marriage and being genuinely happy.

Two weeks later, Jennifer calls you and says, "You were right, it *is* better to be happy than right. Yesterday Daniel started to criticize me about something I bought for my daughter, and I started to argue with him about how she needs it. It was turning into the usual argument—you know, both of us being right and angry—when I remembered what you said about choosing to be happy or right. I decided I just didn't want to be angry and miserable anymore, so I said, "Daniel, I should have talked to you about buying this before I did it. You've asked me to do that a hundred times before, and I haven't done it. This is all my fault." When I said that, Daniel stopped talking, stopped frowning, and relaxed. Finally, he said, "Well, I shouldn't have gotten angry. I'm sorry." The argument was *over*. Can you believe it? And it all happened because I said I was wrong."

If you and I are arguing, and I tell you I'm wrong, what's left for you to say? But we have such a hard time admitting we're wrong. We hate to look foolish. We hate it that our partners might then feel smugly superior to us. But being wrong only creates an opportunity for us to learn, to feel loved, and to grow. It's far better than continuing an argument with your partner and guaranteeing that you'll feel unloved and unhappy. The cost of being right far exceeds its rewards.

When we tell the truth about ourselves to other people, we need to be very clear about it, and we need to avoid involving our partner in any way. Imagine, for example, if Jennifer had said any of the following as she told the truth about herself to Daniel:

- "I shouldn't have bought that stuff the other day without telling you, but sometimes you do the same thing." Daniel would have heard only that she was attacking him.
- "I admit, I'm not perfect about helping you with the finances." Admitting to a flaw in a vague, general way is fairly useless. We need to specifically describe what we did wrong.
- "I know I should have told you, but you don't have to get angry about it." Another attack directed at Daniel.

Tell the Truth about Yourself to a Wise Man or Woman

Jennifer calls you a week later.

Jennifer: Remember how well I handled that argument with Daniel last week?

You: Sure.

Jennifer: I have not done well since then. I don't know what happens. We start disagreeing about something, and I get angry and just keep going when I know I should be quiet. When it's all over, I'm sorry I did it—but then it's too late.

You: Pretty stupid when we keep doing things that make us so unhappy, isn't it?

Jennifer: It really is, but at the time, I don't know how to do it differently.

You: Do you want a suggestion?

Jennifer: Sure, why not?

You: You get angry because you still expect Daniel to love you—but he doesn't, not unconditionally. We get angry when our expectations don't get filled, so remind yourself that he *can't* give you what you're expecting. Continuing to expect it then becomes foolish. But that doesn't mean you have to live without the love you need. You just need to get it from people who have it to give. So when you feel angry, you can call someone right then and get a moment of the acceptance you need.

Jennifer: Like right in the middle of an argument?

You: Sure. I know that seems a little strange, but *anything* is better than continuing a conflict that's destroying your happiness and your relationship. It's worth it to do whatever it takes to eliminate it. So if there's an argument where you just can't be honest and loving, tell him—right in the middle of the argument—"Daniel, when I'm angry, I never say the right thing. *That's my fault,* not yours. Can we continue this conversation in a few minutes?" Then call someone who can listen to you and accept you. When you feel more loved, you'll be able to continue the conversation with Daniel and be much more loving.

Tell the Truth to Yourself

There may be occasions when you won't have the courage to tell the truth about yourself to the person you're arguing with, and you may not have access to a wise man. But you can at least admit *to yourself* that you're wrong when you're angry—or lying or using other Getting and Protecting Behaviors. When you remember that, it's difficult to remain angry, and you may be able to make a conscious choice to see and accept your partner.

Tell the Truth About Your Partner

We all make lots of mistakes, so it's easy to find fault with our partners. But it's rarely productive to focus on the mistakes themselves. What we do need to see is that when our partners don't have enough Real Love, they're drowning (pages 7-8), and to save themselves, they use the Getting and Protecting Behaviors that hurt themselves and others—including you. When you understand that a partner is drowning, how could you be hurt or angry? Who would be offended by the splashing of a drowning man? Or angry at him? But we do that all the time. We're irritated because people who are empty and afraid reach out and use Getting and Protecting Behaviors to save themselves.

It's not usually wise to offer our observations about someone else's behavior—especially their Getting and Protecting Behaviors—unless we've been asked to do that, and we'll not likely get such requests until we've demonstrated a level of acceptance for others. Jennifer continued to tell the truth about herself and receive the acceptance of wise men and women. As she became more loving toward Daniel, he became curious about what she'd been learning, and eventually he read *Real Love*. One day he asked her if she had seen him using Getting and Protecting Behaviors lately, so she gently described a few examples. Because he felt accepted by her, he asked her to help him see when he did those things in the future.

Occasionally, we have the responsibility or opportunity to tell the truth about the behavior of others without being asked, as in the following example.

Juan has been working at a mid-sized corporation for two years now, and he's well known for getting offended easily, snapping at people, and resenting authority. He's lost two jobs in the previous three years, and on each occasion he said he was terminated because his supervisors just "didn't like him."

Tim is Juan's immediate supervisor and has seen his attitude on many occasions. Because Tim understands the principles of Real Love, he knows that Juan isn't intentionally being difficult. He's just drowning and using Getting and Protecting Behaviors to save himself. If Juan were a personal friend, Tim could accept Juan's behavior and simply make a decision about how much time he wants to spend with him. But Juan is an employee whose behavior is detracting from his productivity and causing tension among other employees, so Tim calls Juan into his office.

> Tim: Juan, you make a valuable contribution to this company. Just last week I was impressed with your creativity as you solved the problem we had with the Wilson account. I'd like to help you be even more productive. Would you be willing to hear some observations and suggestions?
>
> Juan: Sure.

Tim: You have some characteristics that are interfering with your ability to be an asset to us. When you're working on a project of your own and don't have to interact with other people, you do fantastic work. When you have to work with others, though, it's often quite a different thing. When co-workers get in your way, you're impatient with them. I don't think you do this intentionally, but your irritation is obvious and makes people back away from you. Unfortunately, that means the work suffers, because everything happens more effectively when we're all genuinely cooperating. You also get annoyed when supervisors—myself included—give you a job you don't like, or when you disagree with the approach we're taking to something. Have you noticed any of this?

Juan: Sometimes I do get annoyed when people aren't helping me out, but who wouldn't? I don't think it's a big problem.

Tim: I'm sure you don't, or you would have stopped it. But your anger and resistance *are* interfering with your performance. We're often blind to the things we do—we've been doing them for so long we don't notice them anymore.

Tim is in a position where he's *responsible* for telling Juan about his Getting and Protecting Behaviors—not to control him but to help him stop behaviors that are interfering with the productivity of the company. Although Tim unconditionally accepts Juan as a person, he can't continue to allow Juan to affect the business in a negative way. If Juan refuses to listen, and his behavior stays the same, he may lose his job. Tim makes an appointment to talk with Juan about his progress in two weeks. We'll discuss more about follow-up later in the chapter.

When you do have the responsibility of helping someone see their Getting and Protecting Behaviors—as a friend, parent, employer, wise man in a group meeting, or just because you've been asked for your opinion—clearly state what you see. Don't be hesitant about it. If you're obviously nervous about the discussion and say something like, "Now, don't be offended, but . . ." or "I don't mean to be critical, but . . ." the people you're speaking to will unconsciously make one or both of two conclusions: First, you're hesitant because you don't really know what you're talking about. In that case, why should they listen? Second, you're afraid. Fear is the most common reason for people to be reluctant to speak. With fear you communicate that you see the listener as a perpetrator, and then he or she will often be offended by the implied accusation.

Recognize What You Really Want

We introduced this subject on page 68, and on page 70 we talked about the folly of the man who cut down his apple tree. He insisted on having more apples in a particular moment, and the price he paid for his choice was the loss of every apple in the future. Similarly, if you choose the short-term gratification of earning Imitation Love, you will get it, and you'll pay for that by forfeiting the Real Love and happiness you could have had. It's important to see exactly what you're choosing, because what you decide will determine what you get, as was the case with Luke and Deborah.

Like most couples, Luke and Deborah got married because they'd fallen in love, but over the years, their idealism has been replaced with disappointment and unfilled expectations. Increasingly, they've been finding fault with each other—about many things—and now they're in the process of detailing one another's shortcomings to you. You ask Deborah to focus on just one complaint, and she says, "Luke wants to have sex all the time, and I don't."

"I'm not an animal," he says. "I don't want sex *all* the time. But you *never* do. It's like I have to beg you every time, and then it's no fun for me."

They begin to argue about the exact frequency of their sexual activity, but you interrupt: "These are just details. Let's talk about what you both really want from sex. It's pretty obvious that you (gesturing to Luke) want to have sex much more often than you do (gesturing to Deborah). Agreed?" They nod their heads.

"So let's talk about *why* that is," you say. "Deborah, do you have sex as much now as you did earlier in your marriage?

Deborah: No.

You: Why is that?

Deborah: (pause) I just don't enjoy it as much.

You: How do you feel toward Luke during the times you do have sex?

Deborah: Usually irritated. I only give in because he keeps pushing me.

Anger is a response to the emptiness and fear that result from a lack of Real Love, so the next question is easy. You ask, "Do you feel like Luke cares about you when you have sex?"

A light goes on in Deborah's head as she replies, "No. That's it—I feel like he's just interested in *himself.* He doesn't really care about *me.*"

You: Feeling unloved is painful, so it's natural that you'd protect yourself from that. When it comes to sex, then, your goal is to protect yourself from being used and feeling unloved. Do you see that?

Deborah: I hadn't thought of it quite like that before, but yes.

You: Now, Luke, why do you want to have sex?

Luke looks at you like you're stupid. He's thinking, "Have you never *had* sex?"

You: Because it feels good, right?

Luke: Sure.

You: So when it comes to sex, your goal is pleasure.

Luke's silence and frown are a clear communication that he agrees but doesn't like how it looks. You ask them both what they see as their greatest goal in life, and after a couple of minutes of discussion, they both agree that they want to feel unconditionally loved by each other and be happy.

Deborah and Luke *say* they want to be loved, loving, and happy, but with their *behavior* they demonstrate that they want safety and pleasure, respectively. *With their ideal goal in mind,* you ask them to tell the truth about themselves and their relationship. This is a sobering moment for both of them, and after considerable discussion and reflection, you write down in two columns what each of them has concluded:

Deborah	Luke
Luke partly wants sex for pleasure, but he also sees it as evidence of my love for him.	Deborah doesn't hate *sex*. She just hates it that I don't show her I love her in other ways, and then she feels used when I want sex.
I'm protecting myself instead of trying to make our relationship happier.	I'm manipulating Deborah instead of thinking about what she wants.
I'm being selfish.	I'm being selfish.
What I'm doing isn't helping either of us to be really happy.	I'm not helping Deborah to be happier, and it's not working for me, either.

As they tell the truth about themselves and each other, they experience several consequences almost immediately:

- They feel more accepted and loved by one another. When we tell the truth about ourselves, whatever we get afterward feels unconditional and genuine.
- Their anger vanishes. How long can you stay angry at me when I admit that I'm being selfish?

- They begin to see how they can change their behavior in ways that will contribute to what they really want. They can offer these changes as genuine gifts to each other—making contributions to their real and shared goal—instead of feeling like they're forced to give what their partner wants.

Later in the chapter we'll discuss how Deborah and Luke continue to resolve their conflict.

Always ask yourself what you really want—not just in your marriage, but at work, as a parent, as a friend, and so on. Ask yourself, Do I want to win this argument, *or* do I want to establish a long-term relationship that will benefit both of us? Do I want to win this contest of wills *or* have a happy marriage? Do I want to get money, power, praise, and safety for myself in this situation at work, or do I want to benefit the company as a whole, which in the end will help everyone? Do I want to be loving and happy, or right and miserable? Do I want to cut down the apple tree or nourish it, prune it, and enjoy its fruit for a long time?

The Truth About What We Want in a Given Moment— Our Getting and Protecting Behaviors

Sometimes we *say* we want the genuine happiness of everyone around us, but we reveal our self-deceit (which by definition is unconscious) by how we behave, specifically our Getting and Protecting Behaviors. In any interaction between you and someone else, I suggest asking these questions:

- Am I using Getting and Protecting Behaviors?
- Is my partner (spouse, child, co-worker) using Getting and Protecting Behaviors?

If you can identify your Getting and Protecting Behaviors, you'll immediately know you're trying to get something for *yourself*. You can then tell the truth—at least to yourself—and create the opportunities to change your behavior and also feel accepted and loved. It takes real honesty to recognize and admit these behaviors.

On occasion, we also need to identify the Getting and Protecting Behaviors in *other people*, but, as we discussed above, the goal is not to criticize them or accuse them, just to recognize their need for our acceptance.

Determine *How* You and Your Partner Can Get What You Want

Now that you and your partner have decided what you really want, you can make much more meaningful progress toward realizing your short- and long-term goals.

In the three years since the Alpha Corporation started operations, it has grown quickly, from three people in a small office to one hundred fifty employees today. Although the company initially offered limited benefits, and wages slightly below the average for the area, people were eager to get in on the ground floor of a company that was filling a new niche and promising the possibility of advancement and exciting work.

Most employees, have now become impatient, however, with the failure of the company to deliver adequately on the promises of more benefits and better wages and salaries. A team of employee representatives is appointed, and they confront management about their demands. Management insists that satisfying these demands will consume capital needed for expansion and could affect their ability to meet the demands of the developing market, a key factor in the company's survival. After several meetings, no consensus has been achieved, and the tension is increasing. One of the employees asks you to serve as a mediator, and although you have little business experience, you accept, solely on the basis of your understanding of the principles of Real Love and conflict resolution. As you attend a meeting between the labor and management teams, you immediately see that neither "side" understands the principles we've discussed thus far:

- It's always about Real Love. It may seem strange to think about Real Love in a business setting, but it's imperative to do that, because everyone in a business is a *person*, usually with an enormous unfilled need to be seen and accepted. When two people are in conflict, they communicate in myriad ways that they don't genuinely accept one another. That lack of acceptance is quite different from disagreement. You and I can deeply disagree about many issues, but our differences will become a conflict only when we show—through words or the many non-verbal forms of communication we discussed in Chapter Five—that we don't genuinely care about one another's happiness. Both labor and management were indicating with their impatience and demands that they did not care about the welfare of the other team.

- Listening. Neither negotiation team is really listening to the other and is minimizing the other's concerns. As a result, the painful fires of lifetimes of emptiness and fear are being fanned into an uncontrollable blaze, and both parties are reacting with the Getting and Protecting Behaviors they've always used: They attack each other, exaggerate their positions (lying), act like victims, and call a halt to any session when they feel backed into a corner (running). No true agreement can be reached in that environment.

- Never speak in anger. As each side senses the other's lack of understanding and acceptance, they become more irritated and insistent on their position. Of course, this is perceived as an attack, and the Protecting Behaviors accelerate.

- Tell the truth about yourself. The people on neither side are admitting their fears, nor their Getting and Protecting Behaviors. Few people do.

- Tell the truth about your partner. They're both telling the truth about the other's failings and selfishness, but they're not telling the truth about the needs and fears of the other team—nor are they seeing the positive intentions of each other.

- What do you really want? Each group is clear about what they want *right now*, but they're not addressing long-term goals.

- How can we get there together? This is impossible when the other principles are being ignored.

You ask each side to lay down for a moment every individual component of the conflict and to focus on something else entirely. They agree, so you begin to apply the principles you understand.

- What do you really want? You ask both teams to go to opposite ends of the room and imagine that they're starting a new company of their own. What would their goals be for the entire company, including productivity, safety, management, employees, and so on. When they reach consensus within the group, they write their conclusions on a large piece of paper, and when they return to the table, the goals of the two groups are virtually identical. They both want a company that is creative, growing, and responsive to the needs of the customer. They also want a place where employees and management are sensitive to one another's needs, and where, as a result, everyone loves to come to work. All this will naturally lead to the goals of greater productivity, safety, job security, and the possibility of advancement.

- Tell the truth about yourself. You go through the goals one at a time and alternately ask each group to be completely honest as they describe anything they're doing that could interfere with that goal. You stay with each goal until both teams can name at least two of their own unproductive attitudes or behaviors. This is difficult in the beginning, and for the first few goals, you have to provide examples. With the goal "Company growth," for example, you ask management if their present insistence on lower benefits and wages will enable them to continue attracting the high quality employees that will make real growth possible. With some hesitation, they agree that their present position *would* have a negative effect on growth. Labor agrees that a stubborn position on sudden and dramatic increases in benefits could hamper the ability of the company to make use of limited capital for expansion. With each goal, each side becomes increasingly honest, partly because their trust grows as they see the honesty of the other side.

- Tell the truth about your partner. Again the two groups go to opposite ends of the room and discuss what they see as the principal concerns or fears of the other group. They begin to see one another much more clearly. Among other comments, management says, "We see that our reluctance to raise pay and benefits communicates a lack of concern for you, and you would naturally be concerned that we'd continue to disregard your needs." Labor says, "When we insist on immediate increases in our pay and benefits, you're concerned that we're willing to destroy the company for our own interests." As they do this, they begin to understand why the other group would tenaciously defend its position.

- Listening *and* It's always about Real Love. The more they talk and genuinely listen to one another, the more accepting they become, and that greatly facilitates their willingness to share their feelings and consider new options.

- Never speak in anger. In this environment, anger disappears and is no longer the huge obstacle to productive conversation that it had been.

- How can we get there together? Now that the real goals are on the table, and everyone understands the other side's concerns, and both parties admit the potential harm in their demands, they're able to describe what can be done to reach their goals. Management realizes that benefits and wages must be increased to keep attracting good people and keep those they already have. Labor agrees that immediate satisfaction of their original demands would limit the ability of the company to grow, or even survive. Other agreements are reached fairly quickly. Management agrees to provide much more information to labor about the exact financial picture of the company, and to allow a representative from labor to be paid while he or she goes through the raw data to verify the report. With this information, both sides will be able to accurately determine at the next meeting—in four months—how their joint efforts are contributing to their shared goals, and what can be done to adjust their course.

Let's return to Deborah and Luke and see how working together to get what we want also works in personal relationships. They've already told the truth about themselves and agreed on a common and higher goal, so now working toward their goal becomes much easier. "Deborah," you say, "now that you see what you really want—to have a loving and happy relationship, not to be right or defend yourself—tell Luke exactly what you'd like from him."

"I want to feel like you care about me all the time, not just when you want sex."

Luke asks her to be specific about what she wants, and she talks about touching, talking, cuddling, and so on.

> Luke: So if I do all those things, you'll have sex with me?
>
> Deborah: Well . . .
>
> You: (smiling) If you do the things she wants just *so* she'll have sex with you, she'll still feel used instead of loved, and you won't have a loving relationship. And Deborah, if you *expect* Luke to do the things you described, you won't appreciate them or feel loved when he does them.

As they keep in mind the goal of making one another genuinely happy, they begin to work out the details of what they can do for each other.

Remember the Law of Choice

Several days later, Deborah calls you in a state of agitation.

> Deborah: When we talked to you, Luke said he understood that I needed more non-sexual attention from him, but he hasn't changed a bit. And he still expects me to have sex with him. He didn't learn a thing.
>
> You: Do you remember the Law of Choice?
>
> Deborah: Yes.
>
> You: Remember that he gets to make his own choices, after which you can always make *your* choices, preferably the ones that lead to your real goal. Are you willing to think about that and give me a call later?

A week later Deborah calls you again.

Deborah: We got into one of our arguments about Luke not being affectionate, and I was getting angry, as usual. But this time I remembered the Law of Choice. I *want* him to show me more affection that's not sexual, but I don't have the right to *demand* it, and that's what I've been doing. He really gets to choose what he does, even if I don't like it, and when I remember that, my demands just seem selfish and controlling.

You: You've really learned something.

Deborah: That's not all. You told me that *I* always have my own choices to make. I can be loving and happy, or demanding and angry and miserable. So instead of insisting that he give me all the attention *I* want, I decided to do whatever I could to love *him*. I started *initiating* sex with him, and it's become a whole different experience for both of us. He's much happier, obviously, and I *like* being more loving toward him. Sex is even better for me *physically* now that I feel loved. He's more tender with me during sex, and he pays more attention to me at other times, too. I can see why he wasn't affectionate before—I was nagging him all the time. Why would he *want* to be with me when I'm like that?

You: You're amazing.

In order to be genuinely happy, we need to feel Real Love, but while we're acquiring that feeling, we can be greatly assisted by an intellectual understanding of principles—the Law of Choice, for example. When we really understand that law, our expectations vanish, and we're much better able to offer our love to other people. Deborah learned that. She allowed Luke to make his own choices, instead of pressuring him. She then made her own choice, to love him as well as she could without his changing in any way. He could feel her unconditional love, and he responded with more love of his own.

Unfortunately, many conflicts are "resolved" only when both parties give up something they want. They make a compromise, a trade that fails to entirely satisfy anyone. Or they surrender out of the necessity of weakness, only to regret and resent their decision. It's compromise, trade, and surrender that characterize most human interactions: politics, business, and personal affairs.

It doesn't have to be that way. Notice that Deborah didn't trade affection with Luke. She didn't give him sex *in exchange* for what she wanted. There was no compromise in which they both gave up something, nor did she *give in* and surrender to his demands. Instead she freely offered him a gift, without expectation of anything in return. As a result, the conflict instantly disappeared, and she enjoyed both the gift she gave and the one Luke later offered.

Conflicts can be eliminated when you decide that you will simply offer your contribution freely to a relationship. If your offer is unconditional, you will not be disappointed or angry— key ingredients in any conflict—regardless of the response of your partner. But what if your partner isn't satisfied with your gift? What if he or she is still angry and demands more from you? Then you can make a *choice* to give more, not because you're being pressured but because you wish to be more helpful or loving. *Or* you can choose *not* to give more, knowing that you're still not responsible for the response of your partner. No matter how angry he or she becomes, *you* can still choose to be loving and happy. Although your partner is making a conflict *possible* with his or her anger, the conflict—which requires two or more participants—cannot happen.

In any interaction you can always choose to be loving and happy, regardless of the behavior of your partner. When you remember that, you'll realize you can always create a world in which you never lose. That pretty much eliminates feeling like a victim, or being angry, or running.

Certainly, it would have been nice for Deborah if Luke had immediately begun to be affectionate after your first meeting with them, as he'd agreed. But he didn't. Before a relationship can change, *somebody* has to start making loving choices—and it might as well be *you*. That takes faith. And even if your partner doesn't respond in kind, simply *being* loving feels great. Deborah, for example, began to enjoy sex more just because she was offering it unconditionally.

Refuse to Be in Conflict

Conflict is always a choice. You can't determine the behavior of another person, but you can refuse to defend yourself or struggle to win Imitation Love. When you refuse to do those things, you don't have a conflict, just a partner who is angry or otherwise manipulative.

Imagine that a co-worker, Stan, approaches you with what he believes is a mistake you've made that has enormously inconvenienced him. He's furious and quite eager to take the hide off your flesh. As it happens, you *have* made some contribution to the mistake he's talking about, but other people are also responsible.

"Two days ago," he says, "I asked you to get that information for me by the next day—which was yesterday. I still don't have it, and now that's really going to cause me a lot of trouble."

Stan's anger is supplying plenty of potential fuel for a lively conflict. If you defend yourself—by lying, attacking, acting like a victim, or running—you'll instantly have a bonfire that will consume both of you. But if you make a conscious decision not to defend yourself, you won't be burned, even though Stan may turn *himself* into a pile of ash.

You'll find it much easier to make the choice to stay out of conflict if you remember the other principles we've discussed:

- It's always about Real Love. Stan is angry because he doesn't feel accepted and is protecting himself and getting a sense of power with his anger. It's acceptance he needs.
- Never speak in anger. Anger will only inflame Stan's emptiness and fear, which would be unproductive for both of you.
- Tell the truth about yourself. You actually *did* make phone calls two days ago to get the information Stan wanted, but you couldn't give him everything he needed because some of those people did not return your calls. The rest of the truth about yourself, however, is that you did not call yesterday to check up on those unreturned phone calls, and you didn't call Stan to tell him that his information would be delayed.
- Tell the truth about your partner (silently in this case). If Stan had really wanted that information by yesterday, he would

have called you about it yesterday, which would have given you additional motivation to complete the task on time. But it won't help to point out his faults. It's more important to identify for yourself that Stan is using Getting and Protecting Behaviors—not to accuse him, but to help you recognize his emptiness and fear and enable you to respond to him in a more productive way.

- Recognize what you really want. You could win this argument, by attacking Stan with anger, by acting like an incensed victim, or by presenting volumes of evidence to indict other co-workers and prove your own innocence. Or you could simply walk off and win some kind of draw in your battle. But do you want to win this one encounter, or do you want to have a long-term, productive relationship with Stan that will benefit both of you and the company as well?

- Determine how you and your partner can get what you want. Is there a way you can approach this problem *with* Stan, a way that will be better than having a duel?

- Remember the Law of Choice. Stan really does get to be angry. It is not your business to stop him from expressing that. But now *you* have your own choice to make.

Let's apply all these principles in your answer to Stan.

"I had to gather information from several sources," you say, "and I failed to get all that done. My mistake entirely. I also didn't call you yesterday to tell you I hadn't done the job. I can probably have all that information within the next two hours. Would that be all right?"

You just refused to participate in the battle Stan was starting. Without a co-combatant, Stan suddenly feels a little embarrassed to be the only one standing there with a sword in his hand. But he also feels accepted. It may seem strange to talk about such a concept at work, but you're giving him a moment of unconditional acceptance, and he feels that. He still needs a moment or two, however, to cool the fires from his initial attack.

"Well, I suppose that would help," he says, "but I'm still behind my deadline, and I'm going to get in trouble over this."

You could easily respond, "You wouldn't be in trouble if you'd followed up on this yesterday. You just want to make *me* responsible for your problem." But you're much smarter and more loving than that, so you say, "I'm sorry I made this harder for you. Is there anything else I can do to help?

Now that you're helping Stan, instead of defending yourself and providing Stan with even more evidence that nobody cares about him, the two of you work out something to accomplish the job as quickly and effectively as possible.

Occasionally, a partner will continue to attack you even though you refuse to participate in the conflict. It might get to the point where you don't feel sufficiently loved or loving to continue the conversation. Do not give in to your natural tendency to defend yourself. Make a conscious decision to physically remove yourself from the situation. Although this appears to be the Protecting Behavior of running, it's actually quite different, because running is motivated by fear.

What exactly can you say to someone when you want to withdraw? Some examples:

- My mistake. I'm not listening very well and need to try again. I'll come and get you shortly so we can finish this discussion.
- I'm not responding well to you, and that's not your fault. Let me collect my thoughts here and come up with a way to better address what you're saying.
- I'm just not loving enough to continue this conversation. Can I come back to you in a few hours (or minutes, or the next day) and talk some more?

When you speak in this way, it's very difficult for most people to continue pushing for an argument.

Avoid the Details

An old saying goes, "The devil is in the details." That is especially true in conflicts, as we'll see while we watch Linda take a phone call from her mother.

Mother: You'll be spending your Christmas holiday with us, won't you?

Linda: Well, I thought I might go with some friends to the mountains and do some skiing.

Mother: But we've always been together for Christmas, and you haven't been home in a long time.

Linda: Mother, I was there just four months ago.

Mother: Oh, it's been longer than that, and you never call, either.

Linda: I have my calendar right here, and it *was* four months ago. And I call you all the time. We just talked last week.

Mother: You can go skiing with your friends anytime. Why can't you spend the holidays with *us*?

For every explanation Linda offers, Mother can come up with an objection of some kind. As you know, this kind of conflict can go on forever. After Linda has spoken with her mother for ten minutes—arguing the whole time and becoming more angry—she says she'll get back with her mother the next day. Then she calls you for advice.

You: Linda, you have those awful conversations only because you choose to.

Linda: But she just keeps pushing me, and eventually I don't know what to say, or I just do what she wants to get her off my back.

You: You do not have to answer her objections. *She* has made a choice to browbeat you into doing what she wants. You can now choose what *you* will do, and you do not have to keep explaining your choice. Each time you offer an explanation, she attacks the details of what you're saying, and that can go on forever. Do not respond to the attacks. Simply tell her what you are going to do—lovingly, but directly.

Linda: She'll get mad.

You: She's already mad. You won't make that much worse. The whole reason you're frustrated is that you feel responsible for making her happy. You're not. You're not responsible for the happiness or unhappiness that results from the choices *she* makes. Love her, don't speak to her when you're angry, and simply tell her what you'll be doing.

The next day Linda talks to her mother again.

Linda: I've decided that I *will* be going with my friends skiing.

Mother: I thought we'd talked about that. You *said* you'd come home.

Linda: Mother, I love you. I love being home with you for the holidays, but this year I'll be spending time with my friends.

Mother: But why? You've always come home for Christmas.

Linda resists the pressure to answer the deadly *why* question, knowing that if she provides an answer, it will only be followed by more objections and questions, all intended to make her change her mind. "That's just what I've decided to do, Mother," she says. "I'll miss you and Dad, but I'll be having a great time—and so will you. When I get back, I'll call you. Is Dad there? I'd love to talk to him."

You do not have to engage in the details which only fuel the fire of a conflict.

No Boundaries

When I state that we can always choose not to participate in a conflict, someone invariably says, "So sometimes I just have to set boundaries with my partner, right?"

No. It *is* healthy when we make choices not to participate in a conflict. In that case, we feel self-directed and even loving. When we "set boundaries," however, we're *reacting* to the behavior of others instead of making our own decisions. We're also defending ourselves, which promotes a feeling of fear. You need to remember that with the exception of occasions when you're physically in danger, other people can't really hurt you if you feel loved, so you rarely need "boundaries." If the Real Love you have is not sufficient for a particular situation, you can choose to *withdraw* from it because it would be unproductive, which is quite different from *running* or otherwise using Protecting Behaviors in response to your fear. Don't protect yourself with boundaries. Simply make your own choices about what you will or will not do.

CONFLICT PREVENTION

You now have the tools for eliminating conflict in your life, but you'll be even happier if you can also *prevent* conflict. You can do this as you apply the principles above *before* a conflict, and also by making clear requests—a subject we introduced on pages 59-63—and having no expectations.

Back to Deborah and Luke. After the conversations above, their relationship has improved a lot. But at times we all forget the true principles we've learned, and then we set ourselves up for conflict. Deborah calls you to complain about Luke.

Deborah: Luke really does express more affection to me outside sex than he has in a long time. But sometimes he just ignores me. Right now he's in there playing a video game on the computer, and he hasn't talked to me since he got home from work.

You: What exactly would you like him to do?

Deborah: Well, I guess spend some time with me.

You: Have you told him that?

Deborah: Of course. I've told him lots of times that I want him to pay more attention to me.

You: No, have you told him that *tonight*?

Deborah: No, not exactly, but he should know that.

You: Luke does have things in his life other than constantly trying to read your mind. If you want him to know what you want, you have to tell him.

Deborah: Okay, I'll go talk to him right now.

We often fail to tell people what we want—sometimes we don't even know ourselves what we want—and then we lie in wait, like predators, waiting for them to make a mistake, and then we pounce on them with criticism of what they've done or not done. That's not a great way to nourish a relationship. As we make our requests, we also need to be careful to make them specific, and not to turn them into veiled attacks, which you now explain to Deborah:

You: Exactly what are you going to say to him?

Deborah: I'll tell him that I wish he'd spend more time with me.

You: That approach will almost certainly lead to an argument.

Deborah: Why?

You: If you say, "I wish you'd spend *more* time with me," you're telling him that the time he's already chosen to give you is not enough. You're criticizing him, and people don't like that. Instead, just tell him what you want.

Deborah: Okay, I'll just say I'd like to do something with him.

You: Better, but it's lazy. Again you're making him read your mind. I've heard you do this before. You ask him to do something with you, and then when he suggests you watch football together, you don't like that. Then he feels criticized, and your conversation goes straight into the sewer. If you want something specific, tell him what it is. What do you want?

Deborah: To talk to him, to feel close to him.

You: Not specific enough. You're still making him do the creative work and to partially read your mind. I know you don't have much practice at making specific requests without being accusing, so let me suggest some words, and you tell me if they'd work for you. You could say, "Luke, I'd like to talk to you for a few minutes, but I don't want to interrupt your video game. Do you know when you'll be at a place where you can stop?"

Deborah: He won't know when that is. He could play all night.

You: Keep being specific. If he doesn't give you a time, ask him if you can come back and check on him in fifteen minutes, or whenever. Then you keep that up until you arrive at a time when he'll be done—even if that's hours away.

Deborah: Then what?

You: When he's done playing, tell him you'd like to talk to him in the living room about what you've done that day. Hold his hand while you talk, ask him about his day, and whatever else you'd like. You'll feel much closer to him than if you expect him to read your mind.

Deborah: What if he just doesn't want to talk to me at all?

You: He might not. Be careful that you don't have *expectations* that he'll do what you want, because then you're really delivering a demand, and he will *feel* that, which will make it far less likely that he'll want to spend time with you. And if you have expectations, you won't feel loved even if he *does* what you want. Communicating a lack of expectations involves more than the words you speak. You have to honestly be prepared to accept a *no* from him before you can have a loving interaction. And remember that if he does say *no*, that doesn't limit your choices in any way. You can still do an infinite variety of things by yourself or with others.

In some situations, expectations are acceptable. When you ask people at work, for example, to fill a necessary assignment, you have every right to expect them to do as you've requested. They're paid, in fact, to do just that. But you still need to make your requests clearly. If you ask someone to "take care of that problem pretty soon," you're doomed. In most requests, you need to be specific:

- Who. Exactly who is going to do this?
- What. Exactly what do you want done? Name the steps and parts involved. I once asked one of my children to do the dishes by the time I got home. When I returned, the dining room table was still covered with dirty dishes, and when

I asked why they weren't washed, he said, "I thought you meant the ones in the sink." If you're not crystal clear about your request, it's not likely you'll get what you want. You could, for example, describe what the completed assignment would look like.

- When. If you don't specify an exact time for completion of an assignment, people will naturally work at a pace convenient for *them*, which is rarely the pace you had in mind. Remember when Stan asked you to complete the assignment by "the next day?" You probably would have responded more reliably if he'd asked you to complete it by 11:15 a.m. the following day. And you would have gotten better results from the people you called for information if you'd told them exactly when you needed it. The lack of specificity greatly increases the likelihood that any assignment will fail.

- Follow-up. One reason Stan didn't get what he wanted from you is that he didn't say how he'd follow up on the assignment. He could have said, "I'll need that information from you by 11:15 a.m., and if you can see that you won't have it by then, I need to hear from you by 10:00 a.m." You, in turn, could have given a similarly clear assignment and description of follow-up to the people who were supposed to get back with you.

Who, what, when, and follow-up can be applied to personal relationships as well, although not always as rigidly. Luke and Deborah agreed on who needed what from the other, but they didn't specify exactly when they would give each other the kind of affection desired. On some occasions, *what* and *when* can be inappropriate. Some people don't like to be given a detailed schedule for sex, for example. However, Luke and Deborah did talk about follow-up. They agreed to talk with each other again in two weeks, at which time they would both discuss how their needs were being met.

RESOLVING DIFFERENCES

As Deborah and Luke have learned to feel loved and loving, their interactions have changed significantly. "I'd like to go out to a movie tonight," says Deborah. "How about you?"

"I hate the crowds," says Luke. "I'd rather stay home and watch a DVD."

Not long ago, Deborah would have shot back, "We never go anywhere, and the crowds aren't that bad on a weekday anyway." But she's learned how to care about her partner while still stating clearly what she wants. "I'd still prefer to go out," she says. "I just want to get away from the house for a bit. I could go alone, but I'd much rather be with you. Maybe we could go out for just a little while to get a bite to eat at someplace quiet, and then you wouldn't have to deal with the crowds."

In the past, Luke would have become irritated and told her to do whatever she wanted, but he's begun to understand that what he really wants is a loving relationship. "I just changed my clothes to something more casual," he says, "and I just feel like slouching around here at home. But I don't want to ignore what you want, so tell me, on a scale of one to five how much you want to do this."

Deborah has a real opportunity here to push her short-term goal by exaggerating her desires, but she remembers what she really wants, and replies honestly, "Probably a three."

Luke: I probably have a desire to stay home that's about a three or four.

Deborah: So what if you run with me to the store for a few minutes—you can go just like you are—and we'll get something we can throw in the microwave, and we'll watch a movie here.

Luke: I could do that.

As they drive to the store, they plan an evening later in the week when they'll go out to a movie together.

Coming up with a scale of desire, as above, isn't binding. It just gives people a relative idea of how much they each want to do something so they can make better decisions about lovingly satisfying one another's needs. If Deborah's desire to go to a movie had been a four out of five, and if Luke's interest in staying home had been a two, he might have considered doing what she wanted. Of course, people need to be careful about inflating their ratings in this approach.

With human beings, there will always be differences in preferences: what we eat, how we dress, how we spend our time, and so on. Because we always get to make our own choices, we'll never eliminate differences, but when we understand the principles that reduce or eliminate conflict, *and especially when we feel loved*, differences—or disagreements—will not become conflicts.

Chapter Summary

- When disagreements or differences involve Getting and Protecting Behaviors—most notably anger—they become conflicts.
- Conflict arises out of scarcity—or perceived scarcity—of Real Love and Imitation Love.
- We can eliminate and prevent conflict from our lives if we understand and apply the following principles and actions:
  - Realize that it's always about Real Love
  - Listen
  - Never speak in anger
  - Tell the truth about yourself
  - Tell the truth about your partner
  - Recognize what you really want
  - Determine how you and your partner can get what you want
  - Remember the Law of Choice
  - Refuse to be in conflict
- In the presence of Real Love there are only differences and disagreements, not conflicts.

The Miracle

The Healing Power of Real Love

From birth, children's bodies grow with astonishing speed. Each day, millions of cells grow and divide, adding to the length and breadth of bone, muscle, and sinew. To accomplish that remarkable physiologic feat, a minimum of water, protein, fat, calories, vitamins, and minerals is required. Most of us are familiar with many of these essential elements—we read lists of their minimum daily requirements on containers of the foods we buy. If any one of these basic building blocks is restricted, the building process stops. If children are deprived entirely, they become seriously ill and eventually die.

As parents, we generally provide more than enough of these physical requirements for our children, and, as a result, our children grow up with bodies that are relatively healthy and strong. Children, however, are more than just muscles and bones. They have minds, or spirits, or souls—use whatever word you wish to describe that which distinguishes us from trees and refrigerators—and this soul also has minimum requirements which must be satisfied. The most important of these soul-needs is Real Love. It is also the most challenging requirement to satisfy.

THE EFFECT OF GROWING UP WITHOUT REAL LOVE

At literally thousands of moments in our childhood, we needed Real Love to develop the next building block in our character. We needed to feel loved consistently in order to acquire the qualities of responsibility, faith, forgiveness, and the ability to love other people. But in those critical moments, many of us didn't get what we needed. Instead we were neglected, or criticized, or given a morsel of conditional praise. As a result of these unhealthy substitutions, the muscles and sinews of our soul became weak and twisted. Sure, we were given plenty of food, water, and shelter, so our bodies grew up healthy enough, but without unconditional love, we felt empty and afraid, and we learned to respond to the world with Getting and Protecting Behaviors.

Many people have a difficult time understanding just how difficult it is for us to function in a healthy way as adults when we didn't get Real Love as children. "Oh, come on," they say, "that all happened so long ago. You can't blame everything on your childhood. Just get over it and move on." A child's need for Real Love is just as critical as his or her need for physical nutrients. Deprived of Real Love, children *cannot* be as emotionally healthy and strong as children who are loved. If that deficiency is not corrected, they *will* leave childhood in a relatively crippled condition. These children will then become adults who might look normal on the outside— even appearing to function well in some aspects of life—but they're empty, wounded, and unable to be genuinely happy. They can't just "get over" the absence of the Real Love essential to their emotional and spiritual health.

As wise men, we need to understand that almost everyone around us grew up with insufficient Real Love. They're trying to be happy and trying to respond productively to the people around them—including us—but they're missing what they need to do that. As I explained on pages 81-4, however, our past does not entirely determine our future. We can still make some decisions about restraining our use of Getting and Protecting Behaviors, and we can always begin to take the steps that lead to feeling loved and being loving.

Physical and Spiritual Health

We spend billions of dollars every year on our health—nutrition, exercise, and campaigns to stamp out cancer, heart disease, AIDS, and other scourges. Certainly these are worthwhile efforts, but in the midst of all this concern for our bodies, we often forget that our bodies simply create the possibility for us to experience the profound pleasures of emotional and spiritual joy. Without that happiness, our physical health means little.

Every day we feed our bodies, and if we forget to do that, our physical hunger reminds us of the need for nourishment. Our *souls* also communicate their need to be fed. Our emptiness, fear, and Getting and Protecting Behaviors all tell us that we're starving for Real Love. But we rarely feed our souls what they need. Instead we get Imitation Love and use more Getting and Protecting Behaviors, which only guarantees that we will feel even more empty, alone, and afraid. We feed our bodies but starve our souls. Our neglect is not intentional. We just don't realize there's an alternative. We're doing only what we've seen other people do all our lives.

THE HEALING EFFECT OF REAL LOVE

Fortunately, we don't need to go back to childhood and be rebuilt from the bottom up. As we learn to tell the truth about ourselves and feel loved, we can begin to eliminate all our emptiness and pain. Real Love heals all wounds, destroys fear, and replaces misery with a happiness we can scarcely imagine until we've experienced it.

Healing the Past

Therapists often unearth, dissect, and categorize the many wounds their patients have suffered in the past in an attempt to bring some measure of understanding to the present. But these efforts are expensive and time-consuming and rarely produce genuine happiness. I've counseled with people who have suffered a wide array of injuries—physical, sexual, emotional, and spiritual—and

I've learned that no matter how different these individual injuries appear to be from one another, they all distill into a single common wound: a lack of love. In the end, it does not matter much whether people were beaten, yelled at, lied to, abandoned, sexually violated, controlled, or simply ignored. They still suffered most from a lack of Real Love. We do not have to go back into their childhoods and re-create their injuries again and again, nor make monsters of the people who hurt them.

In order to be healed from our wounds, we just need to be loved—by anyone. As adults we do not require the love of our parents, and we rarely need the help of a trained professional. We just need Real Love from anyone capable of seeing and accepting us—from someone like you. As a wise man, you are capable of applying the healing balm that heals the wounds of the past and present. The effect is miraculous.

Over the years Robin had read dozens of self-help books and had been in therapy with several counselors. She was a walking basket of "issues" she'd collected from her reading and her therapists. She'd been wounded by her emotionally distant mother, her alcoholic and sexually abusive father, her alcoholic grandparents, and her verbally abusive siblings. Virtually every week she remembered another traumatic childhood event that explained her miserable adulthood and justified her "trust issues" and "abandonment issues." She'd been divorced once, after a marriage of three months, and had never been successful in establishing a meaningful relationship with a man—or with anyone, for that matter.

Although Robin had been given many explanations for her misery, none of them made her any happier. A wise friend suggested that she come to a meeting of loving men and women, and there she detailed many of her wounds, especially the sexual experiences with her father. She talked about that at length, and with considerable bitterness.

Wise woman: You didn't feel loved unconditionally as you grew up, did you?

Robin: That's an understatement.

Wise woman: What I'm suggesting is that *not feeling loved* is the main reason for the problems you've experienced since childhood. The details of *how* you didn't get loved—what exactly your mother or father did—are not as important. You simply needed to get Real Love from your parents, which is more important to a child than anything else, and you didn't get that.

Robin: You're saying it doesn't matter that my father sexually abused me? How can you say that?

Wise woman: I'm not saying it wasn't awful for you, just that the real pain came from seeing that your own father didn't *love* you. *That* was the worst wound in your life, not the sexual abuse. To a child, not being loved is a living death. It doesn't really matter how death is delivered—whether it's with a gun, a knife, or whatever. Dead is dead. Some people were yelled at, some beaten, others ignored. It all ends up feeling pretty much the same. Your mother criticized you and withdrew from you. Your father sexually abused you. But what matters *most*—by far—is that they both *failed to love you.*

Robin: Aren't you making this too simple?

Wise woman: A child without Real Love is like a plant without light and water. Without love, there was no way you could have come out of your childhood happy and healthy.

Robin: So you expect me to pretend the abuse didn't happen?

Wise woman: Not at all. I'm saying that you'll benefit most from identifying the *real* problem—that you feel unloved and alone—because then you can do something about it. You don't want to waste the rest of your life describing the *details* of your wounds, but that's what you're doing when you keep talking about how your parents treated you. Has that ever made you genuinely happier?

Robin: Not really.

Wise woman: So you have two choices: You could *talk* about how you're starving, or you could just *eat*. You can learn the process of finding Real Love, which is simple and works every time if you're willing to do it. Which choice seems smarter to you?

Robin: (pause) I've been in therapy for twelve years, and nobody has ever talked to me like this. It makes sense, but I don't know if I can do it.

Wise woman: You *won't* know until you try it, but what have you got to lose if the things you're doing now haven't worked?

Robin learned to tell the truth about *herself*, instead of talking about what had been done to her. She talked about her anger, her fears, and her Getting and Protecting Behaviors. She talked about how selfish she'd been, and how she'd often used her wounds to justify her anger and make people feel sorry for her. As she told the truth about herself, she could see that the people in the group genuinely accepted and loved her. With that love, her emptiness, pain, and anger began to evaporate. Her wounds healed, and she quit talking about all her "issues." When we're consistently full and happy, we simply lose any interest in thinking or talking about the times in our life when we were hungry and miserable.

Healing Racism, Sexism, and All the Other Hates

George was raised around people who had numerous prejudices, and he was taught that people who were black, gay, Hispanic, female, short, fat, stupid, poor, jobless, ugly, and crippled were inferior and deserved his disgust and even hatred.

George learned to tell the truth about himself in a group of wise men, and over a period of months, he felt the results of being accepted and loved. At a group meeting, he spoke to Randall, a black man.

George: Randall, I'm a little embarrassed to talk about this, but I want to tell you something that's been bothering me. When I first started coming to these meetings, I was uncomfortable around you.

Randall: Why?

George: Because you're black. I was raised to think that black people were a lot less than me, and I believed it. So I didn't like you when I first saw you.

Randall: (smiling) How do you feel now?

George: You're my friend. I was wrong about how I felt, and I've been wrong to think badly of other black people, too.

Randall: Not a problem. Prejudice and hatred are just ways of attacking people to protect yourself and make you feel stronger. It's not hard to understand.

For thousands of years racism has torn millions of people apart. But *race* is not the cause of racism. Racism is caused by a lack of unconditional love. When people feel loved by those around them, their pre-judgment of other people goes away.

When we don't feel loved, we eagerly find anyone we can label inferior to us in some way, and we learn this at an early age. Children in grade school have already learned to pick on the child who is shorter, fatter, and slower than they are. They're already mocking the children who don't dress as well, can't speak as clearly, wear glasses, or walk with a limp. Throughout history we've judged people, joked about them, hated them, imprisoned them, and even killed them because of their race, sex, religion, and beliefs. We do not have to address all these prejudices individually. As people feel unconditionally loved, their need to feel superior to *any* group disappears.

Healing Shame

For several weeks Scott has been attending group meetings with you and other wise men and women. He hasn't spoken at all in the meetings. Finally, you say, "Scott, you don't have to say anything here if you don't want to. I just remember that it was hard for me to start talking when I first came here. But once I did, I felt accepted, and that's made a big difference in my life."

Scott: I guess I'm just nervous.

Wise man: The only way you can know what it's like to feel accepted is to have a little faith and talk about yourself. Everyone in this room was afraid in the beginning. You're sitting next to Jim, for example, who was embarrassed to tell us he'd spent time in prison for dealing drugs and embezzling funds from the company he worked for. He thought there was no way he'd ever be accepted by anyone after they knew he was an ex-con, but he told us anyway. Does he look unhappy?

Scott: No.

Wise man: That's because people here accepted and loved him after he talked about himself. If you keep hiding your warts, your life will stay the same, but this is still your decision—if you decide to say nothing, I won't be disappointed.

Scott: I don't think anyone here has done the things I've done.

Wise man: Maybe not. You might've done the worst things of anybody in the room, but that still wouldn't make you unacceptable. There's no pressure here. If you don't want to talk, don't. If you'd rather talk to people one at a time outside the meeting, do that.

Scott: (pause) I've never talked about this, not to anyone. I even moved away from the town where I used to live, because a few people there found out, and I couldn't stand the thought of ever facing them. (long pause) Eight years ago, I sexually abused my daughter.

Scott hangs his head and looks at the floor.

Wise man: Were you married at the time?

Scott: Yes.

Wise man: Were you happy in your marriage?

Scott: No.

Wise man: Were you happy in anything?

Scott: No.

Wise man: You've been in the group long enough to know something about Real Love. At the time you abused your daughter, did you feel loved by anyone?

Scott: No.

Wise man: You were so miserable that you were willing to do anything to get a moment of relief from your own pain—even though it hurt your daughter. You already know that what you did was terribly wrong, and you know it had an awful effect on her, and you quit doing it long ago, so we don't need to keep going over that. You just need to understand *why* you did it and what you can do now to change the rest of your life. Everybody in this room has used something to make them feel better when they didn't have enough Real Love—money, power, sex, praise, approval—and we've hurt the people close to us. We've ignored our children, said unkind things to them, and hurt them in ways we're just beginning to understand. The different *ways* we hurt our children—hitting them, yelling at them, sexually abusing them—are just details. We're all guilty, but you simply chose to hurt your child in a different way than I hurt mine—and you chose a way that's much less socially accepted. But we both failed to love our children, and I don't see your behavior and mine as so different.

Scott has agonized over this serious mistake for years and is clearly touched that his friend is accepting and loving him.

"Now you have a choice," says the wise man. "You *could* spend the rest of your life feeling ashamed about this, *or* you could just get the Real Love you need and be happy. Which would you rather do?"

Over the following year, Scott's happiness continues to grow. A little guilt is useful when it motivates us to change our behavior, but excessive guilt and shame are destructive. Scott's shame has kept him from reaching out in a healthy way to the daughter he molested years ago. As he accepts the love of others, he's freed from the chains of his shame and is finally able to share his love with his daughter, now a teenager. Their relationship is becoming healthy and richly rewarding for both of them.

THE ABUNDANCE OF REAL LOVE AND HAPPINESS

Many people are skeptical that Real Love exists—understandable when they've never seen it. Of course, if they persist in nourishing their doubts, they won't see Real Love even when it's offered. We tend to see what we believe. There are other people who initially feel the offers of Real Love, but they still back away, sometimes saying, "I'm afraid to be loved." That's not true. No one is afraid of being unconditionally loved. We're just afraid that the promise of love won't be real, or that it will somehow go away, like so many other good things in our lives.

All this fear is supported by experience. There is so much fear, emptiness, anger, loneliness, and despair among us that we've come to believe these conditions are unavoidable, even normal. The truth is, Real Love is infinitely available. When people truly love you without conditions, why would that ever have to stop? It's *conditional* love that must be earned and therefore has a limited supply. Real happiness does exist, and it's as freely available as the air we breathe. We only need to learn how to find it and feel it.

Removing the Obstacles

My father was raised on a farm where the rainfall was insufficient to sustain the crops. But they always had enough water. All winter, snow accumulated on the nearby mountains, and during the spring and summer, the melting snow fed the streams that ran through the valley below. The farmers used a series of irrigation ditches to carry water from the streams to the fields. As a boy, it was my father's job to get up early in the morning and open the gates in the banks of the ditches to allow the water to run into the fields and orchards where it was needed.

The water flowed in an endless stream from the mountains. To benefit from it, my father only had to *eliminate the obstacles*—the gates—between the water and the fields. Similarly, there is an endless supply of happiness all around us. It flows by like a mighty river, and to experience it we need only to reach out and tap into it by removing the obstacles between us and the source. There is no need for any of us to die of thirst when a cool, life-giving stream runs close by.

Fear

Fear is the greatest obstacle to joy. When we're afraid, we're blindly occupied with filling our own emptiness and protecting ourselves. We can't see clearly. We can't feel loved, nor can we love other people. Fear leads to selfishness and anger. It destroys faith and our ability to grow. Living in fear is a terrible thing, and the solution is love. Real Love removes the fear that keeps us from the infinite river of joy we all want, and we find it as we tell the truth about ourselves.

Getting and Protecting Behaviors

Getting and Protecting Behaviors are a huge obstacle to feeling loved and happy. Real Love can be felt only when it's freely given and received, without manipulation. If we do anything at all to influence other people to give us what we want—which is the purpose of Getting and Protecting Behaviors—we can feel what we're given only as payment for our manipulation. Even if we're actually offered Real Love, we turn it into Imitation Love. I talk more about that in Chapter Three of *Real Love.*

Imitation Love

When we're learning to feel Real Love and genuine happiness, the temporarily satisfying effects of Imitation Love can be very distracting, as we see in the life of Brian.

Brian had been telling the truth about himself in a group of wise men and women for several months, but he was not happier. He was still angry and withdrawn, and was blaming his wife for his problems. I concluded that he must be doing something wrong. The definition of *wrong*, as you recall, is anything that interferes with our ability to feel unconditionally loved and to share that love with others (page 84). It includes Imitation Love and any of the Getting and Protecting Behaviors. One day I talked to him about it.

Me: Brian, you still seem unhappy most of the time.

Brian: You're right, and I don't know what to do about it.

Me: How often do you call people from the group?

Brian: Almost every day.

Me: That's what I thought, and I've seen you be honest about yourself many times. I have a thought: When someone continues to be unhappy despite telling the truth and making regular contact with loving people, as you've been doing, they're often doing something wrong, something that's distracting them—maybe using a form of Imitation Love—and they're hiding it. You might be doing something you're ashamed to tell people about, or maybe you're hiding something from the past. I may be mistaken. I'm just suggesting that this might be an obstacle to you being happy.

Brian hung his head and said, "Since I was fourteen I've been addicted to pornography. It was the one thing in life that made me feel good. For years I snuck around in porn shops, and then the Internet came, which made it real easy for me. Every day I look at porn on the Net and do what guys always do when they're looking at that stuff. I can't believe I'm telling you this, but I have to tell somebody. This is killing me. I just couldn't tell you before, because I was sure you'd think I was a complete loser, and then you'd have nothing to do with me.

There were two reasons that Brian's secret was keeping him from feeling loved. First, he couldn't feel loved while he was hiding the truth about himself. Second, pornography is a drug, just like all the other forms of Imitation Love. If I give you a dose of narcotics, it will certainly dull your pain, but it will also dull your ability to fully participate in everything else in your life. In a similar way, emotional drugs—Imitation Love—temporarily distract us from the pain of not feeling loved, but they also distract us from feeling and doing anything good.

Of course, Brian felt a huge relief when he was still accepted and loved after telling me the truth about himself. He shared his secret with another member of the group, and then he chose to tell the entire group at a meeting. Everyone expressed their acceptance of him, and several men in the group shared similar experiences. Like Brian, many of us are not initially comfortable sharing ourselves with large numbers of people—nor should we feel any pressure to do so. We might begin with one person, and as our faith is rewarded with acceptance, we can be honest with more and more people.

But Brian didn't feel the full effect of the love he was receiving, because he was still using his drug. It was just too distracting. I suggested he make a commitment to stay completely away from pornography for two weeks and call someone in the group to talk about how he was doing every day during that period. He did that, and the longer he stayed away from the numbing and distracting effects of his drug, the better he was able to feel the love he was receiving. Of course, the more Real Love he felt, the less *need* he had to use any form of Imitation Love. As I suggest on p. 83, there is a powerful synergy between Real Love and self-control. As we make conscious decisions to avoid whatever form of Imitation Love we use as a drug, we'll feel the love we receive much more powerfully. And then, with a greater sense of Real Love, we can better avoid our drug.

Faith

A lack of faith is an insurmountable obstacle to feeling loved and happy. We discussed how to address that in Chapter Six. We have only a limited number of moments to be alive. Why waste any of them feeling afraid, angry, and alone when profound joy is always available? It doesn't take brains to be happy, just faith. It also takes courage and persistence in doing whatever is required to find the Real Love that always leads to genuine happiness. The river is there. All we have to do is open the gate on the bank and let the joy flow in our direction.

Clinical Depression and Other Mental Illness

Imagine that you have a serious illness and a high fever. In that condition, the chemistry of your brain is dramatically altered, so obviously you will say and do things differently than you normally would. You'll be confused and quite unable to show any concern for the people around you. You might even say unkind things to people. You won't *intentionally* be unloving; you're simply not able to make loving choices with a high fever.

Many people suffer from other clinical disorders that affect the chemistry of their minds. With depression—perhaps the most common example of mental illness, affecting as many as nineteen million Americans—people just cannot respond in an entirely healthy way to anything.

Depression and a lack of love have a strong effect on each other and on our ability to be happy. An insufficient supply of Real Love will often cause or worsen depression. On the other hand, genetically-determined, clinical depression can significantly worsen feelings of being unloved and can make it impossible for people to feel the love they're offered. Each condition—depression and a lack of Real Love—contributes to the other.

Over the years, I've observed many examples of the following:

- People who have not responded optimally to their anti-depressants. With Real Love, their depression goes away, and many of them are able to stop taking their medication.
- People who remain unhappy despite being surrounded with Real Love. With anti-depressants they begin to feel the love they're offered.

In individual cases it can be difficult to determine whether people need medical assistance in addition to Real Love. With most people I first recommend taking the steps to find Real Love, and if that is ineffective after they've really done all they can—including removal of the obstacles we discussed above—I suggest they see a physician.

Some people stubbornly resist the idea that they might need medical assistance for their problems. They're frightened of the social and personal stigma still attached to any form of mental illness. They "hate to take a pill" or want to just "handle" their own problems. Those are not productive attitudes. We don't try to handle diabetes or a heart attack without medical help, and sometimes we also can't handle alterations in our brain chemistry without help. When that help is available, we're foolish to suffer without it.

CHANGE

I have seen people make profound changes in their lives so many times that it no longer surprises me. Real Love has the power to do that. When people are freed from the crippling effects of emptiness, fear, anger, their Getting and Protecting Behaviors, and their past wounds and mistakes, they often describe their transformation as a rebirth—as we see in the case of Andrea.

After several months of experiencing the effects of Real Love, Andrea said to me, "I used to be angry all the time. I was always trying to control people, and when they didn't do what I wanted, I was irritated that things didn't go my way. It was pretty terrible."

Me: You've changed a lot since I've known you.

Andrea: More than I ever would have imagined. I used to hate getting up in the morning. Now I love it. I look forward to being around people. I don't get angry like I used to. I actually like being with my husband—can you imagine that? Remember how I used to complain about everything he did?

Me: I remember it well.

Andrea: And remember how my children were such a mess? I thought they'd never stop being rebellious and difficult, but then I saw they just didn't feel loved. The other day I was talking to my seventeen-year-old daughter, and she told me that she actually likes being around me now. She used to avoid coming home just because I was there. Before I learned to tell the truth about myself, I didn't understand that the problems with my children were *my* fault. Now that I've learned to be more loving toward them, they're so much happier—everyone in the family is. My husband and I still disagree about some things, but we never fight like we used to. I feel like a different person.

As you share your love with other people, you too will see the power of Real Love, but you won't always see the effect as quickly or dramatically as in the case of Andrea. When people have been doing the same old things for a lifetime, doing something new can be frightening. Many people change very slowly, and when you expect otherwise, you'll tend to become impatient and manipulate them to do what you want. You don't have the right to do that, even if you're trying to help them do the "right thing" that would be "good for them."

Although Real Love is a powerful force, some people cannot be reached at all by the love you offer. My son Michael lived in South America for two years. Several times he helped an elderly woman carry some large plastic bags from the middle of town to her house, about two miles away. One day he looked inside the bags and was stunned to see that they were filled with garbage. He learned that every day, for years, she'd rummaged through garbage cans in town to find her food, which she then took home in bags.

People tried to give her fresh bread and other food, but she preferred to pick her dinner from the garbage. She was used to it. As horrible as that sounds, we all do things like that. We prefer to use Getting and Protecting Behaviors and Imitation Love—we eat the garbage we're accustomed to—rather than change our lives and experience the joy that's available and infinitely preferable. We keep doing what we're familiar with, even when it's disgusting and harmful to us and the people around us. As wise men, we need to love and teach people as they cling tightly to the garbage bags in their hands.

People without sufficient Real Love are literally sick and dying, and in most cases they are surrounded by people who are also empty and afraid and therefore quite incapable of giving them what they need. If you feel loved—even a little—and have a willingness to share that with someone, you may become the only person in his or her world who can help. That puts you in rather powerful— almost indispensable—position, but don't take upon yourself the responsibility for changing people. When you remember that, you won't feel burdened or disappointed when people change slowly or not at all. Just have faith in the power of the truth and in the power of Real Love, and allow miracles to happen.

Some people either can't or won't tell the truth about themselves. They don't exercise the faith necessary to feel the effects of Real Love. Even with Real Love and medical help, some people seem utterly resistant to happiness. As a wise man, you must accept that and be willing to move on when interacting with some people. What I can't tell you is *when* to move on with any given person. You'll have to learn that with experience.

Chapter Summary

- If we receive insufficient Real Love as children, and that condition is not corrected, we *will* be severely impaired in our ability to be happy and make loving choices.
- The primary wound of our lives is not the individual injuries that have been heaped upon us, but the lack of Real Love we've received.
- As we feel Real Love from anyone, we can heal all the wounds of the past.
- Real Love eliminates anger, shame, racism, and all forms of prejudice.
- There is an infinite supply of Real Love available to us. We only need to remove the obstacles—fear, Getting and Protecting Behaviors, Imitation Love, and a lack of faith—between ourselves and the sources of that love.

≈ Chapter Eleven ≈

Practicing

Exercises

In Chapter Four of *Real Love*, I describe four exercises to help people tell the truth and find Real Love, and now that you've read *The Wise Man*, you should have an increased ability to use those exercises in more effective ways. The following exercises will begin with Exercise 5, continuing from the four in *Real Love*.

EXERCISE 5: TELLING THE TRUTH ABOUT FEELINGS

The participants in this exercise interact in pairs. They alternate the roles of speaker and listener, followed by a discussion in the group about what everyone has learned.

For one or two minutes, the first speaker talks about specific events in his or her life and the associated feelings he or she experienced. The listener then becomes the speaker and the exercise is repeated. The group reassembles to talk about what they've learned from speaking and from listening.

Comment

This is an expansion of Exercise 2—about fear—in *Real Love*. Most of us—especially men—have little experience talking about how we really feel, so we tend to disguise our feelings with socially acceptable words. To minimize that distraction, before the exercise someone could encourage the group to use more direct and expressive words as they describe their feelings, like *angry, afraid, empty,* and *happy*—as we discussed on pages 177-8.

It might help to share some examples of feelings before splitting the group up into pairs:

"When my wife complains, I get mad."

"When people criticize me, I hear them saying that something is wrong with me, and then I'm afraid they won't like me."

"I realize I've felt empty most of my life, but I never knew how to put that in words. I suppose if I had, I would still have been too embarrassed to say it."

"I'm constantly afraid of what people will think of me: how I look, the job I have—it goes on and on."

Lessons

When the group reassembles, people share what they've learned from doing the exercise. Following are a few examples:

"When I was honest with my partner (in the exercise) about being afraid, she didn't look down on me. I felt like she saw me and accepted me. I feel less alone when I can do that. I didn't even realize that all these years I've been lying to people about myself."

"People have always told me not to be angry, so when I am, I feel like I'm bad. But I didn't feel guilty here as I talked about being angry. It's a relief to be myself and not pretend to be something else, you know?"

"When my partner shared his fears with me, I felt closer to him and less afraid of him. I like that."

"I was really afraid to talk about being empty and afraid—it's not very flattering—but I love feeling accepted. I've never done this before, and it feels pretty good."

After discussing the feelings of people in the group, some people gain the confidence to share additional feelings. Because of that, you might consider repeating the exercise after the group discussion. See Chapter Seven for more examples of helping people to tell the truth about their feelings.

EXERCISE 6: SEEING OTHER PEOPLE

The group splits into pairs. One person is designated the speaker, while the other is the listener. The speaker talks about himself—how he was raised, his feelings, his failings, his joys, his Getting and Protecting Behaviors. This brings Exercises 1-5 together. The listener asks *occasional* questions. This takes perhaps fifteen minutes or more—as long as the speaker and listener are comfortable with it—and there is no switching of speaker and listener.

The group reassembles. Each listener then introduces his partner (the speaker) to the group, sharing what he or she learned as he listened to the speaker. Members of the group are encouraged to ask questions about the speaker, but only the *listener* may answer them. If he doesn't know the answer, he says so.

Comment

Speakers and listeners don't switch during their initial pairing, because the exercise requires the complete concentration of the listener, who will be sharing with the group the information he's gathering. The listener cannot be distracted by thoughts of what he or she will be saying when it's his turn to be the speaker. After the group has learned about every speaker, and if there is time remaining in the meeting, speakers and listeners can switch roles and repeat the exercise. Or they could switch roles at a subsequent meeting.

Following are some common things said by listeners as they've introduced their partners. I'll use the names of John and Mary to illustrate.

"John's parents loved him when he did all the right things, but they were critical toward him when he didn't do what they wanted. So he's always been afraid to make mistakes, and he works hard to impress people and do the right things. In other words, he's always felt conditionally loved. He always knew something was missing in his relationships, but he could never quite describe it."

"Mary was divorced a year ago, and since then she's been blaming her ex-husband for all her problems. In the past couple of months she's begun to see that she's been unhappy for a long time, probably all her life. She never felt loved— even before she met her husband—so she's beginning to see that her husband was not the whole problem."

"John has a serious problem with anger. He gets angry at his wife for being late, for not having sex with him, for not cleaning up the house, for almost everything she does. That makes their relationship pretty terrible, and then he blames her for it."

"Mary has a hard time talking about her feelings. She says she's frustrated and annoyed about things, but she has a hard time using words like angry or afraid. She's always been around people who made her feel guilty for using words like that."

Members of the group can ask questions about the speaker at any time. Following are some examples of questions often asked:

"How does John communicate his anger at his wife? What does he say and what does he do? And how does it all affect their relationship?"

"What Getting and Protecting Behaviors does Mary use with people?"

"You said John is nervous and anxious a lot. Does he see now that he's just afraid of not being loved?"

Lessons

These exercises give the listeners a wonderful opportunity to see and accept their speaker-partners as they listen to them and introduce them to the group. People in the group also get an opportunity to practice being wise men as they ask questions, and as they see, accept, and love the speakers. The group should discuss lessons they've learned from their experience. Following are some examples:

Listener: "I learned more about my partner in fifteen minutes than I know about most people I've known for years."

Listener: "I don't listen to people as well as I thought. When you (referring to the group) asked me questions about her, I discovered I'd forgotten a lot she told me."

Listener: "Nobody's ever told me as much about themselves as my partner just did. It felt like a gift."

Speaker: "I was afraid to let my partner get to know me, but the more I talked, the more relieved I felt, and less alone. I liked it."

Speaker: "It felt great to have someone know me like that. When he introduced me and answered questions about me, I felt like he really cared about me—and this is someone I barely knew before tonight."

EXERCISE 7: THE NEXT RIGHT THING

The group stays together. Each person describes the next step he or she is going to take toward being truthful, seen, loved, and loving. The group discusses that proposed step, sometimes making suggestions. The next week, group members report about the steps they took. What happened? How did they feel? What did they learn?

Comment

The more action we take, the more quickly we feel loved, and learn to love other people, and experience the joy available to us. A life of profound happiness is a natural consequence of steadily doing the next right thing. Each such step in the right direction is an act of faith. As with most things in life, the greater the risks we take, the greater the reward.

Following are some examples of next right things people have committed to do, along with comments of wise men and women in the group:

> "I'm not doing enough to be seen and accepted. This week I'll call somebody in the group every day and tell them how I'm feeling."
>
> (Someone in the group then suggested that the speaker commit right then to name three specific people she would call in the next three days. Being specific increases the likelihood of our doing any task.)
>
> "I'm always getting angry at my wife when she criticizes me. This week I'm going to remember that she only does that because she feels unloved and empty and alone. I think that will help me to not feel angry."
>
> (A wise man said, "That could be difficult to do at first, so I suggest you might remember your promise better if you know you'll be talking to someone else about how you did. What if you make a commitment to call a specific person in the group in two days to talk about whether you actually *did* remember to see your wife differently on some occasion when she criticized you? Would you be willing to do that?" It's more likely that people will do the next right thing when a clear time is set for follow-up.)
>
> Mike: "I've enjoyed other people loving *me* for a long time, but I haven't done much about giving anything to anybody else. This week I'm going to call another man in the group and ask what *he* needs."

(A wise man then asked if there was anyone in the group who could use a friend, and Brian said, "Sure, I could." Brian said he'd call Mike if he needed someone to talk with, and Mike committed to calling Brian whether he got a call from him or not.

"I need to sit down with my son and take responsibility for the mistakes I've been making with him. I know he feels hurt and angry, and I also know that one conversation won't fix all that—but it will be a start. I'll tell him I haven't loved him as he needed, and that I know how painful that's been for him. And I'll tell him that all I can do now is learn how to love him."

(Someone in the group said, "When you have that conversation, you'll want to feel as loved as possible. If you want to call someone in the group for support before you talk to your son, don't hesitate.")

Glenn: "I've noticed that when I get nervous, I drink. I don't drink every day, but I often take a drink or two when I get home from work. It's a quick and easy way to feel good, when I really should be finding someone to see me and accept me. This week I'm not going to drink anything, and I'll see how that works."

(Seth said, "You'll find it easier to keep that commitment if you talk to someone about it every day. Do you want to talk to me on the phone every day about how you're doing?")

Alice: "I've been avoiding telling my husband what I've been learning here in group. I'm afraid he'll laugh at me. But this has become an important part of my life, and I want to share it with him. But I don't want him to think I'm preaching at him or accusing him of something."

(Louise suggested that Alice call her right before she talked to her husband, so that Alice would feel accepted and loved before she talked to him.)

Lessons

As we consistently do the right things, our progress toward feeling loved, loving, and happy is assured. This exercise gives people an opportunity to commit themselves to taking steps in the right direction. After you've done the exercise, follow-up of some kind is helpful—perhaps by phone in the following days, or at the next week's meeting. People are not being graded. Follow-up is just a way of allowing people to talk about what they've learned.

Following are some examples of things people have reported learning after making their commitments to do the next right thing:

> "Now I understand what you guys mean when you're always saying, 'Make your phone calls.' When I made my commitment last week to talk to people every day, that gave me the motivation I needed to do it. It really did help to talk to people. I haven't been doing that often enough."

> "I can't believe what happened with my husband. Last week I told you I'd listen to him differently, and sure enough, the next time he started criticizing me, I remembered that I'm loved by the people here, and then I didn't feel afraid or angry at him. I remembered that he's just feeling unloved and empty and needs me to accept him, not demand things from him. What a difference that made. I didn't defend myself, and there was *no* argument. Unbelievable. It's the first time we've had a positive interaction while he's criticizing me. I need to do it this way more often."

> "I talked to my son like I said I would last week. I told him that all the problems in our relationship were my fault. I told him that I just haven't loved him like he needed. And I told him that I was going to do my best to learn how to love him. He was really touched, and when I hugged him, my seventeen-year-old angry son cried. I never thought that could happen in my lifetime. I wish I'd done this a long time ago."

> "I didn't have a drink all week. It's not like I was an alcoholic or anything, but I can tell a difference in how I feel now. Instead of drinking, I've been calling people in the group every day. This idea of doing the next right thing was good."

"Last week I said I'd tell my husband about some of the things I do here in the group. He didn't exactly warm up to anything I said, but it feels good to be honest with him."

When people do the next right thing, they feel an increase in their faith. They feel stronger and more likely to take more positive steps. They feel more loved and loving. Making a public commitment to do something right tends to motivate people to move forward.

EXERCISE 8: GROUP INTERACTION

People in the group are given an opportunity to describe their interactions with other group members in the past week. They talk about how they felt and what they learned.

Comment

Our lives don't change much if we gain only an *intellectual* understanding about Real Love. We change most as we tell the truth about ourselves and actually *feel* loved. We need to create these opportunities to feel loved as often as possible. You can have loving interactions with anyone, but the likelihood of feeling loved and sharing Real Love is much higher with a group of wise men and women, because these people understand the process.

As a speaker describes his interaction with a group member, wise men in the group have opportunities to teach and love that person.

Jack: I called Miron this week.

Wise man: What did you learn?

Jack: Nothing, really. We just talked for awhile.

Miron: Actually, you talked about some important things. You told me you were worried about your marriage and admitted that you've been a pretty selfish husband. And you told me you don't manage money very well. Do you remember that?"

Jack: Yes, I guess so.

Wise man: Jack, did you get any sense from Miron that he was disgusted by you when you talked about yourself?

Jack: Well, no.

Wise man: You had the courage to let Miron to see you with your fears and flaws, and he accepted you. You haven't seen that kind of acceptance much in your life, so maybe you didn't even see what was happening when he did it. I'm just suggesting that you might have missed what you could have learned—and felt—from that phone call.

Jack: You're right. I did miss it. I'll probably get more out of the next call.

Wise man: Keep calling people, and you'll have more experiences like that. As you feel accepted by the people here, it will make a difference in other relationships you have, like with your wife.

As people discuss the interactions they've had during the week with people in the group—on the phone, by e-mail, and in person—wise men will ask them questions like the following (left-hand column). In the right-hand column are common answers.

"How did you feel as you talked with the person you called? Were you afraid? Of what?"

"I put off calling for several days. I was afraid I'd look stupid, or he wouldn't have time for me."

"As you talked with her, what changed for you?"

"She just accepted me and made me feel at ease. The more I talked, the more accepted I felt. I didn't feel nervous anymore."

"Why didn't you call anyone all week?

"I just didn't have time." (In almost every case, the truth is, they were afraid, and this is an opportunity to talk about that.)

Lessons

"I tend to avoid calling people and being with them. I'm afraid of what they'll think of me when they really see who I am."

"I discovered that other people have the same fears and flaws I do. I felt accepted and less alone when I talked about myself and listened to other people talk about themselves."

"When I finally exercise a little faith and tell the truth about myself, I love that feeling. I just have to keep doing this."

"I'm seeing that when I feel alone, it's always my fault. There are people out there who will love me if only I'll reach out and take advantage of it."

"Sometimes when I talk with people from the group, I find myself being critical and judgmental. I'm not as accepting as I want to be."

USING THE EXERCISES

Your group might want to go through all the exercises, or just a few of them. If they jump into telling the truth and accepting each other without the exercises, you may not need to use them at all. They're only here to help you.

After you've used the exercises initially, you'll discover you can use just parts of them. You can also have a single person in the group do an exercise to help that person be seen. Some examples:

A wise woman asks Dennis, who has said nothing for weeks, "Is there anything you want to talk about?" After Dennis says no, she suggests that he will never feel seen and accepted until he talks about himself. She further suggests that he might be reluctant to talk about himself because he's afraid, and then she asks him if he'd be willing to talk about some of the things he's afraid of. Essentially, the wise woman is doing Exercise 2 from *Real Love*, the one entitled "Fear." Dennis is the speaker while everyone else in the group is a listener.

A woman has been coming to group meetings, but hasn't been speaking. A wise man suggests that she commit to doing something—anything—to find some of the happiness she's been looking for. This is a one-person version of Exercise 7, "The Next Right Thing."

If someone doesn't have anything to say after check-in, you might ask her what contacts she's made with group members that week. You're doing a version of Exercise 8, "Group Interaction." If she *has* interacted with members of the group, there will be feelings and behaviors to discuss. If she *hasn't* interacted with anyone, that's almost always an indication that she's running from people, and then you can discuss why she uses that Protecting Behavior.

More About Real Love
and
Being a Wise Man or Woman

There is so much material available to help you in the process of becoming a Wise Man or Woman. You can

- read the book, *Real Love—The Truth About Finding Unconditional Love and Fulfilling Relationships*, available at www.RealLove.com and retail bookstores.
- read the books
  The Real Love Companion — Taking Steps Toward a Loving and Happy Life, available at RealLove.com
  Real Love in Dating — The Truth About Finding the Perfect Partner (Unabridged audio book also available) at Real Love.com
  Real Love in Marriage — The Truth About Finding Genuine Happiness Now and Forever available at www.RealLove. com and retail bookstores.(Unabridged audio book also available) at RealLove.com
  40 Days to Real Love and Happiness in Your Marriage — A companion Workbook for Real Love in Marriage
  Real Love in Parenting — The Truth About Raising Happy and Responsible Children (Unabridged audio book also available) at RealLove.com

Real Love in the Workplace — Eight Principles for Consistently Effective Leadership in Business

Real Love and Freedom for the Soul — Eliminating the Chains of Victimhood

Real Love and Post-Childhood Stress Disorder — Treating Your Unrecognized Post-Traumatic Stress Disorder

Under the Bridge — a novel

- watch the six-DVD series, *The Essentials of Real Love*, available at www.RealLove.com (also available on CD).
- read *The Essentials of Real Love Workbook*, which is a highly effective companion to the DVD series above.
- go online to www.RealLove.com where you can
  - watch the archived Daily Video Coaching sessions with Greg.
  - participate on the Real Love Forum.
  - receive live coaching from a certified Real Love Coach.

Index